Paths to International Political Economy

Paths to International Political Economy

Edited by
SUSAN STRANGE
London School of Economics & Political Science

London
GEORGE ALLEN & UNWIN
Boston   Sydney

George Allen & Unwin (Publishers) Ltd,
40 Museum Street, London WC1A 1LU, UK

George Allen & Unwin (Publishers) Ltd,
Park Lane, Hemel Hempstead, Herts HP2 4TE, UK

Allen & Unwin, Inc.,
Fifty Cross Street, Winchester, Mass. 01890, USA

George Allen & Unwin Australia Pty Ltd,
8 Napier Street, North Sydney, NSW 2060, Australia

First published in 1984
Second impression 1986

British Library Cataloguing in Publication Data

　　Paths to international political economy
1. Economic history—1971–
2. World politics—1975–1985
I. Strange, Susan
330.9'048　　　HC59
ISBN 0-04-382041-7
ISBN 0-04-382042-5 Pbk

Library of Congress Cataloging in Publication Data

Main entry under title:
　　Paths to international political economy
Includes index
Contents: 1. Perspectives and theory / by Roger
Tooze—2. Why economic history? / by David Wightman
—3. World politics and population / by Nicholas Demerath
—[etc.]
　　1. International economic relations—Addresses,
essays, lectures.　I. Strange, Susan.
HF1411.P3195　　　1984　　　337　　　84-10996
ISBN 0-04-382041-7 (alk. paper)
ISBN 0-04-382042-5 (pbk. : alk. paper)

Set in 10 on 11 point Plantin by Spire Print Services, Ltd, Salisbury, Wilts
and printed and bound in Great Britain by
Biddles Ltd, Guildford and King's Lynn

Contents

Preface

Once upon a time, the prairies of the American West were a vast, wide open range. It was there, according to the cowboy song, that

> . . . the deer and the antelope play,
> Where seldom is heard
> A discouraging word,
> And the skies are not cloudy all day.

So it was until the present century with social science. That too was once a vast, wide open range where anyone interested in the behaviour of men and women in society could roam just as freely as the deer and the antelope. There were no fences or boundary-posts to confine the historians to history, the economists to economics. Political scientists had no exclusive rights to write about politics, nor sociologists to write about social relations.

All that has changed. In the past century a series of enclosure movements have progressively fenced off the open range in the West, and in the social sciences. Both have been subdivided into exclusive territories where trespassers meet with plenty of discouraging words, ominous warnings and keep-out notices. For the social sciences at least – whatever may be the case for the prairies – there have been serious losses to set against the gains from specialisation.

Yet one small corner of social science is still open and unenclosed. This book is dedicated to the hope that it may long remain so. International political economy is still unfenced, still open to all comers. It ought, we believe, to remain so. It would be fatal to its development if it were ever to become the exclusive preserve of economics, of international relations, or of political science. Only by remaining alertly attuned to a variety of special insights and concerns will it remain vigorous, alive and adaptable to the changing needs of world society. It must, moreover, remain open to the special contributions to be made not only by academics, but by bankers, journalists, corporate managers, diplomats and government officials, and practical people of all kinds. One of the fatal weaknesses of social science during the enclosure movement has been the tendency of each specialism to become a closed shop, a self-perpetuating secret society of the initiated, ever less able to talk to, or listen to, ordinary people in the rest of society. Openness within the social sciences is the best defence against the natural academic inclination to pretentiousness, pomposity and obfuscation.

In that belief, what I have collected here is a selection of somewhat unconventional views of what modern teachers of politics, or – in schools – of civics or current affairs, ought to know if they are to venture – as surely they ought to – beyond the confines of their own national scene into the open prairie of international political economy. Each of the contributions I have included offers the reader a new angle, a fresh perspective on some of the most contentious unsolved problems of the modern world.

It is not quite a random selection in that I have tried to include those elements or aspects of international political economy – history, population studies, money, trade, technology and law – that it would be wrong, in my view, for any would-be student or teacher to overlook or ignore. Each of the contributors was asked to try to explain the reasons why his particular ingredient in the mix was valuable and important, and to provide a kind of pocket-guide to some of the basic concepts (and where appropriate the key books or articles) in his special field. None of them, it is worth noting, even tacitly implies that any of the others are expendable or unnecessary ingredients, or even that their particular specialism plays a dominant role in the development of the subject.

Such a claim, I fear, is one that some economists might be tempted to make, and that I think is one reason why none has been included in this collection. The economic theorists who specialise in macro- or micro-economics are too often apt, in their pursuit of purity and internal logical consistency, to pretend a false detachment from those value judgements which none of the other specialists venturing into the study of political economy, whether national or global, would dream of claiming. And if there are would-be 'enclosers' lurking about, they are more likely to be found in departments of economics than elsewhere.

That comment does not apply to the economic historians, nor to the development economists and exponents of other kinds of applied economics like transport economics or labour economics. Indeed, had time allowed, I would have been happy to have included a tenth chapter by a development economist. They have undoubtedly made some very special and important contributions to the subject (I would instance particularly the work of Hans Singer, Gerald Helleiner, Paul Streeten, Constantine Vaitsos, Michael Lipton, Carlos Diaz-Alejandro, Osvaldo Sunkel). And the reason is precisely that they have stressed the plurality of values necessary to a full understanding of the political and social organisation of systems of production, exchange, distribution and consumption. They have consistently talked about justice, as well as efficiency; about order and national identity and cohesion, even self-respect, as well as about cost and price. Indeed, there is by now a well-developed literature of development economics and most serious students of international political economy will be aware of it. But it is necessarily concerned only with a part of the world economy, the developing countries, and not with the whole system. Almost as strong arguments could be found for including contributions from the study of socialist economies, or of the European Community. Whereas part of the strength and interest of international political economy is that it is the antithesis of 'area studies', and deliberately sets out at least to look at the system as a whole.

That certainly was the focus of the discussions from which this book originated. These took place at an annual conference of the (British) Political Studies Association, and I must gratefully acknowledge the political scientists' awareness of the subject of international political economy, their interest in finding out more about it and their invitation to me to commission papers on it. Other acknowledgements are owed to the Social Science Research Council, who provided travel expenses for participants as part of the support given to the International Political Economy Group of the British International Studies Association; and to the United States Embassy in London, whose Cultural Attaché's office provided funds to enable us to consult with our American contributors. My thanks also go to Arthur Kilgore, for his editorial assistance.

SUSAN STRANGE

I

Perspectives and Theory:
a Consumers' Guide

ROGER TOOZE

International political economy (IPE) is very much in vogue. Over the past few years we have seen a deluge of literature – theory, general analyses, issue analyses, reports and recommendations – on, or purporting to be on, the subject. Joan Spero's popular introductory textbook which uses a very narrow conception of IPE contains a bibliography stretching over twenty-five closely printed pages (Spero, 1977). Those who wish to understand the issues and problems of IPE, or even find out what it is all about, are confronted with a galaxy of writings, each of which views IPE from a particular perspective and each of which embodies a particular interpretation of how the world 'works'. As each one of us reading this literature also views the world from our own perspective, how can we make sense of it all and take advantage of the insights IPE offers without falling foul of its many pitfalls? This chapter provides a 'consumers' guide' to the literature through a focus on its basic perspectives and central theory.

Every guide, however, contains its own assumptions about how the field of knowledge has developed and how it is currently organised. In the nature of the social production of knowledge this chapter cannot be any different. But it will, it is hoped, provide a set of explicit criteria by which one should be able to identify and utilise the IPE literature and perspectives that are relevant to the questions we are asking.

International Political Economy: What Is It?

The nature and content of the study of IPE is itself contentious. Hence the present discussion reflects a particular perception of IPE: one that is drawn from within the perspective of international relations, rather than directly from economics or politics (Strange, 1970). As such it reflects an initial emphasis on the international (or world) level, if only because both economics and politics, and their respective forays into 'political economy', have been bounded by the state as the unit-of-analysis. They have in the past taken little account of the international context of state activity.[1] At a time when states are characterised by degrees of penetration by other social, economic and political entities, the lack of attention to international factors is misleading.

International political economy is here a focus of inquiry. It denotes an area of investigation, a particular range of questions, and a series of assumptions about the nature of the international 'system' and how we understand this 'system'.[2] These three criteria clearly overlap, but taken together they define the field.

'An Area of Investigation'

In a contemporary sense the focus is initially defined by the areas, issues, and problems under investigation. In general, we are concerned with that area formed by the merger of the previously separated areas of 'international' economics, 'international' politics, domestic (that is, national) economics and domestic politics.[3] Specifically this produces a concern with problems and issues such as international trade, international monetary relations, North–South relationships, transnational corporations, global economic problems, the foreign economic policies of states and a whole host of other specific topics (R. J. B. Jones, 1981). The general domain created constitutes the focus of IPE, where economics and politics at international and domestic levels are integrated and cannot be understood independently of each other (Gilpin, 1975a; Bergsten *et al.*, 1975).

However, the extent to which each of these conventionally separate areas is, in fact, separate, and can be understood as such, is a moot point, and forms part of the intellectual and political debate within IPE at the moment. Much of the international politics literature focuses solely on questions of international security and military affairs, and relegates both domestic and international issues and concerns to the 'non-political' and unimportant.[4] And economics too has conventionally, and conveniently, ignored E. H. Carr's warning that 'The science of economics presupposes a given political order and cannot be profitably studied in isolation to it' (Carr, 1942), and has developed a whole literature which is sadly deficient when the 'given political order', whether it is international or national, undergoes change. So the very use of the term 'international political economy' or 'political economy', and the adoption of an IPE focus, is a mark of dissatisfaction with the conventional definition of the issues and boundaries of international relations, political science and economics (Strange, 1975). This dissatisfaction comes from a growing realisation that many of the world's problems – poverty, inflation, the nuclear arms race – and conflicts – over trade and services, in international money, in industrial bargaining and within conventional governments – cannot be understood within the conventional framework of knowledge whereby historically defined academic disciplines each have their own exclusive area of inquiry. We need better intellectual tools not only to cope with more complex questions, but to direct us towards different questions.

The definition of a subject area of inquiry – *what* is considered legitimate within a field of study and *how* it is best studied – is never fortuitous. The boundaries and methodology of a subject are set by the wider assumptions that form the social and political context of that subject area. Hence Marxist scholars have always used the term 'political economy' in line with their perspective and latterly to differentiate their understanding from 'conventional economics', which early on separated out the politics from 'political economy'. Perhaps the important question is, therefore, how and why economics and politics became separated in the first place and how, in a similar process, the field of international relations came to be defined in a particular way.

One way we can move towards an answer to this question lies in our understanding of the nature of the social production of knowledge.[5] Knowledge, in the form of theory (here simply a set of propositions which explains the world), is never free from value. As Robert Cox puts it: 'Theory is always *for* someone and *for* some purpose. All theories have a perspective . . . There is . . . no such thing as theory in itself, divorced from a standpoint in time and space' (Cox, 1981, p. 128; emphasis in original). A statement such as this, however, goes against the mainstream conventional interpretation of social science theory. In this, theory is supposed to be objective and value-free, and could therefore give an explanation of situations drawn from widely different historical and social contexts. The perspective values inherent in theory were 'defined out' in the attempt by social scientists, most evident in economics, to emulate the 'value-free' and 'objective' status of theory in the physical sciences. A value-free social science is, in our conception, neither ultimately attainable nor, in fact, desirable, because it cloaks the necessary value content of theory in an 'objective' disguise. The principal function of 'objectivity' is precisely that it *denies* the historical context and ideological nature of theory in its claim to a universal validity.

In this conception of theory the separation of economics and politics can be traced to the particular historical period which produced a conceptual separation between the state (or political society) and civil society: the eighteenth and early nineteenth centuries. The separation broadly corresponds to two distinct spheres of human activity, 'to an emergent society of individuals based on contract and market relations which replaced a status based society, on the one hand, and a state with functions limited to maintaining internal peace, external defence and the requisite conditions for markets, on the other' (Cox, 1981, p. 126). This conception reflects a particular historical distribution of power, as did the notions of mercantilism before it,[6] in which the interests of an emergent middle class are served by the separation and legitimation of an economics free from political (state) intervention. The interests of

this group are further served by the institutionalisation of the separation, in the form of a dominant ideology (liberalism), as well as in state
political processes and norms of behaviour.[7] Liberalism became the
defining perspective, the mainstream of Anglo-Saxon society, that
shaped our conceptions, to the extent of setting the parameters for the
establishment, maintenance and understanding of the postwar international economic order (Gardner, 1956; Ruggie, 1982). The incorporation of a particular notion of economics and politics into a prevailing
ideology subsumes this notion as a given or fixed aspect of the social
definition of reality. In this way it becomes the only legitimate way to
define the field.

In a similar process the content and 'proper' concern of international
relations also reflected the distinction between state and civil society.
As political society is defined by the state, then 'politics' is state action,
particularly to ensure internal peace and the maintenance of the 'requisite conditions for markets'. Only one major political outcome,
the achievement of security from external attack, required the state to
engage in foreign intercourse, and depended on how successfully it did
so. Hence a special mode of thinking was developed in order to understand the processes and outcomes of the 'anarchic' international society.
Given the presumption of separability from politics, the resultant study
of international relations developed a separate set of theories, requiring
particular knowledge, which explained and clarified the outcomes of
state external action, principally in the context of war.

However, much like the separation of economics and politics, the
separation of international relations from politics only makes sense
within the context of this distinction. If conditions change or if we can
demonstrate that the original presumption of separability is historically
and ideologically determined (as we have seen it is), then it becomes
much harder to argue that the study of international relations is separate from the study of politics and that each can be pursued independently of the other. And if international relations is not in general
separate from politics, then the area of inquiry of international political
economy must necessarily include domestic politics and economics.

This theoretical conclusion is easily supported by our experience of
international reality. Here the 'boundary-crossing character of political
processes challenges the assumptions of the autonomy of political processes within their own sphere of competence' (Leurdijk, 1974). The
permeability of state authority is clear. Whether we understand this as
'the domestication of international politics' (Hanrieder, 1978) or the
internationalisation of domestic politics, as implied by Katzenstein
(1977), is for the moment secondary to its theoretical impact. If we
have, as it seems, 'penetrated systems whose boundaries do not conform to the divisions between national and international systems'
(Leurdijk, 1974), the study of international relations in general, and

international political economy in particular, must encompass this reality. Moreover, as Hans Schmitt points out in one of the few analyses of this problem, 'The boundaries of the modern nation-state reflect the interaction of three separately bounded phenomena: the nation, the state, and the economy' (Schmitt, 1972). Any change in the nature and extent of these phenomena or in the nature of their interaction will affect the area of inquiry.

The original definition of international relations produced an emphasis on international *politics* with war and the diplomacy of war (its avoidance and/or successful conclusion) as the principal processes and issue, and the state as the key political entity. Later characterised by Robert Keohane and Joseph Nye as 'state-centric realism' (Keohane and Nye, 1977), the core assumptions of this definition successfully resisted the intellectual attacks of Marxism, from the late nineteenth century onwards, idealism in the 1920s and, in a different sense, behaviouralism in the 1960s (Lenin, 1939; Carr, 1942; Vasquez, 1982). But even though 'state-centric realism' came under increasing criticism from academics in the 1970s, it remained then, and is still today, very attractive to government policy-makers.[8]

Over time the basic assumptions of conventional international relations have been added to or modified. Reacting to and encouraging the forces of nationalism, the state expanded its economic role nationally and internationally through the late nineteenth century, and this modifies the conception of state embodied in the literature. 'State' increasingly becomes equated with 'government', with important implications both for the implicit conception of politics utilised and the notions of political economy absorbed into the assumptions – a point to be further discussed later in the section on the 'Assumptions of international political economy'.

The study of international relations also takes on national characteristics and reflects particular aspects of national concern and perception. We see the academic dominance of the subject by American scholars not just by their production of more books than anyone else, but in the way the field is defined by American writings and policies. Some of the major assumptions and concepts of these American scholars are not shared by others just as 'liberal'. The existence of an independent and traditional 'English school' of thought in the subject is illustrative (R. E. Jones, 1981). Yet as with the so-called 'great debate' between behaviouralism and traditionalism (Wight, 1966), these national differences were initially perceived as differences in method, in line with the 'social science' thinking of the time, rather than political challenges to the prevailing definitions. The gradual change from the post-1945 'state-centric realism' to a 'world politics' perspective introduced concepts and frameworks such as interdependence,[9] issue analysis and regime (Keohane and Nye, 1977; Krasner, 1982) and enlarged the area of inquiry to include new actors, processes and issues, particularly economic ones. Such developments largely reflected changing American perceptions of the world role and capabilities of the United States. But they also sensitised us to the importance of non-state entities and transnational processes and, importantly, prepared the way for a re-emergence of IPE itself.

'Mainstrean' work in international relations now confronts and contains much that is economic, albeit in a particular way. Kenneth Waltz's *Theory of International Politics* (1979) represents a 'state of the art' discussion of the field. His explicit concerns for the nature of thinking and explanations, the problems of encompassing a totality of relationships and his desire to integrate economic relationships all demonstrate that, to a certain extent, the 'conventional' study has taken on board the challenges of the IPE critique.[10] However, much of the dissatisfaction with mainstream definitions of the field still remains. The dissatisfaction is expressed by those who work within a completely different perspective and those who remain broadly within the mainstream but who urge redefinition of the field. One of the first, and best, of such redefinitions was Robert Gilpin's *US Power and the Multinational Corporation* (1975a) in which he discusses the need for a political economy approach and subsequently develops a 'mercantilist' type of explanation. More important, he develops an integrating conception of international political economy that is still relevant and widely used, as 'the reciprocal and dynamic interaction in international relations of the pursuit of wealth and the pursuit of power' (Gilpin, 1975a, p. 43). As you might expect, even this conception can be criticised for its assumptions – that behaviour is rational; that politics imply action; and that international political economy is limited to the international level. The perceived collapse of the postwar economic order produced other analyses that attempted to redefine the area of concern (Bergsten *et al.*, 1975), but the majority of these still incorporated the basic assumptions of mainstream international relations.[11]

The Range of Questions

We have seen how the perspective inherent in theory defines the area of investigation, although we have not yet considered the full range of perspectives on international political economy that have evolved. Perspective also sets what some call the 'approach', and this term can normally be used instead of 'perspective'. Each reflects the overall social and political context of inquiry – the what and the how. Perspectives also contain a range of questions about the field. The range of questions implicit in a perspective is sometimes called (after the French *problematique*) its 'problematic': every perspective contains value judgements as to what is important in the world, what processes are critical and what outcomes are preferable. Its problematic translates these into an analytical framework, which describes and explains, and more important, into a rationalisation of the perspective. Rationalisation gives direction and meaning to the perspective and also enables those who work within it to understand the perspective on its own terms. Each perspective can only be judged on the basis of whether or not the individual accepts its problematic. Does one see the world in terms of the 'liberal', 'Marxist', 'mercantilist', or any other problematic? The choice eventually comes down to the individual's own values because there cannot be any logical *a priori* reasons for selecting one perspective over another, or indeed for developing your own.

International political economy as a focus of inquiry extends beyond the problematic of conventional international relations, although we have seen that this itself has changed. Questions of war and security are clearly of fundamental importance, but these questions are part of an international political economy and are meaningful in as much as they relate to both politics and economics. An IPE problematic will initially ask questions about assumptions and values. IPE developed as a critique of existing orthodoxy through exposing the implicit assumptions and values in accepted perspectives (Gilpin, 1975a; Blake and Walters, 1976). Consequently most of the perspectives of IPE are consciously critical approaches which link empirical study much more explicitly into an analysis of basic assumptions and values. IPE *starts* from an awareness of the centrality of perspective in setting the problematic: what you ask is often more important than the answers you get. Because what you ask and how you go about getting the answer nearly always determine that answer for you. If your problematic identifies, say, questions of regime and regime change as important, you might be tempted to assume that contemporary IPE consists of myriad and complex processes of regime construction and change. Yet, another problematic may see regimes as peripheral to the major concerns of IPE, as particular and limited instances of the attempt by a declining hegemonic power to maintain control (Strange, 1982). What one problematic categorises as a central question needing urgent resolution, another ignores.

An IPE problematic also asks questions about the relationship between politics and economics at the international level and about the link between domestic policies and processes. Concepts such as hegemony and imperialism link politics and economics and require an examination of the precise nature of the relationship (Hirsch *et al.*, 1977, ch. 1). Individual policies and events are questioned for their implications for other areas, for example, the impact of the Vietnam War upon the unchallenged supremacy of the dollar as an international currency, or the effect of today's rapidly changing international monetary situation upon general world political and economic stability. No process, policy, or event is unquestioningly accepted as either purely economic or political or, for that matter, as purely international or domestic. We have seen that the traditional definition of international relations (IR) precludes international political economy from inquiring into domestic processes, but now the problematic reflects the superfluous character of the IR/politics distinction for most issues and problems. For many processes of IPE, the distinction is simply irrelevant.

Finally, the problematic also directs attention to preferable outcomes and ways of attaining these outcomes. Perspectives of IPE embody a theory of change, however implicit, and in some cases, however simplistic, which prevents a past, present and future image. Analysis of the present is sustained by historical understanding of change, and action is directed towards achieving the future according to the particular image presented by the problematic. In the prevailing conventional problematic change, action and the future are reflections of the present distribution of power and wealth. The operations of the International Monetary Fund (IMF), for example, clearly reflect a 'liberal' problematic; economic problems in countries are defined as those of increasing efficiency, pushing up levels of production, increasing capital investment, and so on. They are problems of 'technical' change within the existing framework.

Other non-conventional problematics focus on questions which challenge the basis of the existing system of world economy – questions of justice, questions of the distribution of wealth, education and technology, and questions about food. These basic questions are linked to further analyses of how the present situation arose and what can be done to move out of it towards some preferred alternative goal. The various 'structural' perspectives of IPE, particularly those concerned directly with the creation of a New International Economic Order (NIEO), contain an imperative for change based on historical analysis and a critique of existing structures and processes (Cox, 1981). In this respect the crucial part of the problematic is that which links analysis to action, that part which produces specific questions, particular political policies and bargaining positions from generalised statements. The link between theory and practice, and in some perspectives the *unity* of theory and practice in the concept of praxis, transforms an intellectual position into a political force – whether it be for a continuance of the existing state of affairs or for a fundamental change in those affairs.

Assumptions of International Political Economy

The third set of criteria for identifying the field of IPE presents many problems in itself. Whereas it has been reasonably straightforward to lay out its area of inquiry and its problematic *in very general terms*, it is part of the nature of the study that no clear set of assumptions exists. As we have seen, the field is perceived from several perspectives each of which offers a different and contending view. But why not take bits from each and construct a correct – or at least a comprehensive – view? At first this sounds sensible and attractive, but we quickly come up against problems. First, our 'correct' view is almost always not someone else's, in other words, there is not necessarily any one 'correct' perspective. Secondly, what 'bits' do we select? And thirdly, every 'bit' we take from a perspective comes with its own specific assumptions which give it meaning and value. Every concept takes its meaning from the context of its perspective. This means that the development of a comprehensive perspective which combines elements of disparate approaches is not a very difficult task (R. J. B. Jones, 1982).

Each perspective not only embodies an explicit analysis of how the international political economy works, but also contains an epistemology, that is, a view of *how* we know what we know. A comparison of liberal analyses with Marxist perspectives reveals a different methodology of investigation, and almost a different way of defining what is evidence and what techniques of investigation are acceptable. Differences in perspectives go much deeper than just different views of how the system works. Given the difficulties involved in the synthesis of a comprehensive perspective on international political economy, how do we evaluate the perspectives and 'modified' perspectives we actually have?

Our analysis so far suggests a possible criterion: the ability of a theory, derived from a particular perspective, to 'stand outside of itself' and explain events different from those assumed in its perspective. In the context of a review of dependency and development Jacob Reuveny (1982) has called this quality 'theoretical openness' and this is a good way of seeing the criterion. Reuveny develops three elements of 'theoretical openness' which can also be applied to IPE theory:

(1) substantive aspects – the capacity of the framework to explain situations which essentially differ from those which shaped the original premisses of the perspective, accounting for both similarities and differences;

(2) analytical aspects – the extent to which concepts, analogies and metaphors enhance or impede understanding of new situations;

(3) ideological aspects – the degree to which a certain perspective is inherently tied to a definite ideological argument, leading to a consistent interpretation of a given reality in a way which fits the premisses of the ideology. Ideological closedness implies a rejection of both data and modes of explanation which are inconsistent with the ideological tenets (see Reuveny, 1982, pp. 6–7).

We shall look at each of these aspects starting with the most important, the ideological.

Robert Cox has extended our understanding of the ideological nature of theory in international relations and his arguments are used here (see Cox, 1981, pp. 128–9). Theory, for Cox, has two distinct purposes which give rise to two different kinds of theory. The first purpose is 'to be a guide to help solve the problems posed within the terms of the particular perspective which was the point of departure'. This gives rise to 'problem-solving theory' which works within the given social and political framework primarily to 'solve' policy problems or problems within particular specialised activities. Realism as currently portrayed in IR is problem-solving theory, as is monetarism and neo-classical theory. The second purpose of theory is 'to become clearly aware of the perspective which gives rise to theorising and its relation to other perspectives (to achieve a perspective on perspectives)'. This leads to 'critical theory' – critical 'in the sense that it stands apart from the prevailing order of the world and asks how that order comes about'. Critical theory challenges the very 'framework of action' that problem-solving theory works within and takes for granted. Critical theory is concerned with the overall 'process of historical change'.

Reuveny's category of 'ideological openness' can now be broadly interpreted as the question of whether (or to what extent) a perspective is problem-solving theory or critical theory. Perspectives often contain elements of both, but are normally dominated by one type of theory. One is not necessarily 'better' than the other in political terms. If we consciously or unconsciously agree with the prevailing distribution of wealth and power, then we would tend towards problem-solving theory, if not, then critical theory is more attractive. But using these categories it is important to establish whether and to what extent theory is 'problem-solving' or 'critical' because we then begin to understand the capabilities, limitations and problems of the perspective outside of its own social, political and historical context. We are then in a position to judge the worth of a theory independently of the criteria the theory itself puts forward.

'Problem-solving' theory of IPE, for example, takes the current framework for action as a given and derives meaning and policy from this context. In particular, it assumes a future very much like the present and does not consider problems of historical change in any real sense. Current 'problem-solving' analyses of the problems of the international political economy involve the assumption of the same goals – economic efficiency leading to 'full' employment at low rates of inflation – and the same mechanisms to achieve these goals – increased investment, higher productivity, interstate regimes of free trade and directed movement of capital – as the circumstances that brought us these problems. The recipe is more of the same. On the other hand, we could equally see how the radical perspectives on international political economy may be too committed and too closed in the ideological sense. Most radical perspectives *assume* that economic relations, that is, capitalist relations, are inherently exploitative. This assumption cannot be examined within the perspective itself. Hence it is important to look for the basic assumptions contained within each theory: assumptions (*a*) of the nature of economic relations (harmonious, exploitative, or sometimes both?); (*b*) of the relationship between politics and econom-ics (separated with one dominating the other, or integral as 'political economy'?); (*c*) of the nature of the international system (static equilib-rium, or inherently dynamic) leading to assumptions of change (how achieved?); and (*d*) of the basic units of analysis (world system, world economy, international economy, state, firms, classes, social groups?). These assumptions taken together identify the ideological context of the perspective and signify the extent to which the perspective is locked within this context (Gilpin, 1975a).

The 'analytical openness' of theory is related to ideological aspects in as much as the perspective defines, through its problematic, the units and modes of analysis, as well as the general concepts of the theory. Let us consider the problems involved. First, the unit(s) of analysis. Con-ventionally the state is the unit of analysis in international relations with a consequent distinction between the level of analysis – at the level of the international system or at the level of the state itself. The choice of each level changes the analysis. How far is our analysis helped by focusing solely on the state as the unit of political economy? Marxists identify social class as a prime unit of analysis. Those who adopt a transnational or pluralist perspective will include a range of entities and non-state processes, while mercantilists argue that a focus upon the state is an essential, and unchanging, element of the international power structure. And in analysing international economic relations the terms 'international economy' is commonly used as a unit of analysis to describe the sum of economic interactions (normally exchange trans-actions) between national economies and is, therefore, a state-based concept.

We have to question each perspective for its ability to enhance under-standing of a whole range of new developments, such as the emergence of a 'world' economy. A 'world' economy has been defined by Charles-Albert Michalet in terms of production and service structures which extend beyond national territorial boundaries, in contrast with the international economy based on flows of goods, payments and capi-tal (Michalet, 1982). Michalet's thesis is that both structural models coexist in the world today: 'international' (old and of declining impor-tance); and 'world' (new and of growing importance). Hence the term 'world political economy' is often used instead of 'international political economy' to denote a much broader concept of political economy, one not necessarily defined and limited by the state. A perspective that focuses on the state, such as the mercantilist, or a liberal transnational perspective would not identify such a development.

Secondly, how open are the specific concepts derived from various perspectives? To what extent do existing concepts enhance or impede understanding of the new situation? Without going through each perspective concept by concept, we would find it difficult to give any assessment of this question. But several common problems exist, which suggests that existing concepts of international political economy are not as open as they might be; that is, they impede analytical understanding.

The key concept in IPE is the nature of political–economic relations, which is derived from notions of the nature of politics itself. In most non-Marxist perspectives politics is conceptualised in a particular way: politics is concerned with the state – but not just the state in general, but the state as defined by Max Weber. Weber defines the state as an organisation – government – which claims a monopoly on the legitimate use of force. This conception, as David Sylvan so ably shows in his analysis of the 'newest mercantilism' (1981), gives rise to a particular notion of political–economic relations. 'From a theoretical standpoint economic activities are linked to politics insofar as they involve the government as actor or object of action. From a methodological standpoint, then, the way to study political–economic relations is by looking at actions' (Sylvan, 1981, pp. 388–9; also Strange and Tooze, 1981, ch. 1). The first implication is that politics is defined narrowly with the result that political economy is defined as government economic activities and international political economy as the attempts by governments to regulate and manage international economic relations (Spero, 1977).

Alternative conceptions see political economy as much wider – economics is never above or below politics – economics *is* politics. A narrow conception of political economy precludes understanding of many new situations and skews the overall description of the world political economy itself towards government activity and policy, rather than at the totality of political–economic relationships.

The conception of politics as action is inherent in liberal, transnational, mercantilist and some other non-structural perspectives. Politics as 'actions' takes no account of the broader framework within which action takes place. This framework is rarely institutionalised, particularly at the international level, but encompasses a wide range of social relationships which set the parameters for action and inaction. Again Robert Cox puts this very succinctly: 'action is never absolutely free but takes place within a framework' which has the form of an historical structure, a particular combination of thought patterns, material conditions and human institutions which has a certain coherence among its elements. These structures do not determine people's actions in any mechanical sense but constitute the context of habits, pressures, expectations and constraints within which action takes place. (Cox, 1981, p. 135; cf. Sylvan, 1981, pp. 388–93)

Clearly, a conception of political economy which fails to take account of this broader framework is essentially limited in its explanatory potential. It can only describe and, perhaps, explain actions and issues within the terms of the actions and issues themselves. It can never explain why some actions are never taken or how some issues never achieve even discussion. The major weaknesses of such important analytical concepts as 'issue analysis' and 'regime analysis' is precisely that they fail to take account of the historical structure of the world political economy. And, in so doing, they incorporate certain values, which in the main reflect the present American position in and attitudes to the world economy, which makes them 'problem-solving' analyses rather than critical concepts.

The extent of analytical and conceptual openness is critical in assessing the worth of a perspective. We have seen that just in respect of two basic areas – the definition of the units of analysis and the concept of political economy – many problems arise because of the values contained within the concepts themselves. The third element of openness, the 'substantive', is even more of a problem. Substantive openness, as suggested by Reuveny, is 'the capacity of the framework to explain situations which essentially differ from those which shaped the original premises of the [perspective], accounting for both similarities and differences' (Reuveny, 1982, p. 6).

The origins of 'conventional' economics, politics and international relations were all within the similar general social and political context of the late eighteenth and nineteenth centuries. All three have had to face new situations and problems which were essentially different from and could not be explained in terms of the conditions prevailing in those times. The enormous differences between then and now just, say, in the growth of the world economy or in the power of the state, confront these historically located perspectives with great difficulties. A particular difficulty for 'radical' as well as 'conventional' perspectives has been the emergence of the Third World, and the problem of explaining the Third World with a single set of concepts based on Western experience and values. The cultural values implicit in most perspectives quickly reveal their limitations in explaining other Western and especially non-Western experiences.

The combination of historical change and geographical, non-Western expansion of the world political economy produced problems for existing perspectives and generated a whole new range of perspectives at the same time. Dissatisfaction with the apparent inability of perspectives based on the previous historical experience to describe and explain brings with it a desire for alternative approaches as it brings about a new problematic. These new problematics focus on a different range of questions than established perspectives, and suggest different descriptions, explanations and policies. Typical of the non-traditional perspectives is the 'structuralist' approach to international relations (which will be briefly discussed later), which does not suffer from the assumption of the ideological separation of economics and politics and is generally concerned with specifying and describing world structures of dominance and dependency, rather than focusing on interstate relations.

If the necessity of coming to terms with new situations has led to the growth of new perspectives, we are still left with the question of how well these perspectives, old and new, explain situations. No one perspective at this moment provides an adequate description and explanation of contemporary world political economy. And no body of empirical research is sufficient to sustain or falsify any one perspective. Some perspectives highlight certain areas, some others.

Much good and useful work has been done on a wide variety of important problems, areas and issues, including monetary problems, trade relations and, increasingly, the service structure. But as yet we do not know enough of the actual workings and processes of change in the structure as a whole to support any one coherent description, let alone a single explanation, of the world political economy. Specific questions related to particular structures of the world economy, such as security, production, trade and transport, credit and money, and the communication and knowledge structure, can be analysed in a problem-solving sense that, if done with an explicit awareness of assumptions and values, can be very useful. But we cannot assume that such studies necessarily add to our overall understanding unless they are conducted in a critical way, in the sense we have discussed. Better than producing value-laden and culture-bound studies would be a move towards such a critical perspective that is explicitly aware of its own cultural and value assumptions.

The moral for the student of international political economy, as we are all aware, is to be truly sceptical of all claims and analyses in the entire literature. Only then is one in a position to begin to evaluate what is useful, and what is not, along the lines suggested here.

Perspectives on International Political Economy

In conclusion, it may perhaps be helpful briefly to review the major current perspectives on IPE. The intention is to indicate the basic literature within each approach, rather than to explicate and then offer a coherent critique. Others have reviewed and analysed the main perspectives already (Gilpin, 1975a, 1975b; Petras, 1978, esp. ch. 1; Baldwin, 1978; Cox, 1979). What is perhaps worth emphasising is that the perspectives reviewed here are none of them fully worked-out bodies of theory with clearly articulated ideas and propositions. Rather, more often than not, they represent clusters of opinions and shared values which form a basis for analysis. Individual authors often cut across perspectives in such a way as to produce a unique view and we do not mean to force here any of the literature into a category. The 'labels' given to the perspectives are not categories imposed by us, they are the means by which authors identify themselves and through which they communicate with others.

'Liberal' Perspectives

The 'liberal' perspective is considered the basis for 'conventional' or 'mainstream' approaches, and we have already discussed its historical basis throughout the chapter. It is, above all, problem-solving theory of a fairly recent kind. Its basic assumptions include the essentially harmonious nature of economic relations (which are still analytically separated from politics); a prime value of efficiency above all other social values; a concept of the world economy based on equilibrium processes; a goal of global welfare and a focus on the state, which provides secure political frameworks for markets.

The IPE critique of 'state-centric' international politics and neo-classical theory of international economics, based on notions of comparative advantage, has produced two distinct approaches. The weaknesses of international economics have been criticised by political 'scientists' and this has led to an approach known as 'the politics of international economic relations' which has attempted to marry world politics and international economics.[12] And if the marriage has not been completely successful, it is because both partners brought with them critical assumptions from their individual pasts. Although much interesting work has been done within this approach, it is essentially limited by its conceptualisation which is based on an analysis of the politics of economic interactions between *national* economies. In other words, the perspective is limited by the assumptions of state-centricity which give it its 'political' content.

A critique of 'state-centricity', however, provides the basis for the second approach within the liberal perspective. This is IPE as 'the politics of interdependence and transnational relations', organised around what Robert Gilpin calls 'the sovereignty at bay model' (Gilpin, 1975b). Transnationalism proposes a decline of the state and an image of IPE consisting of a multiplicity of actors, the most important of which is the multinational corporation, set in the context of a web of state-boundary crossing 'transnational' processes which engender 'interdependence'. This perspective is also limited by its assumptions of the potency of economic forces. It severely underestimates the importance and power of the state (Waltz, 1979) and overestimates the degree of ideological neutrality of economic processes and institutions. That is, it takes little or no account of its historical context (Cooper, 1968; Morse, 1976; Keohane and Nye, 1977; Michalak, 1979).

'Mercantilism' and 'Neo-Mercantilism'

The contemporary mercantilist perspective is partially a revival of the mercantilism of the sixteenth and seventeenth centuries, in response to the declining ability of the liberal perspective to provide both explanation and a basis for policy. The essence of mercantilism, as defined by Gilpin, is 'the subservience of the economy to the state and its interests – interests that range from matters of domestic welfare to those of international security' (Gilpin, 1975b). The assumption is that economic relations are inherently conflictual and dominated by national self-interest and extensive governmental involvement. Economics is determined by politics and only makes sense in the context of the state (Gilpin, 1975b; Block, 1977; Krasner, 1978; Viner, 1948).

Mercantilism is very attractive to government policy-makers faced with demands for protection from their constituents but it incorporates a narrow 'statist' view of international political economy that is incapable of registering major changes presently occurring in the world economy. It is also made less useful because of its narrow conception of political economy based on a particular definition of the state (Sylvan, 1981).

'Structuralist' Perspectives

Although a distinct perspective, mercantilism shares with liberalism an ethnocentricity derived from its historical origins. As with all ethnocentric theory, the explanation of phenomena outside of the culture base is biased and inappropriate. In this case both liberal and mercantilist perspectives fail to provide satisfactory explanations for the conditions of life for the majority of the world's population.

Structuralism is a perspective which analyses the development of the world political economy as a whole. Its main concern 'has been with the manner in which those nations located at the center of the global economy created and continue to maintain structures and patterns of exchange that systematically benefit these center nations at the expense of those in the periphery' (Petras, 1978, pp. 23–4). This analysis contributes much to an understanding of global political economy and contains many individual statements within it – particularly Galtung and Prebisch, as well as others (Galtung, 1971, 1981; Prebisch, 1964; Hveem, 1973; Targ, 1976) – and has given rise to a whole movement for change in the world political economy. The political manifestation of the movement for change has been the demand for a 'New International Economic Order' and this has generated much literature (Cox, 1981). Structuralist thinking is based on a series of abstractions that relate directly to specific historical processes. In this way structuralism explains at the level of generalities but cannot handle instances of specific historical dominance.

'World Systems' Perspective

The 'world systems' perspective also analyses the development of the world political economy as a whole, but takes as its major unit of analysis the world system (of capitalism) itself rather than nations within the system, as do the 'structuralists'. Like the 'structuralist' perspective, however, the literature does not form a single, coherent theory. Its basis is found in the critique of the 'developmentalist' view of liberal political economy (Gunder Frank, 1979; Baran, 1957; Cardoso, 1977), but has more recently been articulated by Immanuel Wallerstein and other major 'dependency' writers. The general direction of the perspective is very simple: specific events within the world system can only be explained in terms of the demands of the system as a whole. Action is related to the system.

Many problems arise from this perspective which are impossible to summarise here but can be attributed to problems with a far-reaching holistic view of the world, which can be very superficial, and a focus on exchange relations, as distinct from the production relations of the structure of world economy.[13]

Marxist and Radical Perspectives

Again we find great difficulty in locating the literature on these perspectives within a single theoretical corpus of work and even greater difficulty in summarising it briefly here. What is distinct from all the other perspectives except for the 'world systems' work, is that the intellectual basis of these perspectives is historical materialism (Mandel, 1968; Marx, 1947a, 1947b). So instead of the focus on the state, as in mercantilism, this perspective focuses on the production process and its dynamics and structures. Writers such as Frank and Baran are within both the 'radical' and 'world system' perspectives and, in many cases, the two perspectives are complementary. The common assumption of these perspectives is 'a relational interpretation of development and underdevelopment' (Reuveny, 1982, p. 3). The concept of imperialism is central to this relational interpretation, as is the notion of the 'internationalization of capital'.[14] Classical Marxist concepts and theories have undergone change as new varieties of theory have been developed out of them: most important has been the work of Arghiri Emmanuel, Samir Amin and Ernest Mandel.

A simple listing of the literature only serves to illustrate the intellectual variety and proliferation of work within this perspective. Because it is written from a different intellectual tradition with totally different assumptions about the nature, structures and processes of international political economy, any critique or assessment of this perspective from the 'liberal' mainstream position involves an ideological statement of one's own world view. In the nature of the fundamental differences in the perspectives it is not possible either to explain or deny one perspective from the point of view of the other, without invoking basic assumptions that cannot be falsified. Hence evaluation of this approach is a question of basic values and assumptions.

The questions and procedures outlined in this chapter are intended to help with such an evaluation of this and other perspectives on IPE. But the guidelines outlined here can only be useful if we, as individuals, can recognise and be aware of the way in which understanding IPE reflects our own values and assumptions. The choice is up to us.

Notes: Chapter 1

1   Economists have only recently developed theories of the 'open' economy; see Rudiger Dornbusch, *Open Economy Macro-Economics* (1980), while variants of 'political economy' based on the political–business cycle or political theories of rational choice usually ignore the international dimension; see Bruno S. Frey, *Modern Political Economy* (1978).
2   Even the notion of 'system' contains assumptions that affect its possible use. 'System' implies equilibrium and a tendency to return to equilibrium.
3   Karl Polanyi was among the first 'modern' writers to link these domains in *The Great Transformation* (1944).
4   For an early critique of 'security politics' see R. Keohane and J. S. Nye, 'Transgovernmental relations and international organizations', *World Politics*, vol. XXVII, no. 1 (1974), pp. 39–62.
5   My own thoughts on this problem have been greatly aided and stimulated by: Robert Cox, 'Social forces, states and world order: beyond international relations theory', *Millennium, Journal of International Studies*, vol. 10, no. 2 (Summer 1981); and John Maclean, 'Political theory, international theory and problems of ideology', initially given as a paper to BISA Theory Group and later published in the same edition of *Millennium* as the Cox article, pp. 126–55.
6   For an analysis of classical mercantilism see Jacob Viner, 'Power versus plenty as objectives of foreign policy in the 17th and 18th centuries', *World Politics*, vol. 1, no. 1 (1948), pp. 1–29.
7   Friedrich List, writing from outside the ideology, clearly identified the political nature and intent of the separation, in *The National System of Political Economy* (1928).
8   For why this should be so see Robert L. Rothstein, 'On the costs of realism', *Political Science Quarterly*, vol. XXXVII, no. 3 (1972), pp. 347–62.
9   The initial discussion by Richard Cooper, *The Economics of Interdependence*

(1968), paved the way for an enormous literature, part of which was well summarised by David Baldwin, 'Interdependence and power: a conceptual analysis', *International Organization*, vol. 34, no. 3 (1980), pp. 471–506.

10 For an incisive critique of Waltz see Rosecrance, 1981, 'International theory revisited', *International Organization*, vol. 35, no. 4 (Autumn 1981), pp. 691–713.

11 One way of moving out of state-centred analyses without falling into the pitfalls of transnationalism is to use a 'sectoral political economy' analysis. See Roger Tooze, 'Sectoral analysis and international political economy', in R. J. Barry Jones (ed.), *Studies in Political Economy* (1982).

12 Petras, 1978, pp. 17–20, has an excellent discussion of this approach, typified by Spero, 1977, Blake and Walters 1976, and Bergsten *et al.*, 1975. The latter has an extensive bibliography.

13 The best review of the 'world system' perspective I have seen is Bruce Andrews, 'The political economy of world capitalism: theory and practice', *International Organization*, vol. 36, no. 1 (Winter 1982), pp. 135–63.

14 The foundation is V. I. Lenin, *Imperialism – the Highest Stage of Capitalism* (1939), but the best review is Tom Kemp, 'The Marxist theory of imperialism', in Roger Owen and Bob Sutcliffe (eds), *Studies in the Theory of Imperialism* (1972), pp. 13–34. On the internationalisation of capital see, particularly, Stephen Hymer, 'International politics and international economics: a radical approach', in Leon Lindberg *et al.* (eds), *Stress and Contradiction in Modern Capitalism* (1975), pp. 355–72.

References: Chapter 1

Amin, S. (1978), *The Law of Value and Historical Materialism* (New York: Monthly Review Press).

Andrews, B. (1982), 'The political economy of world capitalism: theory and practice', *International Organization*, vol. 36, no. 1 (Winter), pp. 135–63.

Baldwin, D. (1978), 'International political economy and the international monetary system', *International Organization*, vol. 32, no. 2 (Spring), pp. 497–512.

Baldwin, D. (1980), 'Interdependence and power: a conceptual analysis', *International Organization*, vol. 34, no. 3 (Summer), pp. 471–506.

Baran, P. (1957), *The Political Economy of Growth* (New York: Monthly Review Press).

Bergsten, F. C., Keohane, R. O., and Nye, J. S. (1975), 'International economics and international politics: a framework for analysis', *International Organization*, vol. 29, no. 1 (Winter), pp. 3–36.

Blake, D. H., and Walters, R. S. (1976), *The Politics of Global Economic Relations* (Englewood Cliffs, NJ: Prentice-Hall).

Block, F. L. (1977), *The Origins of International Economic Disorder* (Berkeley, CA: University of California Press).

Cardoso, F. H. (1977), 'The consumption of dependency theory in the US', *Latin American Research Review*, vol. 12, no. 1, pp. 7–24.

Cardoso, F. H., and Faletto, E. (1978), *Dependency and Development in Latin America* (Berkeley, CA: University of California Press).

Carr, E. H. (1942), *The Twenty Years' Crisis, 1919–1939* (London: Macmillan).

Carr, E. H. (1945), *Nationalism and After* (London: Macmillan).

Cooper, R. (1968), *The Economics of Interdependence* (New York: McGraw-Hill).

Cox, R. W. (1979), 'Ideologies and the new international economic order: reflections on some recent literature', *International Organization*, vol. 33, no. 2, pp. 257–67.

Cox, R. W. (1981), 'Social forces, states and world order: beyond international relations theory', *Millennium, Journal of International Studies*, vol. 10, no. 2, pp. 126–55.

Dornbusch, R. (1980), *Open Economy Macro-Economics* (London: McGraw-Hill).

dos Santos, T. (1976), 'The crisis of contemporary capitalism', *Latin American Perspectives*, vol. 3, no. 2, pp. 84–99.

Emmanuel, A. (1975), *Unequal Exchange* (New York: Monthly Review Press).

Frey, B. (1978), *Modern Political Economy* (London: Martin Robertson).

Galtung, J. (1971), 'A structural theory of imperialism', *Journal of Peace Research*, vol. 8, no. 2, pp. 81–117.

Galtung, J. (1981), 'A structural theory of imperialism: ten years later', *Millennium*, vol. 9, no. 3, pp. 181–6.

Gardner, R. (1956), *Sterling–Dollar Diplomacy*, 2nd edn (Oxford: Clarendon Press).

Gilpin, R. (1975a), *US Power and the Multinational Corporation* (New York: Basic Books).

Gilpin, R. (1975b), 'Three models of the future', *International Organization*, vol. 29, no. 1, pp. 37–60.

Gunder Frank, A. (1979), *Dependent Accumulation and Underdevelopment* (New York: Monthly Review Press).

Hanrieder, W. F. (1978), 'Dissolving international politics: reflections on the nation-state', *American Political Science Review*, vol. 72, no. 4 (December), pp. 1276–87.

Hirsch, F., Doyle, M., and Morse, E. (1977), *Alternatives to Monetary Disorder* (New York: McGraw-Hill).

Hollist, W. L., and Rosenau, J. (eds) (1981), 'World systems debates', *International Studies Quarterly*, 25 March; reprinted 1982.

Hveem, H. (1973), 'The global dominance system', *Journal of Peace Research*, vol. 10, no. 4, pp. 319–40.

Hymer, S. (1975), 'International politics and international economics: a radical approach', in L. Lindberg, R. Alford, C. Crouch and C. Offe (eds), *Stress and Contradiction in Modern Capitalism* (Lexington, MA: Lexington Books), pp. 355–72.

Jones, R. E. (1981), 'The English school of international relations: a case for closure', *Review of International Studies*, vol. 7, no. 1 (January), pp. 1–14.

Jones, R. J. B. (1981), 'International political economy: problems and issues – part I', *Review of International Studies*, vol. 7, no. 4 (October), pp. 245–60.

Jones, R. J. B. (1982), 'International political economy: perspectives and prospects – part II', *Review of International Studies*, vol. 8, no. 1 (January), pp. 39–52.

Katzenstein, P. (ed.) (1977), 'Between power and plenty: foreign economic policies of advanced industrial states', *International Organization*, special issue, vol. 31, no. 4 (Autumn).

Kemp, T. (1972), 'The Marxist theory of imperialism', in Roger Owen and Bob Sutcliffe (eds), *Studies in the Theory of Imperialism* (London: Longman), pp. 13–34.

Keohane, R., and Nye, J. (1977), *Power and Interdependence: World Politics in Transition* (Boston, MA: Little, Brown).

Krasner, S. (1978), *Defending the National Interest* (Berkeley, CA: University of California Press).

Krasner, S. (ed.) (1982), *International Organization*, special issue, vol. 36, no. 2 (Spring).

Lenin, V. I. (1939), *Imperialism – the Highest Stage of Capitalism* (Moscow: International Publishers).

Leurdijk, J. H. (1974), 'From international to transnational politics', *International Social Science Journal*, no. 1, p. 59.

List, F. (1928), *The National System of Political Economy* (London: Longmans, Green).

Maclean, J. (1981), 'Political theory, international theory and problems of ideology', paper given to BISA Theory Group, published in *Millennium, Journal of International Studies*, vol. 10, no. 2 (Summer), pp. 102–25.

Mandel, E. (1968), 'The contradictions of capitalism', in E. Mandel, *Marxist Economic Theory* (New York: Monthly Review Press), Vol. 1, ch. 5.

Mandel, E. (1975), *Late Capitalism* (London: New Left Books).

Marx, K. (1947a), *Wages, Price and Profit* (Moscow: Progress Publishers).

Marx, K. (1947b), *Wage-Labour and Capital* (Moscow: Progress Publishers).

Michalak, S. J., jr (1979), 'Theoretical perspectives for understanding international interdependence', *World Politics*, vol. 32, no. 1 (October), pp. 136–50.

Michalet, C.-A. (1982), 'From international to world economy', in H. Makler, A. Martinelli and N. Smelser (eds), *The New International Economy* (London: Sage), pp. 37–58.

Morse, E. (1976), 'Interdependence in world affairs', in J. N. Rosenau, K. W. Thompson and G. Boyd (eds), *World Politics: An Introduction* (New York: The Free Press), pp. 660–81.

Petras, J. (1978), *Critical Perspectives on Imperialism and Social Class in the Third World* (New York: Monthly Review Press).

Prebisch, R. (1964), 'Towards a new trade policy for development', United Nations, UNCTAD E/Conf. 46/3, 12 February.

Reuveny, J. (1982), 'Dependency and development: contending positions and a possible alternative', paper presented at XIIth World IPSA Congress, Rio de Janeiro, 9–14 August, mimeo.

Rosecrance, R. (1981), 'International theory revisited', *International Organization*, vol. 35, no. 4 (Autumn), pp. 691–713.

Rothstein, R. L. (1972), 'On the costs of realism', *Political Science Quarterly*, vol. 37, no. 3, pp. 347–62.

Ruggie, J. (1982), 'Embedded liberalism in the postwar economic order', *International Organization*, vol. 36, no. 2 (Spring), pp. 379–416.

Schmitt, H. (1972), 'The national boundary in politics and economics', in R. L. Merritt (ed.), *Communication in International Politics* (London: University of Illinois Press), p. 421.

Spero, J. E. (1977), *The Politics of International Economic Relations* (London: Allen & Unwin); 2nd edn 1981.

Strange, S. (1970), 'International economics and international relations: a case of mutual neglect', *International Affairs*, vol. 46, no. 2 (April), pp. 304–15.

Strange, S. (1975), 'What is economic power and who has it?', *International Journal*, vol. 30, no. 2 (Spring), pp. 207–24.

Strange, S. (1982), 'Cave! hic dragones', in S. Krasner (ed.), *International Organization*, special issue on regimes, vol. 36, no. 2 (Spring).

Strange, S., and Tooze, R. (eds) (1981), *The International Politics of Surplus Capacity* (London: Allen & Unwin), ch. 1.

Sylvan, D. J. (1981), 'The newest mercantilism', *International Organization*, vol. 35, no. 2 (Spring), pp. 375–93.

Targ, H. (1976), 'Global dominance and dependence, post-industrialism and IR theory: a review', *International Studies Quarterly*, vol. 20, no. 3 (September), pp. 461–82.

Vasquez, J. A. (1982), *The Power of Power Politics* (New Brunswick, NJ: Rutgers University Press).

Viner, J. (1948), 'Power versus plenty as objectives of foreign policy in the 17th and 18th centuries', *World Politics*, vol. 1, no. 1, pp. 1–29.

Wallerstein, I. (1974), *The Modern World System* (New York: Academic Press).

Wallerstein, I. (1979), *The Capitalist World Economy* (Cambridge: CUP).

Waltz, K. (1979), *Theory of International Politics* (Reading, MA: Addison-Wesley).

Wight, M. (1966), 'Why is there no international theory?', in Herbert Butterfield and Martin Wight (eds), *Diplomatic Investigations* (Cambridge, MA: Harvard University Press), pp. 17–34.

2

Why Economic History?

DAVID WIGHTMAN

> Nobody can hope to understand the economic
> phenomena of any, including the present, epoch
> who has not an adequate command of the histor-
> ical facts and an adequate amount of historical
> sense or what may be described as historical
> experience.
>
> Joseph A. Schumpeter,
> *The History of Economic Analysis*

The point of this quotation is worth elaboration. As all human societies
are subject to change, they reveal their characteristics not simultaneously, but successively over time. To see them flat is not to see them
at all. A snapshot view will miss the sense of direction and movement;
it will fail to distinguish what is old from what is new, the elements of
continuity from the appearance of change.

Yet ignorance of history is all too common among contemporary
analysts and is compounded, particularly in the United States, by
grant-awarding bodies which advertise their public spirit by concentrat-
ing on the agenda of government. The past is past; what matters is the
mastery of the present and future. In this trend-setting milieu, 'have
concept, will travel', sounds more creative, scientific, forward-looking
and more adventurous. The mere arrival of an apparently novel concept
is sure to inspire a heady rush into print or the nearest academic fair-
ground.[1] That the academic trail is already littered with the rotting
remains of past fads is no reason for caution. The historian, surveying
the scene years later, can only wonder at the innocence of those who
take the intellectual fashions of their day for the true nature of the
world they inhabit.[2] For it is part of the same indifference to past
experience that such ignorance includes the history of ideas, concepts
and theories. Here, for a start, the historian can be helpful in tracing
the historical connotation of terms commonly used in contemporary
thinking. The word 'imperialism', for example, has been used to

describe the government of Napoleon III, the enlargement of colonial empires and the expansion of all capitalist states. It has been transplanted into phrases such as Nazi imperialism and communist imperialism. What then is the reality it is meant to describe? It is perhaps worth noting in passing that the teachings of Marx and Lenin were rooted in arguments about economic history.

The economic historian is interested in the peculiar circumstances of time and place which gave rise to economic theories or ideologies and occasioned their demise. A curious feature of the controversy over classical trade theory, for example, is that its critics, as Myint (1958) has pointed out, are really concerned to show that the pattern of international trade specialisation in the nineteenth century was harmful to the economic development prospects of Third World countries. But instead of demonstrating this directly by the methods of economic history, they concentrate their attack on the theory itself as the responsible factor.

Free trade is still used as an ideal against which to interpret trends in national economic policies. The opposite direction, towards government intervention, leads to mercantilism or neo-mercantilism.[3] Free trade ideology is British by origin and American by adoption. It was never the standpoint from which less powerful nations judged their economic self-interest. In the 1840s a brilliant German propagandist, Friedrich List, pointed out that free trade is not for universal consumption. Studies of wealth and problems of exchange cannot be conceived on one plane, but only in relation to living, changing nations on different and shifting planes. Each stage of economic development through which a nation passes calls for the adoption of a particular policy by that state. In Britain such views were commonly ascribed to the wilful perversity and ignorance of foreigners. But in retrospect it is clear that the historical relationship between government policy, economic development and international trade is more complex than conventional liberal ideology would suggest (Milward, 1981). Even in the case of Britain, notwithstanding Adam Smith's incisive attack on the 'mercantilist system', most economic historians now agree that the system facilitated British economic growth. Industrialisation at home was stimulated by the rapidly expanding demands of protected colonial markets abroad (Davis, 1962).

When after the Second World War smithianismus found a new home in the United States, its policy-makers and businessmen began to propound a theory of development as an act of immaculate private conception[4] and to preach the virtue of fiscal probity by debtors. These convictions owed their strength to a monumental ignorance of American economic history. In the half-century following independence government in the United States played an active role in building canals, turnpikes, harbours, railroads and schools. As for fiscal probity, much of this development was financed by inflation, wildcat banking and depreciating paper money. State bonds were sold to gullible foreign investors, especially in Britain, and later repudiated. As Schlesinger (1965) observed, 'In preaching orthodoxy to developing nations, we were somewhat in the position of the prostitute who, having retired on her earnings, believes that public virtue requires the closing-down of the red-light district'. How much actual development would have occurred, one wonders, if the criteria of the IMF had ruled public policy? Even in that august institution a few economic historians might not come amiss.

After the Second World War, it was hoped and expected that Marshall Plan aid would enable Western Europe to balance its payments directly with the United States and thereby close the 'dollar gap'. But historically Europe had settled its deficit with the United States through transactions with third countries. This pattern of settlements had made possible the evolution of a multilateral payments system. Since American policy was dedicated to the restoration of such a system, the attempt to force a balance between Western Europe and the United States is hard to explain except as a reflection of historical ignorance.

A currently more fashionable preception to which economic history can give a sense of proportion is that of the increasing interdependence of the world economy. This revelation gathered serious academic attention in the United States and has now become a popular cliché. In diplomacy by terminology it signals a newfound sense of vulnerability to external shocks. But what is new and distinctive about the reality it is intended to describe, even for economically developed countries? Before the First World War, a rise in the Bank of England's Bank Rate sent share prices tumbling in New York and could bankrupt Australian sheep farmers. Now European bankrupts blame American interest rates. What then is so peculiar about the nature of economic interdependence today compared with earlier periods, other than the reversal of roles between Britain and the United States? If there is more to the answer, it will only be found through a dialogue between past and present. Many other contemporary observations lend themselves to the same treatment. Much has been written about the leadership role of the United States in the world economy. But what is the crucial test of leadership? Is it, as has been cogently argued, to act as the stabiliser of last resort (Kindleberger, 1973)? If so, how does the American record compare with that of Britain before 1913?

In 1913 Britain held about 3·5 per cent of the world's gold reserves but had the power, as the international monetary crisis of August 1914 demonstrated, to pull in gold from many countries. In 1960 the United States, with over 40 per cent of the world's gold reserves was in a near-panic about gold losses and the stability of the dollar. Kennedy's economic advisers, aware of the contrast, thought the alarm absurd and counselled him to give priority to the promotion of domestic economic growth and employment. In doing so they drew his attention to the cost to Britain in employment and growth of its defence of sterling after 1925. The advisers were drawing an historical parallel to buttress their own conception of the national interest. The comparison did not, however, include the cost of promoting and defending the American way of life and thought abroad. This was simply assumed to be in the interests of its allies also, who should therefore carry a larger share of the burden. In the American catechism the duties of creditors began to replace the probity of debtors. The same change of circumstances saw a traditional American hostility to the sterling area give way to a recognition of sterling as the dollar's first line of defence.

It is also not uncommon for policy-makers to see the future as foreshadowed by historical parallels. During the Second World War the planners assumed that its aftermath would be much the same as after the First World War. Their intention was to avoid the mistakes of the earlier period. Accordingly they anticipated and prepared for deflation as in 1921. Their assumptions collapsed under the weight of an inflationary aftermath which greatly added to the cost of reconstruction. In negotiating an unpopular loan from the United States in 1945 Keynes was forced to accept and justify terms which in the event proved unrealistic, partly because inflation eroded its real value. But in accepting the unpalatable, he no doubt remembered how difficult it was after the First World War to raise any reconstruction loans on commercial terms. The architects of Bretton Woods also built on the lessons of the past as they saw them. But their perception failed to identify unique features, unlikely to be reproduced in the future and so unsuitable as examples to make into rules.

These illustrations make the point: policy-makers are influenced by their beliefs about what history teaches or portends. Their perception of the past helps to shape their current thinking. Once convinced of the relevance of an historical parallel, precedent, or trend, they will see only those facts which conform to the preception. Or, as Arthur Schlesinger puts it in a caustic reversal of George Santayana's aphorism, too often it is those who *can* remember the past who are condemned to repeat it (May 1973). An important function of the historian, therefore, in explaining and analysing the past, is to expose its misuse by those who look to the future.

Economic history has much to contribute to the contemporary debate on growth and development. Years ago Alfred Marshall suggested that the study of contemporary India would enlarge our understanding of Europe's past, from which in turn we should derive a truer insight into contemporary India. One of the best twentieth-century books on China, *Life and Labour in China*, was written by R. H. Tawney, an economic historian steeped in the economy of Tudor and Stuart England. The study of long-term economic change has always been a central theme of economic history, almost its *raison d'être*. Why has a given country developed more effectively than another? How far does the Soviet experience of industrialisation provide a model for less developed countries? There is much to be learned from such case studies. Indeed, development economics with a time dimension is economic history by another name.

Through trial and error economic theorists came to realise that otherwise respectable growth models, built with a few key variables of acknowledged importance in the process of economic change, become unmanageable, inoperable, or nonsensical, as more variables are added (Hahn and Mathews, 1964). Depending on the circumstances, population expansion may stimulate or inhibit economic growth; likewise foreign investment, wars, tariffs, tax structures, political revolution, the merchant and landed class, the demonstration effect of foreign institutions and tastes, and so forth. Hypotheses are subordinate to the context of time and place. No general theory of growth is remotely tenable.

Today international politics is agitated by the demands of poorer nations for a larger share in the benefits of modern industrialisation and by accusations that their deprivation is due to the wickedness, exploitation, or robbery of richer nations in the past and currently. Their sense of grievance is thus deeply rooted in their beliefs about the historical causes of their poverty. A global economic system created and dominated by the industrial West is the responsible agent. This view has received support in the writings of social scientists other than historians, which seek to show how and why the underdevelopment of Third World countries is the result of their historical relations with a metropolitan centre of capital states (Frank, 1969; Wallerstein, 1979; Amin, 1972).

By contrast, the mainstream liberal approach to Third World development sees progress coming from contacts which tend to diffuse capital, technology, skill, organisation and values to poor nations until over time the economy, society and culture become a variant of the economically developed world. Underlying this approach is the conception of a traditional society which undergoes modernisation through incorporation into national and international markets. The classical Marxist position shares much the same approach.

Economic historians are properly sceptical of all-embracing universal explanations of national differences in material development and income. For one thing, they invariably apply key terms, such as 'capitalism', with a generality that robs them of all explanatory power. It is known, for example, that the pre-colonial economy of West Africa had reached a relatively advanced stage of capitalism long before the impact of the Western World was felt in Africa (Hopkins, 1973; Latham, 1978;

Laitin, 1982). The example also brings into question the meaning of 'traditional' society. In some parts of the Third World integration into the world economy was consistent with the maintenance of the established social and political order. The British demand for beef strengthened the already existing class of large landowners in Argentina. In West Africa, in contrast, the development of commodity trade in the nineteenth century posed an acute crisis for the warrior aristocracy, the *ancien régime* which had co-operated so profitably with European slave-traders. Japan offers a still more striking example of the social and political turmoil brought about by integration into the world economy.

In short, the confrontation with European economic expansion overseas – or capitalism, or imperialism – the nature of the interaction and its outcome varied in different parts of the Third World. That is still true today. One of the tasks of history and theory is to account for these differences through detailed case studies. The economic history of a country largely dependent for its exports on peasant production will be different from one where the export economy is dominated by foreign enterprises, such as mining and plantations. The contrast is analogous to that between the prairie wheat belt and the cotton plantation economy in the United States before the Civil War.

A more significant comparison for Third World countries today, which Arthur Lewis (1978) has brought out, is that between temperate and tropical areas of agricultural production in the nineteenth century. In the last quarter of the century a period of falling transport costs, the growing demand of industrial Europe and America greatly stimulated the production and export of wool, wheat and meat from temperate areas of recent settlement and of cocoa, sugar, coffee, vegetable oil and oilseeds, rice, rubber, jute and other tropical products. The world became divided into industrial countries that exported manufactures and countries that exported agricultural products. The international economic order, as we know it today, was then established (Ashworth, 1952; Kenwood and Lougheed, 1971; Latham, 1978).

Agricultural exports from both temperate and tropical areas in the last part of the nineteenth century matched or surpassed the growth of world trade and income. Trade increases the national income and thereby enlarges the market for manufacturers. It then becomes possible to move into import-substituting industrialisation and in due course to join the ranks of exporters and manufacturers. That was the direction taken by Canada, Australia and New Zealand before the First World War. By that time they had joined the richest nations in the world and were producing more manufactures per head of population than France or Germany.

The economies of many tropical countries were also transformed by trade during this period but they did not become industrial nations.

Why not? To this question Arthur Lewis offers a more convincing answer than any of the general theories mentioned.

A popular explanation is colonial status, but it is inadequate. A number of politically independent countries in Eastern Europe and Latin America were just as backward in industrialising. In some tropical countries national income per head in the thirty years before the First World War was almost certainly growing as fast as in Britain and France and faster than in much of Central and South-eastern Europe. This is not to deny the negative effects of colonial rule. What colonial governments neglected to do was often more significant than what they did. It is simply to indicate that colonialism was only one of many varied political, social and economic environments which shaped and determined the rate of economic development. It cannot bear the whole weight of the explanation for the failures of tropical countries to industrialise. The response to trade opportunities, or the lack of it, in any particular country must be analysed in relation to its own circumstances. Nevertheless, one general clue stands out.

In a closed economy the size of the industrial sector is a function of agricultural productivity and income. This is because agriculture has to produce the surplus food and raw materials consumed in the industrial sector and serve as the main market for industrial products. If a large proportion of the labour force consists of low-productivity food producers, it follows that the market for domestic manufacturers is severely limited. In theory it would then be possible to support an industrial base by exporting manufactures and importing food and raw materials. In practice, it is difficult for infant industries to become cost-competitive in international markets without first selling to the more familiar and sheltered home market. Hence countries with low agricultural productivity tend to make slow industrial progress. As all first-year economic history students know, an industrial revolution presupposes a prior or simultaneous agricultural revolution. It is no coincidence that at the end of the eighteenth century the country of the first industrial revolution, Britain, had the highest agricultural productivity. Its productivity in food production was much higher than that of France, for example.

The low food productivity of tropical countries in the late nineteenth century was, therefore, a serious handicap to their development prospects. They could not compete in basic foodstuffs with the much higher productivity of temperate areas. This produced a lopsided development. The areas producing commodities for export prospered relative to the areas producing food crops and livestock products. Furthermore, the rapid growth of tropical exports was not due to more productive employment. It was largely the result of bringing idle resources of land and labour into use. That is how the national income increased. Commodity exports were to a large extent additional to what these countries would otherwise have produced in food. It cannot be said that they were *compelled*, economically or politically, to neglect their own food production. No external relationship prevented tropical countries from raising their own food output and productivity. Moreover, if the bulk of the labour force is in low-productivity food production, the rest of the labour force will get low prices whether it exports agricultural or industrial products; its income will be set by the supply price of the labour reserve in low-productivity food production. Tropical export prices were a function of low living standards in tropical food production.

Ironically the great expansion of exports from tropical countries in the thirty years preceding the First World War confirmed a Western presumption that they had a comparative advantage in agriculture. In fact, as the development of the Indian textile industry soon showed, there were much greater differences between tropical and temperate countries in food production than in industrial production per head. Obviously a revolution in food production in Third World countries is not the only condition for industrial progress; but it is an essential condition, and one within their power to create. The broader conclusion Arthur Lewis draws from his historical analysis is that a transformation of the food sector of these countries will automatically lead to a new international economic order. A question students of political economy should ask, therefore, is: who gains from the failure to bring about such a revolution?

The academic foundations of economic history were laid during the depression of the 1870s and 1880s when economics was in the doldrums, out of touch with reality and held in low public esteem. The parallel with today is uncanny – and possibly, for that reason, should be resisted. But a distinguished British economist, reflecting on a lifetime's experience of his profession as a source of advice, has come to this conclusion:

> The economist who is best equipped to understand the working of the economy around him and to advise on policy, needs in point of analysis the equipment that is needed by the economic historian, and no more. I take this to be the analysis of demand and supply, distribution, international trade and money, as these are developed in a text for undergraduates . . . I doubt whether more concepts or relationships than are contained here will in practice be drawn upon, even by those who can handle them with facility, in work upon particular problems at the highest level of responsibility. The entrant would also receive thoroughgoing training in statistical methods. For the rest his course would include much economic, social and political history: this is essential. The course would also provide for the study in detail of some contemporary societies and their recent changes. (Phelps Brown, 1980)

In short, 'have concept, will travel' is not enough; within every social scientist, and every international political economist, there should be a historian struggling to get out.[5]

Notes: Chapter 2

1 For a timely reminder of the contingent elements, biases and reflected parochialism in much American academic thinking about world politics, see Susan Strange, 'Cave! hic dragones: a critique of regime analysis', *International Organization*, vol. 36, no. 2 (Spring 1982), pp. 479–96.
2 The economic historians of our own time may expect to find their path strewn with rusty Laffer curves, bent supply-siders, busted monetarists and benign neglect.
3 W. E. Minchinton (1969) explains the ways historians have interpreted this term.
4 The phrase is Arthur Schlesinger's: he ascribed this outlook to the Eisenhower administration but it was also shared by leading members of the Truman administration.
5 The first Director of the London School of Economics, W. A. Hewins, was an economic historian; so was W. J. Ashley, the first Dean of Birmingham University's Faculty of Commerce, effectively a business school, which predated Harvard's Business School.

References: Chapter 2

Amin, S. (1972), 'Underdevelopment and dependence in black Africa – their historical origins and contemporary forms', *Journal of Modern African Studies*, vol. 10, pp. 543–60.
Ashworth, W. (1952), *A Short History of the International Economy* (London: Longmans, Green); 3rd edn 1975.
Davis, R. (1962), 'English foreign trade, 1700–1774', *Economic History Review*, vol. 15, pp. 285–303.
Frank, A. G. (1969), *Capitalism and Underdevelopment in Latin America* (Harmondsworth: Penguin).
Hahn, F. H., and Mathews, R. C. O. (1964), 'The theory of economic growth: a survey', *Economic Journal*, vol. 74, pp. 779–902.
Hopkins, A. G. (1973), *An Economic History of West Africa* (New York: Columbia University Press).
Kenwood, A. G., and Lougheed, A. L. (1971), *The Growth of the International Economy, 1820–1960* (London: Allen & Unwin).
Kindleberger, C. P. (1973), *The World in Depression, 1929–1939* (London: Allen Lane).
Laitin, D. D. (1982), 'Capitalism and hegemony: Yorubaland and the international economy', *International Organization*, vol. 36, no. 4 (Autumn).
Latham, A. J. H. (1978), *The International Economy and the Underdeveloped World, 1865–1914* (London: Croom Helm).
Lewis, W. A. (1978a), *Growth and Fluctuations, 1870–1913* (London: Allen & Unwin).

Lewis, W. A. (1978b), *The Evolution of the International Economic Order* (Princeton, NJ: Princeton University Press).

May, E. B. (1973), *'Lessons' of the Past: The Use and Misuse of History in American Foreign Policy* (New York: OUP).

Milward, A. (1981), 'Tariffs as constitutions', in Susan Strange and Roger Tooze (eds), *The International Politics of Surplus Capacity* (London: Allen & Unwin), pp. 57–66.

Minchinton, W. E. (1969), *Mercantilism, System or Expediency* (Lexington, MA: D. C. Heath).

Myint, H. (1958), 'The "classical theory" of international trade and the under-developed countries', *Economic Journal*, vol. 68, pp. 317–37.

Phelps Brown, H. (1980), 'The radical reflections of an applied economist', *Banca Nazionale del Lavoro Quarterly Review*, no. 132 (March), pp. 3–14.

Schlesinger, A. M., jr (1965), *A Thousand Days: John F. Kennedy in the White House* (New York: Fawcett Premier).

Strange, Susan (1982), 'Cave! hic dragones: a critique of regime analysis', *International Organization*, vol. 36, no. 2 (Spring), pp. 479–96.

Wallerstein, I. (1979), *The Capitalist World Economy* (Cambridge: CUP).

3

World Politics and Population

NICHOLAS J. DEMERATH

Barring atomic disasters, the size, growth rate and distribution of the world's population over the next twenty to thirty years will largely determine the condition of man in the twenty-first century. That is to say, demographic factors will influence greatly man's adaptation as one species in nature's larger scheme. Just how, and how well, man will adapt has never been argued more widely by scientists and by 'true believers'; their respective identities not always distinguishable. Human fertility and migration as related to wealth, power, food supplies, energy and environmental quality – these are the modern Malthusian issues.

To be sure, there is optimism in some quarters – especially perhaps among some economists, technological fixers and theists. But hardly a month passes that one more baleful prognostication of man's future is not published. Doomsday authors are among the best-sellers, no matter the dubious nature of many computerised games simulating various scenarios of food, fuels, minerals, materials, environmental degradation, economic growth and population growth. Such studies tend to be flawed by the well-known fallacies of 'Garbage in, garbage out', 'Prejudice in, prejudice out' (Simon, 1981). At the very least, however, one may be certain that continued population growth in most societies entails, as Ridker (1979, p. 121) has pointed out, more local conflicts over land and water use, the need to live with even greater uncertainties and risks of major ecological or nuclear disasters, more dependence on rapid scientific and technological development to reduce the uncertainties and risks and few social options, and the continued postponement of the resolution of other problems, including those resulting from past growth. On the other hand, if rapid population increase can be slowed down, there are political and economic advantages: more time, resources and additional options by means of which to overcome ignorance, redress mistakes of past growth, implement solutions and plan with greater freedom of choice.

As human beings we are all ecologically dependent and substantively demographic – even statistically treatable, however abhorrent that fact may be to Lord Snow's 'literary-humanists'. If the brotherhood of man amounts to nothing more than this, our common membership in nature's web, the consequences are not insignificant, especially today. But there is another underlying aspect of 'world politics and population' to be noted in these introductory pages. And that is power. That population is an ingredient of national power to be inventoried, rulers from Caesar Augustus and the Han Dynasty to the present have demonstrated by taking censuses and surveys of their people. This is not surprising in as much as it is people who both produce and consume. And national political power derives from the quality and quantity of people as contributors, supporters, allies, enemies, voters, as well as from the economy. The powers of nations, I take it, are the very stuff of international politics. Which brings me to the question set for this chapter: 'what should every lecturer in politics know about population as a factor in the political economy of the world?'

Obviously, any answer to this question in a few thousand words must be highly selective. My choice encompasses three topics of particular political economic import. I choose (1) the distribution of the population; (2) urbanisation and migration; and (3) population growth and economic development.

Distribution of the World's Population

Something of the structure of the world's population at present is described in Table 3.1. On every variable tabulated the differences between the more and less economically developed parts of the world, as well as between the major regions of the world, are conspicuous. In size of population the poor, less developed countries (LDCs) outnumber the rich by nearly 3 to 1. But in gross national product per capita, the rich are richer by more than 11 to 1.

The birth rate average of the poor countries is twice that of the rich (32:16), whereas the mortality rates are not greatly different (12:9). This, indeed, is the principal factor explaining the high rates of population growth in poor and predominantly agrarian countries. In the jargon of demographers a 'demographic transition' to low birth rates as well as low mortality rates has yet to occur in these countries. Death control by campaign or organised efforts has been highly successful – at least up to now. Not so with birth control. It was during the Second World War that death control by the widespread applications of cheap and efficient insecticides and vaccines began in Asia and Latin America and, to a lesser degree, in Africa. Government-organised birth control programmes have been far more complex, more costly and as yet largely unsuccessful. Having numerous progeny, after all, is not a disease

Table 3.1 *Population Estimates and Selected Characteristics for the World and World Regions*

	Size (million) (1980)	Birth rate	Death rate	% under age 15	% over age 64	% urban	Per capita gross national product ($)
World	4,414	28	11	35	6	39	2,040
more Developed	1,131	16	9	24	11	69	6,260
less Developed	3,283	32	12	39	4	29	560
Africa	472	46	17	45	3	26	530
Asia	2,563	28	11	37	4	27	760
North America	247	16	8	23	11	74	9,650
Latin America	360	34	8	42	4	61	1,380
Europe	484	14	10	24	12	69	5,650
Soviet Union	266	18	10	24	10	62	3,700
Oceania	23	20	9	31	8	71	6,020

Sources: 1980 World Population Data Sheet of the Population Reference Bureau, Inc., Washington, DC; data from United Nations and US Bureau of the Census; details contained in the Appendix of this book, which is the abridged Data Sheet, including data for subregions and selected countries.

whose prevention is accomplished simply and surely. Habitual ways of life and established institutions still demand high parity in agrarian societies and especially among the poor and uneducated.

The age columns in Table 3.1 (percentages under 15 and over 64) when compared with total population give what is called the 'dependency ratio'. The higher ratios for the poor countries are supposedly associated with smaller amounts of savings available for capital investment. Parents, it is said, must spend more to take care of their more numerous children, and thus they cannot pay higher taxes. That, however, seems to be more guess than fact. And parents just might accumulate more savings *because* they have more children (Birdsall, 1980).

The biosocial profiles of given populations – their composition by age and sex – have long been studied and compared by economists, politicians, human services planners and business entrepreneurs. United Nations statistics permit some rough comparisons of the age–sex profiles of different nations. Given their fertility rates, it is possible to make some guesses about the quality of future generations of adults in developed and developing countries.

How adequately nourished and educated will be the large numbers of children and young people in poor countries? Reports and forecasts which bear on this highly complex and controversial question are not encouraging.

Inspection of the datasheet in the Appendix will show pronounced differences on most variables within each of the seven world regions. One example is temperate South America (Argentina, Chile, Uruguay) with its large European immigrant stock in a favourable climatic and agricultural zone. It has an infant mortality rate of 44, whereas tropical South America (nine states) loses 98 babies under 1 year of age per 1,000 live births. Differences between temperate and tropical habitats are also evident in the data for the rest of the world. This fact suggests that the differences between East and West in socioeconomic fundamentals are less than differences between North and South. Ideological and associated political differences are something else, as Washington and Moscow continue to remind us.

So far we have considered some of the structural characteristics of national and world populations. But look now at world geography and where people are located. The world's population is distributed most unevenly, a fact that is not unrelated to the great differences in density of human settlement and to the corresponding ratios of man to land, with attendant implications for economic productivity and political stability. About nine-tenths of all the people in the world are jammed on to less than a quarter of the earth's land. There are three large clusters of heavy settlement. First and most prominent is Asia. There the most densely populated areas are Japan, South Korea, mainland China and Taiwan, Java (in Indonesia), India and Bangladesh. The second area of heavy settlement is most of the European peninsula, and the rim of the United States from Chicago clockwise around to California. The third area is the Caribbean in part, and coastal South America in part. Non-Soviet Asia, which constitutes not quite 10 per cent of the earth's land surface is occupied by more than 60 per cent of the world's people, and the share is increasing. By contrast, South America, with 13 per cent of the land surface, presently accounts for less than 10 per cent of the world's people but, like all of Latin America, numbers are growing much more rapidly than in North America.

Conditions of climate, topography, land and water have always constrained population distribution and settlement. They will do so in the future. Nevertheless, in the modern world factors of culture are of more importance for population distribution than all but the most extreme geographic conditions. Natural resources may attract initial settlement or even rapid development of certain areas. But in the long run the mere existence of resources is of no real significance unless there is a culture that is technologically, economically and politically able to exploit them.

As for the patterns of residence within nations, village life has dominated most of Asia, Europe and Latin America for centuries. This has been linked with communal or large family ownership of land, as well

as with exchange of labour and sharing of work. Village life also fea-
tured joint defences against thieves and hostile armies. Indeed, there
have been the origins of guerrilla warfare, the tactics of which make
urban targets especially vulnerable today. In North America, of course,
as well as Argentina, Australia, New Zealand and a few other countries,
the predominant settlement pattern has been 'open country'. That is to
say, family farms on separate acreages privately owned or leased, but
with small trading towns and villages accessible, however distant and
difficult the journey sometimes. Where the farm family needed and had
the resources to employ additional labour, as for example in plantation
agricultures and in extensive ranching enterprises, the 'households'
might be as large as some villages.

Behind these varied patterns of residence and of family size are the
institutions of property, production, marriage and the family that
implicate both polity and economy in every society. These institutions
together with the universally vital ratios of natural resources to population to wealth and income are what determine human demography.
Rates of birth, death and migration, and patterns of age, sex, residence,
and so on, by themselves tell us little or nothing. The keys to prediction
and control of population dynamics lie in the institutions and the
resource–wealth–population ratios of each society. Because of this, all
ideas of a 'world population problem' are less grounded empirically
than they are floated theologically or ideologically.

One more aspect of population distribution bears notice because
many believe it to be a significant factor in human welfare, political
unrest and economic development. I refer to crowding or density of
residence, particularly in cities. There has been a good deal of speculation about humans in recent years because studies of 'lower' animals
discovered that overcrowding as well as the other extreme, isolation,
both have negative effects on several species. Galle and Gove (1978)
explored this idea in a review of literature on human populations,
though the data refer to urban populations in the MDCs rather than the
LDCs. They concluded, first, that the concepts of high population
density and overcrowding are more complex in the case of human
populations. Secondly, human crowding is very much related to social
class and to culture. Thirdly, the evidence suggests that although
density probably has some negative effects on health, on human relations in and out of the home, on fertility and on the care of children, the
effects have not been demonstrated conclusively.

Urbanisation and Migration

Most social scientists regard the percentage of any nation's population
resident in urban places as the main indicator of that nation's modernisation or industrialisation or Westernisation. (These last three terms, I

take it, are approximately interchangeable.) While Table 3.1 displays some gross differences in the extent of urbanisation by regions of the world, Figure 3.1 does it more graphically. And it also includes projections on the basis of present trends to the year 2000.

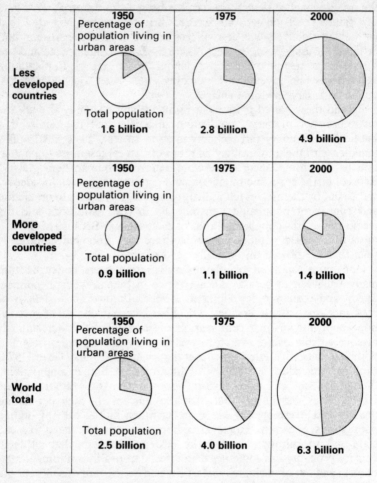

Figure 3.1 *World urbanisation: 1950, 1975, 2000.*

Note: Includes Temperate South America, Northern America, Japan, Europe, Australia, New Zealand, and the Soviet Union.

Sources: United Nations, Population Division, 'Trends and prospects in urban and rural population, 1950–2000, as assessed in 1973–1974', ESA/P/WP.54, United Nations, New York, 25 April 1975, table C, medium variant; Population Reference Bureau (Washington, DC), 'Can Third World cities cope?', *Population Bulletin*, vol. 31, no. 4 (December 1976).

In the LDCs urban populations especially in the biggest cities have increased much too rapidly for human services and facilities to handle. The result is human misery and degradation to an extent that no longer exists in the MDCs. Some LDC cities already have more than 10 million people, and if present rates of growth continue, they will double their size in about ten years. Figure 3.2 identifies the world's largest metropolitan areas in 1980, and also projects their size to the year 2000. Even the casual visitor who has tried to move and breathe in some of these cities in recent years will doubt that they can possibly grow to, say, 31 million in Mexico City, 22 million in New York and 16 million in Calcutta before there is a reversal of the trend. Either limits of a biophysical sort are apt to be imposed or there might be a reshuffling of the 'push–pull' factors, chiefly social, psychological and economic in nature.

The United Nations Fund for Population Activities, when the report on metropolitan areas was released, observed that metropolitan growth had already reached 'proportions which are totally unfamiliar to town

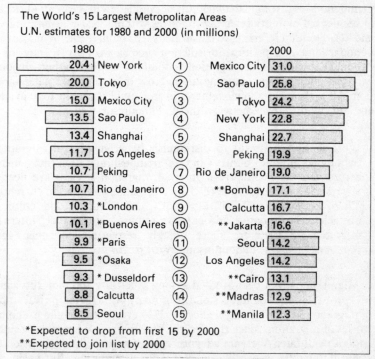

Figure 3.2 *The world's largest cities.*

Source: UN estimates in millions quoted by *New York Times*, 15 June 1980.

planners'. Thirty years ago there were only six cities with 5 million or more inhabitants. Today there are twenty-six and in the year 2000 there will be sixty, with forty-five of them in the Third World.

In Western history urbanisation has been accompanied in the modernised nations by a precipitous decline in the proportion of the people who live on farms. In the United States, for example, farm families made up 95 per cent of the population in 1790 and 3 per cent in 1980. There is some evidence, however, that between 1970 and 1980 this trend may have reversed. In the LDCs cities seem to be growing somewhat differently from the way they did in the West. Whereas industrial jobs and then employment in the tertiary sector attracted streams of migration from country to city in the West, there is evidence from a number of countries in the Third World that the rapid growth of many cities there is attributable as much or more to the natural increase of urban residents than it is to a net immigration from the countryside. In any case urbanisation need not be a result solely of rural–urban migration.

Migration is defined with reference to some geographic boundary. Demographers distinguish two kinds of population movement: (1) local or residential mobility referring to moves within the same community, and (2) migration referring to moves between communities or across the boundary line of a political jurisdiction such as a county, a state, or a nation. The analysis of migration is founded on four rather obvious variables: inmigration, outmigration, gross migration and net migration. All of these refer to movements in and out of areas, the total in and out and the difference between these. Thomlinson writes,

> We also find it useful to distinguish between internal migration (wholly within one country) and international migration (movement across national boundaries). Internal migration streams are nearly always of larger magnitude than are international migration currents. There being fewer legal restrictions and linguistic and cultural obstacles, the initiative and expense required are smaller; internal migration is therefore more quickly responsive to social and economic changes. (Thomlinson, 1976, p. 267)

Migration has not been studied as long as fertility and mortality, and it is probably less well understood. For many years the empirical study of migration has been badly neglected. However, the headline-grabbing stories of migrations since the Second World War, and especially since America's ill-fated Vietnam adventure, have produced an expansion of scientific interest, especially in international migration. But again, as with other demographic phenomena, the question is what does migration tell us about other things, economic and political?

The nature of the internal migration in one nation, its freedom, or restriction may produce admiration or outrage in other nations. It may, therefore, affect foreign economic policies and political events. But it is the movements or migrations of people internationally that have the greatest potential for affecting the international political economy. Thomlinson (1976) writes, quoting the International Labor Office, 'The effects of migration between countries and cultures are of considerable magnitude and import for the individual migrant, for the nation he or she leaves, and for his or her new country. "For many people it has been and still is the only way out of the dead end created in some countries by persistent underemployment." (ibid., p. 283). Many historians and anthropologists, of course, have observed that cross-culture contacts and the diffusion of customs and artefacts are furthered by movements of people across national boundaries, be they political agents, businessmen, scientists, journalists, or the ordinary tourist. At the same time conflicts and misunderstandings arise, mainly due to differences in language and beliefs.

The history of world migration has been divided into three types and three overlapping periods (Thomlinson, 1976). First, and by far the longest, has been *group migration*. This encompasses the wanderings of the Goths, Huns, Vandals, Magyars, Arabs, Turks, Aryans, Muslims and Spaniards. In some cases the natives were forcibly displaced, as in the case of the American Indians who were pushed westward by the European immigrants. In other cases native populations were converted to forced labour or slavery. Between 10 and 20 million black slaves, for example, were taken to the Western Hemisphere between 1550 and 1850. Some kinds of indentured service were also forced migration. Colonisation as a kind of group migration is well and widely known through history.

The second kind of world migration is that of *free migration* by individuals or families beginning about 1500. In this case there is no official mandate; simply the decision of the person, or a family, to move. Although dependable statistics on these first two types of migration are not available, historians have a rough idea of the major intercontinental streams of migration in the modern period. Thomlinson writes that:

> In probable order of magnitude [the streams] have been: from all parts of Europe to the United States and Canada; from southern Europe to Latin America, especially Argentina and Brazil; from Africa to the New World as slaves; from China to the rest of the world; from the Indian sub-continent to the rest of the world; and from Great Britain to southern Africa and Australia. Most of the migrants were of the second type [free individuals], but a sizable minority were type one [group]. (Thomlinson, 1976, p. 285)

Beginning with the Second World War and throughout the decades of the 1960s and 1970s we have witnessed a resurgence of group migration as millions of people fled their homelands in the wake of wars and selective genocidal attacks. Military and political upheavals have triggered group migrations on a much greater scale than would normally occur coincidentally with variations in supply and demand (for labour) throughout the world. Today war and revolution have set off the migration of as much as one-fifth to one-quarter of the total populations of Africa and South-east Asia.

Since 1946, the end of the Second World War, the balance of migration has shifted more and more towards North America and Oceania, as seen in Table 3.2. Indeed, these are the only regions of the world to record a net immigration.

The third type, *restricted* or *controlled migration*, has just about replaced free migration. Thus a source of relief for overpopulated nations has virtually disappeared – that is relief in the form of *legal* emigration. In the twentieth century rules governing migration have increased both in quantity and in degree of restrictiveness. Some nations now prohibit all movement of some kinds of people, while others have set up migration quotas that cannot be exceeded. Exclusion policies are common and limitations on emigration (movement out of a country) are also spreading.

Restrictions on immigration are usually motivated economically as are restrictions on resident aliens. In contrast, the restrictions on emigration seem typically to arise out of political and military considerations.

The public interest in the receiving countries has changed from the places of origin of legal immigrants to the question of 'How many illegal immigrants are there?' Or, in American bureaucratic jargon, numbers of 'undocumented aliens'. Bouvier *et al.* describe the dynamics of

Table 3.2   *Estimated Net Migration Balances for Major World Regions, 1946–57 and 1960–70*

Region	1946–57 (million)	1960–70 (million)
Africa	+0·5	−1·6
Asia	−0·5	−1·2
Europe	−5·4	−0·3
Latin America	+0·9	−1·9
Northern America	+3·4	+4·1
Oceania	+1·0	+0·9

Source: United Nations, *International Migration Trends, 1950–1970*, Conference Background Paper, E/CONF.60/CBP/18, 22 May 1974, table 5.

illegal migration:

> Like legal migration, the illegal movement of aliens is a response to factors both at home and at place of destination. The illegal migrant is faced in his own country with unsatisfactory living conditions, poor job opportunities or other unfavourable situations which he hopes to correct by emigrating, but for one reason or another he cannot legally surmount the obstacles set by the 'target' country. (Bouvier *et al.*, 1977, p. 26)

The United States probably attracts most of the world's illegal migrants, according to Bouvier *et al.* (1977). Estimates of the numbers of illegals range from 6 to 15 million. The fact is nobody knows their numbers or their effects on the society and economy. The only known figures are the numbers of 'undocumented aliens' who are caught. These have quadrupled from about 300,000 in 1970 to 1·5 million in 1980. But the US Immigration and Naturalization Service has estimated that only one of every three or four persons trying to enter is caught. The great majority, perhaps 90 per cent of the illegals, are Mexicans, although the Mexican government does not agree with the American estimates of the numbers who reside illegally in the United States. According to recent surveys, very well done by Mexican agencies, the number is somewhere between 480,000 and 1·2 million as of the 1970s. This likely range contrasts sharply with the American estimates of 3–6 million illegal aliens from all places, the great majority from Mexico. In any case there is no doubt that the stream of illegals from Mexico into the United States has been a valuable safety-valve for a Mexican economy whose rate of growth in recent years has been less than the very high rate of population growth.

The problem of illegal immigration is not confined to the United States. Europe, as well as some parts of Asia and Latin America, are also faced with huge streams of illegals. For example, Michael King writes that,

> Increasingly restrictive immigration policies in Europe have made it more difficult to migrate legally to Western Europe with the result that by the summer of 1973, it is estimated that there were more than half a million foreigners illegally working or living in Europe, mainly engaged in activities such as road construction, building, agriculture, hotels, and the public services. (King, 1974, p. 91)

Illegal migrations from North Africa into southern Italy and parts of Greece and Spain are reported. Shortages of certain kinds of low-paid agricultural labour have developed as a result of excessive outmigration. Hong Kong has become a magnet to thousands of illegal immigrants, mostly from mainland China. The Crown government tries to stem the illegal flow, but scarcely a week passes that the Hong Kong media do not carry news of an overcrowded sampan swamped or lost at sea. And it is doubtful if the projected multilane highway between Canton and Hong Kong can help the authorities.

Particular migration streams across national boundaries are temporary; yesterday Bangladeshi into India, today Afghans to Pakistan, and so on. Migration forces in the world, however, are perpetual. Technological inequalities between nations persist and political upheavals keep occurring. Another force is the tremendous growth of population in the LDCs. One obvious solution to this is emigration to the technologically advanced regions where birth rates are low and, in a few countries, where there are natural decreases in population size. Should it become an objective of some 'new international order' to maintain present rates of population growth, international migration would be one way, maybe the only way, to do it and adapt successfully. The extent of future migration internationally is surely tied to the growth of population and environmental quality. Environmental pressures persist, and if resources become even more scarce, we can expect to see *homo sapiens* continue to migrate in even larger numbers in search of better ways of life and to survive. Throughout history this has been mankind's way of solving resource problems. Why not now? The late President Boumédienne of Algeria might turn out to be an accurate prophet, providing the bombs are not dropped! 'No quantity of atomic bombs could stem the tide of billions . . . who will someday leave the poor southern part of the world to erupt into the relatively accessible spaces of the rich Northern Hemisphere looking for survival' (Bouvier *et al.*, 1977, p. 39). That the emigration from the South has already begun is evident in the advanced countries of Western Europe and North America. Here the presence of large numbers of guest workers/ illegal aliens/political refugees have already strained existing human services and destabilised political orders, no matter how well served are some employers.

Population Growth and Economic Development

The elemental demography of population growth and decline is deceptively simple. Any given population in time will grow or decline or, less likely, remain static as the result of births compared with deaths, plus or minus the net migration (in or out). It is when one tries to get at the causes and facts behind this simple arithmetic that the complexities begin. Especially is this the case with the ups and downs of fertility, a much less straightforward matter than either mortality or migration. At the same time fertility is the most important differential in modern demography. And it is the one variable most likely to be the target of intervention by governments and would-be humanitarians.

Fertility rates are complicated, first, by human biology, by the population's age and sex distribution, and by its fecundity; the biological potential of females to conceive, gestate and deliver offspring. Secondly, there are the complexities of data and scientific method. Fertility is measured by counting the number of children who were born in relation to some base population. Birth rates like death rates come in crude, corrected specific, or standardised forms. But there are also numerous ratios of fertility. Each measure and each kind of data has its advantages and its drawbacks. Thirdly, there are the numerous institutions and structures of any society that shape the biological potentials into the behaviours which give rise to fertility, mortality and migration. It is this third order of complexity, and the values that are attached to demographic behaviour and demographic outcomes, which are especially pertinent to the politics of population growth, not least the growth of global or world population.

Patterns of World Population Growth

The population of the world, estimated at only 599 million in 1800, jumped to 1·6 billion in 1900 and then grew even more rapidly to its present total of about 4·4 billion. United Nations projections to the year 2000 range between 6 to 10 billion, depending upon assumptions. The world's different regions, as the total fertility rates in the Appendix show, are growing at quite different rates: Latin American women were averaging 4·5 children in their lifetimes; East Asia at 2·3 was just replacing its population; South-west Asia had a very high total fertility rate (TFR) of 5·9; and North America along with Northern and Western Europe had TFRs below replacement.

Although demographic influences do not operate alone, the unevenness of regional population growth has doubtless contributed to the changing fortunes of nations and organisations that compete for world power. Thomlinson (1976), for example, thinks that there are at present four political and economic conflicts which have important demographic dimensions: Orient v. Occident, political independence v. colonialism, high living levels v. low/subsistence levels; and the Cold War between the USSR and its adversaries. Two political scientists, Katherine and A. F. K. Organski (1961) stress the importance of population size as a determinant of national power, along with economic development:

There are three major determinants of national power: the size of a nation's population, the level of its economic development, and the skill and efficiency of its government. High standing in one respect may compensate to some degree for lack in another, but no nation can attain first rank without all three. Canada possesses a modern economy and an efficient government and has in addition rich resources, extensive territory, and high morale; but her population of less than 20 million relegates her forever to second rank. India has a giant population and a government of considerable efficiency; but until she succeeds in modernizing her economy she will have trouble even in defending her own frontiers. (p. 27)

No matter how efficient or how troublesome, no nation of small or even moderate size can push its way into the ranks of the great powers of today. Admission to this ever shrinking circle requires a population of at least 45 million; tomorrow the minimum may well be 200 million, for size becomes more important as the years go by. To be a great power, a nation needs many millions of citizens to serve as cannon fodder, labor force, world market and – most important of all – as taxpayers. (K. and A. F. K. Organski, 1961, p. 13)

That even 'small powers' are to be reckoned with when their patrons are great, and the issues are extensively involved, the recent history of Israel, the PLO, and the Arab states makes clear in our interdependent world of today. The same may be said of those organisations which employ guerrilla warfare and terrorism. And once a people have achieved nationhood – no matter how small in size – their demography changes from that of the colonial past. For better or worse population growth, rural–urban distribution, social characteristics, migration, all of these and other patterns are changed by political autonomy.

There is some evidence that racism may be on the increase, due in part to regional differentials in population growth and economic development. There are still Caucasoid racists who see their world imperilled by ever-larger hordes of Asiatics. Believing that race determines intelligence and culture, they are no doubt as frightened, as oriental readers are heartened, by the kind of statement made some years ago by the Raffles Professor at Singapore, Northcote Parkinson. He declared that the twenty-first century will belong to the Asians, the predictably dominating force of the future.

It is true that the remarkable proliferation of the European peoples, which had so much to do with worldwide diffusion of their technology and culture and with their political and economic hegemony, is at an end, at least, for the foreseeable future. And the fear of some Westerners that by the year 2000 Europe and Anglo-America will be overwhelmed by Asian culture may be fed by the fact that in today's world of some 4·4 billion the Asians are 2·5 billion and growing rapidly. Additional facts, however, make such apprehension quite unwarranted. In the first place, there is no one monolithic and dominant Asian culture. A casual reading of any day's political news makes this evident.

Secondly, as Asians make the scientific and economic changes necessary to reduce mortality, and to develop economically, they participate
in the process of Westernisation or, better termed, rationalisation. This
means that the science and modern technology they seek cannot be
borrowed without also, at the same time, taking many Western
attitudes and institutions, including certain features of Western class
structures and belief systems. Thirdly, rates of human fertility have
begun to decrease in Asia and in some LDCs elsewhere. And this is
occurring along with societal changes and economic growth in these
countries; a good omen and a political direction for the future.

Political Intervention and Decreasing Fertility

In matters of world population we have seen an historic first over the
past twenty years. For the first time Western nations sought officially to
reduce population growth in other nations to increase the latter's
economic growth – and their political stability. Until the delegates from
the poor nations under the banner 'Development is the best contraceptive' staged a revolt (at the 1974 World Conference on Population in
Bucharest) against the prearranged 'World Population Plan', the chosen strategy was 'Family Planning'. Western-educated and urban-
oriented family-planners thought that the bioscientific technology of
the pill, the coil, sterilisation, immunisation – even compulsory sterilisation – would be accepted by masses of peasants in predominantly
agrarian societies of the Third World. To promote and to merchandise
this contraceptive technology as a population policy in and of itself was
deceptive nonsense. Barbara Ward called it 'contraceptive imperialism'. Among the more outspoken critics have been these social scientists and physicians: D. Baneji, S. Bergström, L. Bondestam, P.
Pradervand and other authors represented in Bondestam and Bergström (1980) as well as Kleinman (1980), Demerath (1976) and Bachrach and Bergman (1973). Opposition by Indian scientists and others
in the LDCs has embarrassed the American 'population establishment',
but their efforts – still largely one-track contraceptionism – continue to
be well funded even by the budget-cutting Reagan administration
(Simon and Demerath, 1982).

An 'integrated approach' is appearing as a stratagem that would put
family planning where it should be, namely, as just one of several
human services in the betterment of maternal and child health and the
reduction of infant mortality. However, the phrase 'integrated
approach' can be ambiguous. To some it merely means the co-
ordination of multifarious programmes and offices at the United
Nations and the World Bank (Etzioni, 1979; Finkle and Crane, 1976).
To others it means putting population considerations into the making
of economic and social development plans and programmes. At prob-

ably the most inclusive level 'integration' encompasses all of the preceding referents plus ecological and environmental consideration.

There is some evidence that fertility and population growth rates in numerous countries of the Third World have fallen, even though their populations continue to increase quite rapidly. The developing world as a whole from 1945 until about 1968 showed a steady increase in its population growth rate because of a continuous decline in mortality. Then it stabilised at about 2·4 per cent per year. In the mid-1970s the rate fell to 2·3 per cent per annum, in itself not a decline which will have much effect on population size. However, should it mark the beginning of a trend, that fall of 0·1 per cent will be of great importance in demographic and human history. It will be the first time in thirty years that the LDCs' rate of population growth has declined. But why? What is the explanation of this good news for population-watchers?

Figure 3.3, after Roberto Cuca (1980), shows that the decline in crude birth rates, which has caused the decrease in rate of growth is linked with wealth and poverty. In the 'high' per capita income countries all but two (Iraq and Syria) declined, whereas in the 'low' category not one declined. The World Bank studied sixty-three countries with populations of 5 million or more, representing about 95 per cent of the total LDC population and 67 per cent of the total world population (Cuca, 1980).

It is now evident from this and other studies that knowledge and availability of modern contraception will not by itself produce declining birth rates. Is it true, then, that 'development is the best contraceptive'? That depends on what is meant by 'development'. General economic development of a nation as measured by change in its gross national product has less effect on fertility rates than other kinds of development which are less grossly economic and more societal. Hence the greater emphasis among population and development specialists now on 'socioeconomic development'; on changes in the conditions of life, the structures of wealth and power, lifestyles, customs and institutions. Moreover, it seems that there are no simple or universal determinants of demographic variables. Nor do we yet know what *changes* in which *societies* have what effects on demographic variables, or *how* they operate to produce their effects. But the clues increase and so do the refinements of inquiry.

Especially encouraging is the fact that in the field of demography social scientists seem to be sharing ideas and work more and more. The first column of Figure 3.3, taken for the World Bank study, is entitled 'Relative social setting' and denotes an index based upon school enrolments, adult literacy, life expectancy, infant mortality, men in non-agricultural employment as well as on conventional economic indicators. Economist Nancy Birdsall (1980) finds that more recent fertility declines in the LDCs are occurring more rapidly, and at lower average

Relative social setting[2]	Per capita GNP, 1977 (in US dollars)	Government policy on family planning		
		Policy with specific objective of reducing fertility	Policy but no specific objective of reducing fertility	No policy or negative policy
High	More than $1,000	Hong Kong Mexico Turkey	Brazil Chile Iraq Venezuela	Argentina
High	Between $250 and $1,000	Colombia Dominican Rep. Malaysia Philippines Republic of Korea	Cuba Ecuador Peru	North Korea Syrian Arab Rep.
High	Less than $250	Sri Lanka		
Medium	More than $1,000	Iran	Algeria South Africa	Saudi Arabia
Medium	Between $250 and $1,000	China Egypt Ghana Guatemala Indonesia Kenya Morocco Thailand Tunisia	Zambia Zimbabwe	Bolivia Cameroon
Medium	Less than $250	India Pakistan Viet Nam	Zaïre	Burma Madagascar
Low	More than $1,000			
Low	Between $250 and $1,000	Senegal	Nigeria Sudan Uganda	Angola Ivory Coast Yemen Arab Rep.
Low	Less than $250	Bangladesh Nepal	Afghanistan Haiti Mali Tanzania	Ethiopia Guinea Kampuchea, Democratic Malawi Mozambique Niger Upper Volta

Figure 3.3 *Developing countries with a reduction in the crude birth rate of 10 per cent or more, or less (shaded), 1960–77.*[1]

Sources: World Bank, *World Development Report*, 1978 and 1979; Dorothy L. Nortman and Ellen Hofstatter, *Population and Family Planning Programs* (The Population Council, New York, 1978); W. Parker Mauldin and Bernard Berelson, 'Conditions of Fertility Decline in Developing Countries, 1965–1975,' in *Studies in Family Planning*, Vol. 9 (May 1978).

[1]Includes only countries with a population of at least five million in 1977; includes low-income and middle-income countries, capital surplus oil exporters, and centrally planned economies outside Europe with per capita gross national product (GNP) of less than $1,000.

[2]The index of social setting is obtained by dividing the countries into three groups containing about the same numbers of countries, on the basis of the index developed by Mauldin and Berelson (see source reference). Their index includes measures of adult literacy and school enrolment, life expectancy and infant mortality, men in nonagricultural activities, GNP per capita, and urbanisation.

levels of income, than did the European declines which began in the nineteenth century. And they are occasioned by different kinds of development:

> It was once assumed that reducing fertility in developing countries would first require urbanisation, industrialisation, a shift from family to factory production, and attainment of income levels close to those of the West. This view seemed confirmed by fertility declines in the 1960s that were largely confined to the industrialising economies of Taiwan, South Korea, Singapore and Hong Kong. But fertility declines beginning in other developing countries in the late 1960s and spreading to more in the 1970s have moved ahead of this kind of development. (Birdsall, 1980, p. 10)

The older type of development, of course, was in the economic structures associated with higher economic growth, such as higher average incomes and a shift from agriculture to industry. The newer type, Birdsall (1980) says, is 'one defined in terms of the alleviation of poverty and improvement in living standards'.

Robert Repetto (1979), on the basis of extensive research, has made a good case for change in the structure of social classes as the key to lower fertility in the LDCs. 'Economic equality', he calls it. The implication for development policy is that, to reduce birth rates, money is better spent on development efforts aimed specifically at the poor than it is on national economic development across the board. But anything aimed at helping the poor and which is economically intensive probably requires a social revolution within any nation.

Offsetting the heartening signs of new knowledge and humane socioeconomic and population change here and there, may be a more extensive political and ideological differentiation. 'Never have men been so near and so far from each other at one and the same time; the era in which means of communication are multiplying, distances shrinking', as Alfred Sauvy (1961) observed. He was describing the century-old antipathies of neo-Malthusians (who seek to avoid a painful sharing of riches) and Marxists (who would use rising poverty to blow up capitalism). His assessment of the results, so far as the politics of foreign aid and trade today are concerned, applies just as well in 1981 as it did in 1961. Let me quote from Sauvy as a conclusion to this chapter:

> The calculations of both camps are niggardly and unedifying. Helping under-developed countries but confining one's help to war subsidies and malthusian advice is tragically puerile. Trying to blow up a regime, in the atomic age, is a dangerous game. Even a murderous revolution is defensible, on condition that some people remain in the world to apply its principles . . . both camps are neglecting their

common interest: to help people out of the rut . . . neither camp seems to have any real consciousness of this common interest, this common danger [the rise of poverty]. (Sauvy, 1961, p. 228)

References: Chapter 3

Bachrach, P., and Bergman, E. (1973), *Power and Choice: The Formulation of American Population Policy* (Lexington, MA: Lexington Books).

Birdsall, Nancy (1980), *Population Growth and Poverty in the Developing World*, Population Bulletin, vol. 35, no. 5 (December), of the Population Reference Bureau, Washington, DC.

Bondestam, Lars, and Bergström, Staffan (1980), *Poverty and Population Control* (New York/London: Academic Press).

Bouvier, Leon F., with Henry S. Shryock and Harry W. Henderson (1977), *International Migration: Yesterday, Today and Tomorrow*, Population Bulletin, vol. 32, no. 4 (September), of the Population Reference Bureau, Washington, DC.

Cuca, Roberto (1980), 'Family planning programs and fertility decline', *Finance and Development*, vol. 17, no. 4 (December), pp. 37–9.

Demerath, Nicholas J. (1976), *Birth Control and Foreign Policy: The Alternatives to Family Planning* (New York: Harper & Row).

Du Bos, Rene (1965), *Man Adapting* (New Haven, CT: Yale University Press).

Etzioni, Amitai (1979), 'Beyond integration, toward guidability', in P. M. Hauser (ed.), *World Population and Development* (Syracuse, NY: Syracuse University Press).

Finkle, Jason L., and Crane, Barbara B. (1976), 'The World Health Organization and the population issue: organizational values in the United Nations', *Population and Development Review*, vol. 2, nos 3–4 (September–December).

Galle, Omer R., and Gove, Walter R. (1978), 'Overcrowding, isolation, and human behavior: exploring the extremes in population distribution', in K. A. Taeuber, L. Bumpass and J. A. Sweet (eds), *Social Demography* (New York/London: Academic Press).

King, Michael C. (1974), 'The malaise of migrant workers in Western Europe', *Migration Today*, no. 18, pp. 82–93.

Kleinman, David S. (1980), *Human Adaptation and Population Growth* (Montclair, NJ: Allanheld, Osmun).

Organski, Katherine, and Organski, A. F. K. (1961), *Population and World Power* (New York: Knopf).

Repetto, Robert (1979), *Economic Equality and Fertility in Developing Countries* (Washington, DC: Resources for the Future).

Ridker, Ronald G. (1979), 'Resource and environmental consequences of population and economic growth', in Philip M. Hauser (ed.), *World Population and Development* (Syracuse, NY: Syracuse University Press).

Sauvy, Alfred (1961), *Population Problems from Malthus to Mao Tse-Tung* (New York: Criterion Books).

Simon, Julian L. (1981), 'Global confusion 1980: a hard look at the Global 2000 Report', *Public Interest* (January).

Simon, Julian L., and Demerath, Nicholas J. (1982), 'The politics and finance of birth reduction', *American Demographics* (January).

Thomlinson, Ralph (1976), *Population Dynamics*, 2nd edn (New York: Random House).

4

An Ecological Approach

DENNIS PIRAGES

Over the last decade there has been a major transformation of the global political economy. The formerly ignored and powerless members of the Organisation of Petroleum Exporting Countries (OPEC) suddenly asserted themselves in relations with petroleum-importing countries and two resulting massive oil shocks have reverberated for years in the world economy. The industrial countries have been plagued, first, by double-digit inflation, and then a depression supposedly designed to cure inflationary ills. In most OECD countries there has been relatively little growth in real per capita income over the last ten years. The previously developing Third World is now divided into two parts: countries that have a reasonable chance of economic survival, and a never-to-be-developed world composed of numerous small countries with so little to market in international trade that they are consigned to seemingly permanent stagnation. The newly industrialising countries (NICs) have weathered the worst of these economic storms, but are now faced with massive obligations to international banks that may tie up the bulk of export earnings for many years. Given this tremendously convulsive decade, one might ask why conventional political and economic scholarship of the early 1970s failed to predict the events that were to follow.

The perspective offered in this chapter is that explanation of these momentous changes is enhanced by better understanding of the evolutionary relationship among human beings, their societies and the life-sustaining global ecosystem. *Homo sapiens* and the societies in which he lives exist in an interdependent relationship with a global ecosystem that supplies resources that are essential for the continued growth of human civilisation. These resources were once superabundant in relation to human demands, but given the rapid increase in human numbers and demands over the last century, many of them now seem very finite. The most obvious of these important resources are the fossil fuels, the energy source that has been responsible for creating much of the abundance of the industrial period.

Normal scholarly treatment of the international political economy depicts it as being relatively autonomous and a cause of various economic phenomena, rather than as a creation of underlying ecological factors. Existing political and economic structures are a product of the interaction of human societies with the physical environment and with each other. Differential rates of population growth, differing resource endowments and differing technological capabilities within societies have structured the existing global political economy. Understanding how these factors that shape relations among nations interact is essential for both analysis of future changes in the global political economy and for creating more effective alternative international institutions.

Social Evolution

Human social, political and economic institutions are constantly evolving in response to environmental changes (Waddington, 1960; Harris, 1979). Evolutionary principles can also be applied to understanding the evolution of the global political economy. It, even more than domestic social institutions, is driven by ecological factors. Throughout history nations have been the subject of Malthusian dramas in which populations repeatedly expanded beyond the carrying capacity of the land, and then were pruned back in periodic famines caused by changes in climate (McNeill, 1976). When population pressures have become severe and capabilities have existed to get resources elsewhere, nations have devised various strategies to meet their needs. The argument here, in brief, is that the present global political economy is the product of evolutionary pressures from the global ecosystem mediated through social and political institutions.

These evolutionary processes can be analysed on at least three different levels. *Homo sapiens*, like all other species, has physically been shaped by environmental possibilities. In the biological sciences the process of natural selection is considered responsible for shaping the physical nature of human beings. Those genotypes that most successfully adapt to the physical environment reproduce more frequently and thus shape the physical nature of succeeding generations. Over long stretches of history *Homo sapiens* has much more successfully adapted to and modified the physical environment than has most of the competition.

The impact of ecosystem pressures on the structure of human social action and institutions, both within and among nations, is a second level on which evolution can be analysed. It is on this level that changes in social behaviour, institutions, governments, multinational organisations, and so on, related to ecological variables, can be analysed. The social evolution on this level, in which norms and institutions are differentially selected for their survival potential, parallels the physical evolution described above. Social evolution takes place in the structures and behaviour that are responsible for passing survival-relevant information from generation to generation. Those forms of organisation that provide useful guidance in coping with survival dilemmas lead to prosperity for societies that embrace them, at least over the long term. Those forms that are not adapted to physical realities can lead to destruction if they do not change over time. History books are filled with tales of the decline of civilisations that were not appropriately organised to adapt to changing environmental challenges (Pirages, 1978).

Evolutionary pressures also affect the realm of ideas, values, beliefs and ideologies. Ideas about the correct way of doing things are a product of human experience with the physical environment. Capitalist economic ideologies, for example, grew and prospered during a period of rapid industrial expansion. It is not accidental that such beliefs received a great boost as Western European colonial empires expanded and as the frontier in the United States moved inexorably westward to more abundant resources. Nor is it accidental that the present perceived scarcities have given rise to challenges to orthodox growth economics (Daly, 1977). From an ecological perspective, ideas and ideologies reflect, albeit somewhat imperfectly, changes in the physical environment. Without such interactions, ideas would give no relevant guidance for effectively organising societies within different environmental contexts.

The point of view emphasised in this chapter is not commonly accepted in the social sciences because human beings have great difficulty coping with the fact that much of social life is shaped by physical constraints. A human exemptionalist bias masks perceptions of these selection pressures that operate in the social sphere (Dunlap, 1980). But on the other hand, there are limits to the amount of behaviour that can be explained from this perspective. The basic argument, however, is that many of the causes of human behaviour and institutions are anchored in the physical environment and filter into institutional arrangements and human belief systems very slowly over time.

Basic Concepts

A first principle in the ecological approach to global political economy is to recognise that human beings are political animals subject to the same laws of nature that govern other species. For much of human history *Homo sapiens* was involved in life-and-death struggles with other species and was not a terribly successful competitor. Lacking claws, tusks and rapid mobility, the human population of the world grew at an almost imperceptible rate for most of its non-arboreal history. It was not until the period of the agricultural revolution, which began about 8000 BC, that human numbers and activities became significant in competition with other species. And it was not until the technology-driven Industrial Revolution began to gather momentum that human activities became significant in relation to the sustaining capacity of the global ecosystem.

Human beings, like other species, live within groupings called populations. For an ecologist or a biologist, a population is a group of individuals of the same species that lives and interacts together. More technically speaking, a population can be described as 'a dynamic system of individuals that . . . are potentially capable of interbreeding with each other' (Watt, 1973). Thus the human population of the world could be said to number almost 5 billion persons, since it is technically possible for a human being anywhere on earth to interbreed with another human of the opposite sex. But we know that human beings live within and identify with much smaller populations on the nation-state level. Human populations, as opposed to those of other species, can be defined by their frequency of communication, both face-to-face and mediated, which is largely demarcated by the boundaries of nations. While it is theoretically possible for an Australian aborigine to interbreed with a Ukrainian peasant, it is much more likely that communicating and interbreeding will be done within their own respective populations.

While this transfer of biological definitions of population to the social realm might make some biologists uneasy, one of the big differences between *Homo sapiens* and other species is the extent to which communication is highly developed among humans. Human populations can be identified by communication patterns. If we were somehow able to map all of the face-to-face and mediated communications taking place in the world during any one week, it would be obvious that there are clearly demarcated communication clusters that are roughly coterminous with the boundaries of countries. Peoples are marked off from each other by communication barriers, by 'marked gaps' in the efficiency of communication (Deutsch, 1953). For biologists, then, populations can be identified by the objective frequency with which interbreeding takes place. But for social scientists, such boundaries need not be determined by counting offspring.

Recognising nation-states as populations of human beings subject to many of the same laws of nature that govern the behaviour of populations of other species is an important principle of an ecological approach to international political economy. Humans have a tendency to expand numbers and appetites until they reach, or exceed, the carrying capacity of the territory on which they live. Prior to the global spread of the Industrial Revolution there were thousands of isolated groups of humans that could have easily met biological or sociological tests as distinct populations. The dynamics of the Industrial Revolution have forged these smaller populations into a limited number of nation-states which form the population building-blocks for an ecological analysis of the global political economy.

Another basic principle of the ecological perspective is that national populations require large quantities of resources if they are to continue to grow and prosper. In biological terminology a resource is anything needed by an organism, population or ecosystem which, by its increasing availability up to an optimal or sufficient level, allows an increasing rate of energy conversion (Watt, 1973). Put in social science terms, this simply means that human populations, like those of other species, require various kinds of resources if they are to continue to grow in numbers and quality of life. The most obvious resource required by human beings for survival is food. Food is the source of the energy that keeps the human body active. Throughout most of human history the work that has been done by humans has been accomplished almost entirely from animate energy sources, carried by people and beasts of burden (Cipolla). During the Industrial Revolution, however, energy from the fossil fuels has been employed in an ever-greater number of tasks until, at present, most of the work done is accomplished by machines running on fossil fuels.

Although they are not usually thought of as being as important as energy, there are many other resources required by human populations. The global ecosystem, for example, provides waste-dispersal capacity to move toxic waste products away from densely populated areas. The wind, movement of the earth's atmosphere, moves potentially dangerous gasses out of urban areas, dispersing them downwind. Rivers also have been used to disperse liquid and solid wastes for centuries. In addition to these waste-dispersal resources, human populations also need air, water and various non-fuel minerals such as iron, copper and bauxite.

Contemporary nations are experiencing a tremendous growth in demand for larger quantities and new varieties of resources. Most advanced industrial societies are no longer sustained with the resources located within their borders. Since the mix of available resources structures a nation's potential for growth and development, the growth imperative provides the impetus for using various means to seek them beyond national borders. During the period of Western European colonisation resources were acquired from colonies at minimum prices. Since the dissolution of colonial empires and development of sanctions against taking possession of resources by force, needed resources are now obtained by various trading arrangements in an integrated global economy.

Another concept critical to understanding the ecological perspective on the global political economy concerns a key difference between human beings and other species. Human beings use technology to alter dramatically relationships with other species, as well as with supporting ecosystems. Technological innovations have been imperative to sustain the billions of humans now on the earth's surface. They have created demands for a wider variety and greater quantity of natural resources but have also increased the efficiency with which they are obtained.

Technology is a force that has played a critical role in structuring the present global political economy. The impact of technology on power relationships among nations is obvious. Those nations, for example, that possess significant quantities of nuclear weapons are in a different category than those with only conventional arms. Not quite so obvious, but of equal significance, is the economic power associated with technological development. The present international economic hierarchy, with its pronounced differences in standards of living, is in large measure a product of and is sustained by differing levels of technological capabilities. The wealthy industrial countries dominate an international trade system in which technological innovation permits them to develop a comparative advantage in almost any product in which they choose to invest. The United States, for example, which is hardly a country with a climatic advantage for growing rice, uses high-technology growth techniques to remain the world's number-one exporter of rice.

The less developed countries, by contrast, muddle through with technologies transferred from their highly industrialised counterparts. While they are useful in stimulating economic growth in the less developed world, such borrowed technologies do not normally give recipient countries any competitive edge in marketing products in a sophisticated world economy. The presently less developed world, in most cases, is consigned to the export of basic commodities (the resources required for sustained growth in industrial countries) or labour-intensive products for which there is only limited demand.

Technological progress has been a mixed blessing. A heavy price has been paid in terms of disruption of many life-sustaining ecosystems. With no exceptions, technological economic development has entailed increasing accumulations of residues, many of which cause damage to human and non-human populations, and continuing hazards of future damage (Sprout and Sprout, 1978). Technological progress has altered many ecological constraints on human populations, but its by-products threaten long-term damage to the ecosystems that sustain human life.

The Global Ecosystem – Approaching Capacity?

The global ecosystem refers to the planetary total of smaller ecosystems that have sustained the evolution of the human race. *Homo sapiens* shares the physical systems of the earth with as many as 10 million other species. This diverse array of creatures is knit together in highly interdependent biological communities. The total of living and sustaining components of all of these communities grouped together is known as the global ecosystem or ecosphere (Ehrlich *et al.*, 1977, p. 97).

The global ecosystem has a limited capacity to provide resources for all of the dynamic and growing communities on earth. Before the Industrial Revolution, the human impact on the global resource treasury was relatively small. While certain human populations put intolerable strains on regional ecosystems, the pressures were localised and did not threaten the capacities of the entire ecosphere. In the 1980s, however, because of a rapid increase in human population and industrial activity, there is grave concern that the natural resources of the global ecosystem, including its waste-dispersal capacities, will be inadequate to sustain future growth (Meadows, 1972; United States, 1980). The interaction of the growing human population with its complicated demands and the physical limits of the global ecosystem provides a starting-point for understanding many of the issues on the contemporary global political economy agenda.

Ecological factors, starting with patterns of population growth, provide a beginning for analysis of the contemporary global political economy. For most of human history the rate of population growth was very slow. It took hundreds of thousands of years of almost imperceptible increase to reach a world population estimated at only 500 million in 1650 AD. But with the worldwide spread of the Industrial Revolution, there has been a tremendous surge in human population. The 500 million in 1650 doubled to 1 billion by the year 1850, a doubling time of only 200 years. The population doubled again in only eighty years, reaching 2 billion by 1930. By 1970 the global population had doubled again to 4 billion, the doubling time having been cut to less than forty years.

It appears that the 1960s and 1970s will be known historically as the decades of most rapid population growth in human history. During those two decades the growth rate of world population reached a rate of 2 per cent per year which means a population doubling time of only thirty-five years. In the 1980s world population growth seems to have turned a corner and the doubling time is beginning to lengthen due to the slow spread of family planning programmes to the less developed countries. But there are already 4·7 billion human beings and this number is expected to grow to 6·1 billion by the year 2000. Barring some unforeseen catastrophes, world population should reach 7·7 billion by the year 2020 and continue to grow.

A less-noticed aspect of world population growth is its future distribution. Table 4.1 contains estimates of present regional distribution and projections for the year 2020. The industrial countries are expected to approach zero population growth during this period and their populations will increase very slowly. The population of the United States is expected to increase from 232 million to 274 million. The population of the United Kingdom is not expected to increase much at all over the period. In the less developed countries, by contrast, population figures are expected to take a big leap. The population of Latin America is

Table 4.1 *Regional Population Projections*

	1982	2000	2020
Africa	498	847	1,344
Asia	2,671	3,528	4,368
South America	378	549	769
Europe	488	511	508
North America	256	286	308
Soviet Union	270	302	346
United Kingdom	56	57	57
World	4,585	6,082	7,678

Source: UN 1982 World Population Data Sheet of the Population Reference Bureau.

expected to jump from 378 million to 769 million by 2020, and the population of Asia from 2,671 million to 4,368 million during the same period. Africa will explode from a present 498 million to 1,344 million.

When all the projections are added and analysed, a clear shift in the balance of the world's population away from Western Europe and the United States towards the less developed countries is obvious. Of a projected world population of 7,678 million in 2020, only about 11 per cent (816 million) will live in North America and Western Europe. This is due to the demographic momentum inherent in the large numbers of young people in pre-reproductive age groups living in the less developed countries and the failure of the demographic transition to have a significant impact in the less developed countries until well after the year 2000, problems that are discussed more fully by Demerath in Chapter 3 on population.

It is these rapidly growing numbers that put pressures on the global ecosystem and create serious economic development problems for those countries experiencing the highest rates of population growth. In Kenya, for example, the 1982 rate of population growth was nearly 4 per cent, meaning that the economic infrastructure must be doubled every seventeen years just to stay even in per capita figures. Many other less developed countries face similar problems in simply maintaining present development levels.

The anomaly that besets development efforts from an ecological point of view is that successful economic growth in the face of such large population increases requires more resources of all kinds. During the economic stagnation of the early 1980s the pressures on natural resources have remained limited and prices have been stable or even declined. To the extent that development goals are met, however, large price increases for basic commodities, including petroleum, might well reduce the potential for future economic development.

A primary consequence of previous industrialisation has been growing dependency of the industrialised countries on the LDCs for many of the raw materials that are essential for economic growth. Japan, the United States and most Western European countries rely on large quantities of imported non-fuel minerals. Japan has very few mineral resources of any value and almost all its needs must be met by imports from abroad. The United States imports more than 90 per cent of its consumption of strontium, cobalt, manganese, chromium, aluminium, platinum and tantalum, as well as significant quantities of other non-fuel minerals. Western European countries, including Britain, have similar mineral-import profiles.

Industrialisation and economic development have also been accompanied by growing energy dependence. While the United Kingdom has been fortunate in its recent discovery and exploitation of offshore petroleum supplies, most other mature industrial countries have become dependent on Middle Eastern petroleum. Japan imports nearly all petroleum consumed, and the United States imported nearly 50 per cent of its consumed petroleum in the late 1970s before the recent depression cut back on the need for energy. If economic development is to become a reality for the bulk of the world's population living in less developed countries, additional competition for limited petroleum supplies will be an important factor in the global political economy in the twenty-first century.

Industrial growth has historically meant moving beyond the carrying capacity or domestic resource base of each industrialising nation. In the past there have always been less developed countries with excess resources and they have been willing to support the higher levels of consumption in the developed countries. In a sense uneven development has been a requisite for rapid growth in the developed world. But where will imported natural resources come from in a world in which the contemporary LDCs would require their own resource production for domestic economic growth? The actions taken by OPEC in the 1970s to develop their own downstream facilities could well represent initial shots in protracted political-economic warfare stemming from greater consumption requirements on the part of economically developing countries in a world in which natural resources have not been equitably distributed (Fesharaki and Isaak, 1981).

Among the less visible resources essential to industrial growth are the global waste-dispersal systems already referred to above. These include the atmosphere, which disperses the toxic gases associated with intensive industrial activity and the hydrosphere, the world's oceans, lakes and streams, which disperse the dangerous effluents from urban areas. Since these systems are shared in common by all nations, it seems to be in everyone's short-term interest to pollute rather than to internalise costs by requiring polluters to install expensive anti-pollution equipment. In a sense what is happening to these global waste-dispersal systems parallels the tragedies of the commons that took place in mediaeval England. Commons shared by all villagers sometimes collapsed from overgrazing as each individual saw it in his or her own self-interest to pasture as many livestock as possible on the commons. Eventually this rational action on the part of each villager led to the collapse of the overgrazed commons (Hardin, 1968). A similar process is taking place with the global waste-dispersal resources as increasing demands by sovereign nations threaten to destroy their ability to disperse toxic wastes.

The increasing impact of growing populations and per capita living standards on the ecosphere is no longer a matter of conjecture. Two very real environmental problems have already become the subject of international disputes and negotiations. The first is acid rain which results from combustion of fossil fuels. Sulphur dioxide and nitrous oxide combine with water vapour in the atmosphere and increase the acidity of rainfall over large areas. Small-scale industrial activity had little noticeable impact on the generation of acid rain, but large-scale contemporary industrial activity, combined with automobile emissions, has magnified the problem tremendously. In large areas of southern Canada, the eastern United States, Northern and Eastern Europe the acidity of rainfall has changed from a pH of 5·7 to 4·5, which seems to be enough to have a major impact on delicate ecosystems in lakes and streams (United States, 1980, p. 36). Canada and the United States are locked in protracted diplomatic negotiations over the acid rain moving north into Canada from power stations in the Ohio Valley.

A second problem is the increase of carbon dioxide in the atmosphere, also a product of fossil-fuel combustion. While the impact of the slow but steady increase in carbon dioxide in the atmosphere is not yet apparent, there are many studies that project a significant warming of the entire planet because of the 'greenhouse' effect created by increased carbon dioxide concentration in the atmosphere. If fossil-fuel combustion increases at only 2 per cent per year, by the middle of the next century the average temperature of the earth at the middle latitudes could be expected to increase by 2 to 3 degC causing potentially disastrous changes in climate. Some even suggest that such a warming could melt the icecaps and cause a major modification of global climate (United States, 1980, p. 37).

The picture that emerges of the future global political economy based on this ecological perspective is one of increasing domestic pressures to maintain access to cheap resources that have previously sustained economic growth in the developed countries. Choucri and North (1975) have identified demand growth in the face of resource inadequacies as a source of lateral pressure to move beyond national borders in order to obtain resources deemed essential for national prosperity. The form in which such pressures become manifest (that is, increases in trade or creation of rapid deployment forces to defend the Middle East) depends upon a country's physical location, level of technological development, perceived resource needs and the power and perceptions of neighbouring or target nations.

There are a number of ways that these lateral pressures can be expected to affect the future global political economy. The most obvious is increased potential for resource-oriented conflict. Some political leaders in the United States, for example, see the Middle East as a potential target for Russian military adventures aimed at severing petroleum connections to the rest of the industrial world. They also see the Soviet natural-gas pipeline as a grave security threat to Western Europe. European leaders, however, see the pipeline as a method of diversifying energy suppliers and moving away from dependence on the Middle East.

Another obvious impact of population-related lateral pressures from less developed countries is an increase in international migration. Differential levels of economic opportunity serve as a magnet to people from depressed areas of the world and significant international migration to the United States, Britain and Western Europe could become a more severe problem over the next decade because of continued economic stagnation in the non-oil-exporting LDCs.

Global Markets

Lateral pressures that could cause conflicts among nations have also been responsible for creating greater interdependence among them. In the early stages of the Industrial Revolution many European nations met demands for additional resources by using superior technology to support an aggressive outward expansion to colonise large areas of the non-industrial world (Wallerstein, 1974, pp. 39–48). The Portuguese, Dutch, British, Germans and eventually smaller European powers acquired territories for this purpose in distant parts of the world. These territories eventually provided agricultural commodities, fuels, precious metals, other minerals and, in some cases, human labour. At the beginning of the First World War 84 per cent of the world's land was or had been under the control of colonial powers (Fieldhouse, 1973, p. 3).

The Second World War hastened the dissolution of colonial empires and the resources that once were taken from less developed countries became a key ingredient in emerging trade relationships. The direct colonial exploitation of less developed areas of the world is now defined as a malevolent manifestation of lateral pressures. The complex interdependence that has emerged since the Second World War is most often thought of as a more benevolent manifestation. Most scholars who write about interdependence see it as a positive development that eventually will knit members of an emerging global community more tightly together. But the dislocations in the international political economy that have taken place over the last decade have led to a reassessment of the benevolence and malevolence of complex interdependence.

One of the most important impacts of growing resource dependency in the industrialising countries has been the development of resource markets that are global in scope. As the global economy has become increasingly interdependent, some nations have become sensitive to each other, a condition of mutual interdependence by choice. But in increasingly integrated global markets the sensitivity can turn to vulnerability and control of key resources can be used as a weapon in gaining political ends (Keohane and Nye, 1977). Thus more extensive international trade, an increasingly complex division of labour and growth of global markets for critical resources can be seen as both a positive and negative development.

The most critical interdependent global resource market that has developed to date is in petroleum. A world oil market has developed because most industrialised and industrialising countries have inadequate domestic supplies of petroleum and natural gas, preferred energy sources because they are clean, efficient and can be easily transported. In some countries such as France, Italy and Japan petroleum reserves were always limited and dependence upon imports developed several decades ago. In the United States petroleum was once abundant, but early and sustained consumption has resulted in depleted reserves. The Soviet Union, with petroleum reserves of more than 85 billion barrels, stands almost alone among industrialised countries in that it can count on self-sufficiency over the next two decades.

The energy predicament of the United States is typical of many industrial countries. The United States historically has produced more than 130 billion barrels of domestic crude oil, a figure that is not far short of Saudi Arabian reserves. But because of decades of industrial use, the abundance has disappeared and the present 30 billion barrel reserve would disappear in only five years if all domestic petroleum needs were met from existing reserves. As a result, the United States became a major oil importer in the late 1960s and imports reached 50 per cent of consumption in the late 1970s. In the economic depression of the early 1980s imports fell back to about 40 per cent of consumption. Britain is in a much better situation given the recent exploitation of offshore discoveries, but without major new discoveries will be in a similar situation within a decade.

The dilemma faced by most of the industrial and industrialising countries is that sustained economic progress requires increases in energy consumption and, for most purposes, petroleum is still a cheaper and better fuel. In the long run it is possible that world petroleum supplies will be inadequate to sustain industrial growth in all countries and that absolute scarcity will limit growth within a few decades. In the short run, however, it is the concentration of world reserves in the hands of a few countries that has been responsible for upsetting the international political economy.

Table 4.2 indicates present estimates of world petroleum reserves. The pattern of concentration that led to the two 'oil shocks' of the 1970s is very clear. Of the top ten countries in total reserves, seven are members of OPEC. The exceptions are the United States, which is a net importer of petroleum; the Soviet Union, which exports mainly to Eastern Europe; and Mexico, a rapidly rising exporter of petroleum that has co-ordinated its prices with those of OPEC. Saudi Arabia alone possesses nearly one-quarter of present world reserves and has, until recently, been the world's number-two producer of petroleum. Given its relatively small domestic requirements, Saudi Arabia has also been the world's dominant petroleum exporter over the last decade. The remaining OPEC members in the table account for 37 per cent of world reserves. Thus the nine OPEC countries with the largest reserves account for 61 per cent of reserves and the lion's share of world exports.

The global energy market is one of concentration of supply in a handful of exporting countries and growing vulnerability on the part of most other industrially developed and developing countries. There is no reason to fear such interdependence under conditions of abundance with multiple suppliers. But given that petroleum is a finite resource that may not be available in large quantities in only a few decades and

Table 4.2   *Major Petroleum Reserve Countries*

	1981	1977
Saudi Arabia	158	110
Soviet Union	85	59
Kuwait	67	72
Mexico	48	10
Iran	39	47
Abu Dhabi	36	24
Iraq	34	35
United States	29	29
Libya	25	25
Venezuela	20	18
China	19	18
Nigeria	11	12
Indonesia	10	8
Norway	9	5
United Kingdom	8	10
World	660	543

Note: Data in billions of barrels.
Source: World Oil, July 1982 and July 1978.

that the OPEC cartel controls most of the world's exportable reserves, the growing interdependence of the energy market represents a serious economic and political problem for all importers. The Organisation of Arab Petroleum Exporters (OAPEC) legitimised the use of the oil weapon in 1973 by seeking to deny petroleum to hostile industrial countries in 1973. The resulting quadrupling of oil prices sent a shock-wave through the global political economy and resulted in major trauma in the international financial community. The oil shock of 1979, triggered by the fall of the Shah of Iran, found the industrial importers once again in a complacent mood fostered by their perception of an oil glut. It took a reduction in supply of only a few per cent to drive the price of a barrel of oil from $13·00 per barrel to $34·00 per barrel in less than a year.

In the 1980s the importing countries are once again complacent as the world petroleum market appears to be awash with excess oil. While energy conservation accounts for part of the excess supply, the global depression also accounts for much of the lagging petroleum demand. Thus for the moment the ill-health of the world economy appears to have solved the energy vulnerability problem. But should the industrial economies recover, it is very likely that the oil shock syndrome will be played out yet another time. Whether international financial markets could withstand another oil shock in the wake of the massive increase in developing country debt and default remains to be seen.

The growth of global energy interdependence is being repeated in the world food market. While there is presently little comparison between the percentage of petroleum in international trade and that of food, there are disturbing signs that future vulnerabilities are being created. Over the last decade the percentage of grain production entering into the world market has doubled from 10 to 20 per cent. Global population growth has created a larger world market for food, but the modernisation process is responsible for creating new customers. The new customers in the international grain market are found in two categories. The centralised economies, chiefly the Soviet Union, have increased their imports over the last decade in response to both consumer demands and poor harvests. The second category of new customers is made up of the rapidly industrialising LDCs, some of the oil exporters and a few of the least developed countries.

The tight market problem that has been responsible for the oil shocks could also be a factor in the future world food market. World food production has been climbing at a rate that has been just slightly ahead of global population growth for the last decade. This is projected to continue at least through the year 2000. But these global figures disguise serious potential difficulties. For the period 1970–2000 world food production on a per capita basis is projected to increase by 18 per cent. But most of this increase in production will be limited to expensive high-technology production in the industrial countries. Per capita production in the less developed countries is projected to increase by only 11 per cent over the same period. In Africa, by contrast, per capita production is expected to drop by 16 per cent (United States, 1980, tables 5, 6).

These are optimistic estimates and the recent performance of the world food market cautions against complacency. A major worry about a more integrated global food market is that the tight market conditions of the early 1970s could return again in the latter half of the 1980s due to climatic factors. The major grain exporters are even more concentrated than the major petroleum exporters and successive crop failures in the United States, Canada, or Australia could cause serious market disruptions. Under tight market conditions the less developed countries which could not afford to compete for food would be adversely affected and perhaps would fall victim to massive starvation. Those countries dependent upon concessional food aid would be left to fend for themselves. Whereas in the pre-global market era there were certainly significant famines based on local shortages, in a future world food market famine could approach global proportions. While food self-sufficiency need not be a requisite for economic policy in all countries, those that do choose to ignore domestic agricultural development may expect to pay a high price in the future for their neglect.

In summary, from an ecological perspective the increased interdependence of global resource markets represents a matter of concern for policy-makers in countries that are becoming increasingly vulnerable. Ecological scarcity and related tight markets not only represent long-term threats to those most dependent on foreign suppliers, but in the short term these tight markets give political leverage to major exporters who choose to use their commodities as weapons.

Conclusions

An ecological approach to the study of global political economy stresses the impact of population, resource and technology variables on economic, political and social institutions as well as on ideologies and beliefs which guide human behaviour. It emphasises the shaping nature of these ecological variables, as well as the necessity of creating institutions adequate to deal with the type of problems created by demographic and technological changes and a rapidly shrinking global commons. Given the agenda of global issues facing the human race over coming decades, the ecology-based study of global political economy may well replace the traditional agenda of concerns in international relations.

Moving through the 1980s a number of ecology-related trends in the global political economy are becoming more apparent. Perhaps the most obvious is an accentuation of cyclical economic performance related to pressures in tight resource markets. The so-called Kondratief 'long cycles', technology-driven changes in economic productivity, are being reinforced by resource scarcities that may well have an impact on future possibilities for new technological discoveries and related economic growth (see Freeman *et al.*, 1982). For example, it could be argued that the progress of the industrial period has been the result of new technologies focused on cheap fossil fuels. But the so-called fossil find subsidy has disappeared and it now costs much more in economic and net energy terms to discover, transport and refine petroleum (Cook, 1976).

Two related factors accentuate boom and bust cycles; unstable resource prices and inadequate institutions. As tight resource markets have developed, consumer panic has had a destabilising impact on prices. The price runups of 1973–4 and 1979–80 in the world oil market were far in excess of any rational economic response. A similar situation existed in the tight food and non-fuel mineral markets in the early 1970s. A rapid global recovery over the next decade could well induce another massive global inflation in basic commodities.

The institutional responses to rapid price increases indicate the weaknesses of existing structures in dealing with future ecological scarcities. The weapon used to remedy resource-related inflation, tight monetary policy, proved to be much more destructive than the inflation it was intended to cure. High interest rates have forced several large developing countries to the brink of bankruptcy as their debt burdens, acquired in most cases to finance petroleum imports, have overwhelmed their ability to pay in a stagnant global economy. It is clear that new political and economic perspectives and institutions will be required to deal with the pernicious effects of future ecological scarcity on both domestic and global economies.

Aside from the problems associated with accentuated boom and bust cycles, there are very serious questions about the ability of the industrial economies to promote a sustained economic recovery. Economic growth requires technological innovations which, in turn, require significant capital investment. The damaging effects of price and interest-rate instability combined with a double-edged demographic problem makes the source of future technological innovation problematic. In the less developed countries rapid rates of population growth mean that available capital goes into immediate consumption and little is left to provide a surplus for investment in new technologies. But in the industrial countries a population slowdown is causing a shift in population structures towards the older age groups. As a larger percentage of industrial populations moves past retirement, existing entitlement programmes threaten to bankrupt industrial economies. Under projected demographic conditions there may be very little capital surplus to put into the requisite investment activities.

Thus, from an ecological perspective, the future of the global political economy will be shaped by an increasing number of global issues and related sets of problems and discontinuities. Resolving these issues and solving these problems can best be accomplished through an increased understanding of the complex relationships between the changing global ecosystem and economic, political and social institutions and values.

References: Chapter 4

Choucri, Nazli, and North, Robert (1975), *Nations in Conflict* (San Francisco, CA: Freeman).

Cook, Earl (1976), *Man, Energy, Society* (San Francisco, CA: Freeman).

Daly, Herman (1977), *Steady-State Economics* (San Francisco, CA: Freeman).

Deutsch, Karl (1953), *Nationalism and Social Communication* (Cambridge, MA: MIT Press).

Dunlap, Riley (1980), 'Paradigmatic change in social science: from human exemptionalism to an ecological paradigm', *American Behavioral Scientist* (September–October).

Ehrlich, Paul, Ehrlich, Anne, and Holdren, John (1977), *Ecoscience* (San Francisco, CA: Freeman).

Fesharaki, Fereidun, and Isaak, David (1981), 'OPEC downstream processing', East–West Center, Honolulu.

Fieldhouse, D. (1973), *Economics and Empire, 1830–1914* (New York: Cornell University Press).

Freeman, Christopher, Clark, John, and Soete, Luc (1982), *Unemployment and Technological Innovation* (Westport, CT: Greenwood Press).

Hardin, Garrett (1968), 'The tragedy of the commons', *Science*, no. 162.

Harris, Marvin (1979), *Cultural Materialism* (New York: Random House).

Keohane, R., and Nye, J. (1977), *Power and Interdependence* (Boston, MA: Little, Brown).

McNeill, William (1976), *Plagues and Peoples* (Chicago, IL: University of Chicago Press).

Meadows, D. L., and Meadows, D. H. (eds) (1972), *The Limits to Growth* (New York: Universe Books).

Pirages, Dennis (1978), *Global Ecopolitics* (North Scituate, MA: Duxbury Press).

Sprout, Harold, and Sprout, Margaret (1978), *The Context of Environmental Politics* (Lexington, Ky: University of Kentucky Press).

United States (1980), Council on Environmental Quality and Department of State, *Global 2000: Report to the President of the United States Entering the Twenty-first Century* (New York: Pergamon).

Waddington, Conrad (1960), *The Ethical Animal* (Ann Arbor, Mich.: University of Michigan Press).

Wallerstein, I. (1974), *The Modern World System* (New York: Academic Press).

Watt, Kenneth (1973), *Principles of Environmental Science* (New York: McGraw-Hill).

5

The International Political Economy of Technology

ROGER WILLIAMS

From the perspective of political economy, technology is a fourth and possibly now the most important of the factors of production; and the capacity to produce it equals power. It follows that the development and exploitation of technology tends to change power relationships, whether these are social, economic, political, or military. In this chapter the focus will be on certain of the more international aspects of political and economic power relationships affected by technology. A quotation from a standard textbook will serve conveniently to ground what follows in the mainstream of the international relations literature. Thus Holsti (1974), discussing the current predominant indicators of international status, observes that 'Today the primary standard of judgement is technology and all the material things that derive from its application to economic activity'. This Holsti subsequently qualifies, but only slightly; his basic conclusion is really now too commonplace to prompt much dissent.

The exploitation of technology in the modern world is a function of both 'supply push' and of 'demand pull'. The supply of technology is a function of the potential in the current state of the art as determined by research and development, the institutionalisation of this latter activity this century, and especially since the Second World War, constituting one of history's major benchmarks. The 'demand' for technology results from judgements made by private and public decision-makers as to what consumers, that is, the public at large, corporate bodies, the government and the military, will be prepared to buy, the freedom of these consumers being constrained by the options with which they are presented no less than by their economic circumstances. The stream of new technology which has emerged from this 'pull–push' interaction having in recent decades been both qualitatively and quantitatively unprecedented, the ramifications for international political economy have themselves been profound.

It may be noted that the exact relationship between research and development on the one hand, and technological innovation on the other, is not as well understood presently as it was widely thought to be two decades ago. It must also be realised that, with research and development a fully international activity, the hope of comparative advantage and the fear of comparative disadvantage between them mean that there is no realistic possibility, in the prevailing international circumstances, of halting research and development in any sector – even research moratoria will be very few, brief and of limited reliability. This being so, it will be appreciated as well that although predicting technological development is now a much-practised pursuit, it remains nevertheless a highly uncertain one. These three points about research and development and the technical innovation resulting from them do not require expansion in this chapter, but their general implications will be worth bearing in mind in what follows.

Identifying and classifying the main elements in the international political economy of technology must necessarily in part be a matter of definition and of individual opinion, but there are certain items which one would expect to appear in any inventory (Basiuk, 1977). In the first place while it is not quite true to say that technology was respon- sible for creating multinational companies (MNCs), there can be no doubt that technology is procedurally, and often also substantively, central to the operations of these organisations, and therefore largely the cause of their contemporary apotheosis. In the second place there falls to be considered the consequences both of the differential facility with existing technology evidenced by states broadly categorised as industrially similar, and also of the differential access to the newest technology experienced by all states. In the third place there are the facts that the potential of technology has repeatedly in recent decades led governments to collaborate in the elaboration and implementation of new technological projects and programmes; that its dynamic has over an even longer period led them to set up one international organ- isation or regime after another; and that its threat is increasingly driving them to co-operate in determining and controlling risks and hazards which earlier went unrecognised or ignored.

In addition to these three broad areas, there are also several other far from minor issues in the international political economy of technology – two of the more miscellaneous issues considered briefly below are the arms trade viewed as an economic activity, and the emergence of a measure of internationally co-ordinated response, or even opposition, to technology on the part of unions, consumers and the various environmental lobbies. Since one technology – nuclear – overlaps most of the above headings, it seems worthy on this account, as well as because of its inherent importance, of some separate discussion. And underlying all classifications, of course, is the greatly expanded economic interdependence which so characterises contemporary international society. *Technological dynamism was certainly a necessary condition of interdependence on this scale*, and it may even have been a sufficient one, given that few states could be expected, at least for long, to accept the economic penalties which it seems are inescapably concomitant with the political assertion of any independence entailing scientific and technical isolationism.

The Multinationals

To begin with, global reach of MNCs (Barnet and Müller, 1975; Williams, 1979; Madden, 1977; Buckley and Casson, 1976; Curzon *et al.*, 1977; Vernon, 1977) was made procedurally possible by the modern technologies of communication, transportation and computation, and for many of them their substantive activities as well are centred upon technology. This last is naturally most true for manufacturing multinationals, but it is also largely true of resource multinationals, and may even be true, if more marginally, of service ones. Whatever the substantive activities of an MNC, the essence of multinational operation is expertise in the techniques of international organisation, management and finance, and an MNC's independence is ultimately dependent on its skills in these respects, on the exclusiveness of its technology, and on the extent to which its operations are or can be made internationally mobile. The style and methods of most MNCs are now highly sophisticated, as events show, sometimes even in the original sense of that word.

In principle MNCs are economic actors, but in practice, and whether or not by deliberate choice, they commonly play political roles in furtherance of their economic objectives. In addition, the wider social consequences of their activities can be both deep and far-reaching, for they are the incidental importers of what may be alien values. The multinational headquarters and its subsidiaries are a kind of sun-and-satellites system, while the awareness, competence and determination of both the base and the host governments together determine the overall freedom within which the MNC must operate. To the base government the MNC is both something to be controlled, in which case it is not unlike a purely national corporation, though presenting more complications, and also a tempting instrument of foreign policy. On the other hand, the activities of the MNC in its own right will themselves have implications of a general, and sometimes acute, kind for the foreign policy of the base government, as well as leading in particular instances to the MNC seeking to influence the policy orientation of that government or of one of its component bureaucracies. To the host government the MNC, even when it is the bearer of highly desired fruits, in the form of technology, employment, revenue, or the promise of exports, must still remain to some extent an object of suspicion. Always there is the fear that it may so have arranged its affairs as to elude the best efforts of the host government's regulatory provisions, always the possibility that if provoked, or even for reasons quite unconnected with events in the host country, it may simply pack up and take itself off.

It is readily apparent that the great divide among host governments is that between the developed and the developing countries. Admittedly, there are developed countries in which penetration by foreign multinationals is exceptionally extensive – Canada is perhaps the best example, and the case of Lockheed has shown, if this needed showing, that corruption in international commerce can be a serious problem even for advanced industrial states, but the fact remains that it is in developing countries that dependence on MNCs, or possibly on just one MNC, tends to be greatest, and it is also in these countries that the ability of the bureaucracy to monitor and control MNCs is least. A certain amount has been made in recent years (Heenan and Keegan, 1979) of the fact that a few developing countries are now themselves bases as well as hosts for MNCs, and one group of developing countries, the oil producers, has shown that the tiger can be taken by the tail if the circumstances are sufficiently propitious (Turner, 1978). These developments, however, scarcely affect the underlying problem of developing country weakness in the face of MNC power.

American multinationals have tended to be singled out for particular analysis and criticism. Their conduct and objectives were a principal source of the virtual hysteria about the 'American challenge' and the transatlantic 'technology gap' which so affected Western Europe in the late 1960s and their behaviour in the Third World and, above all, in Latin America has continued to generate reprobation. Apart from whatever absolute level of problem through their own actions American MNCs present to the governments of the countries in which their subsidiaries operate, there are two factors at least which do set them apart among MNCs. The first of these is that American MNCs are widely seen as standing in a much closer relationship to American state power, with all that that suggests, than is the case with the MNCs of any other country (Nau, 1976; Bergsten *et al.*, 1978). The second point is that decidedly more information about their activities is normally available, thanks to American law, congressional inquiry and business school research, than is ordinarily the case with multinationals based in Europe. In fact, European multinationals have as a group made big strides in the last decade, presenting the United States, in the eyes of some, with something of a reverse challenge (*The Economist*, 4 February 1978). It also appears that the earlier reluctance of Japan's powerful Ministry of International Trade and Industry to encourage the emergence of Japanese multinationals has now largely been abandoned – as one example, in 1980, in which Japanese manufacture of motor vehicles overtook that of the United States and the profits of Japan's car manufacturers were of the same order as the losses by Detroit's 'big four', several of the Japanese firms were nevertheless on the point of accepting that, to ensure access to overseas markets, their highly successful formula of domestic manufacture and foreign sales would have to be superseded by the multinational manufacturing approach long since adopted by Ford and General Motors.

The striking postwar expansion of MNCs in the manufacturing sector having stimulated increasing political interest in the implications of multinational commercial operations, the 'high-technology' MNCs have been the subject of especial attention (Freeman, 1974; Mansfield *et al.*, 1971; Kelly and Kranzberg, 1978; Utterback, 1978; Baranson, 1978). The American magazine *Fortune* has been publishing its list of the leading American manufacturing and mining companies – a large proportion of which are naturally now multinational – for a quarter of a century. Over that twenty-five years some of the most conspicuous gains in this list have been made by high-technology companies, many of them having been too small to be included in 1955, and several of them not even having existed at that time.

The main foci of concern with manufacturing, and especially high-technology, MNCs have been the location of research and development facilities, the consequences of the specific manufacturing arrangements which such MNCs choose to make, and the implications of technological near-monopoly where this appears in prospect. The geographical distribution of MNC research and development is important for several reasons – because of its effects on that highly emotive phenomenon, the 'brain-drain', because of the restrictions it indirectly introduces on the diffusion of technical ideas and personnel, because the presence or absence of the kind of staff employed in research and development has a bearing on the local socioeconomic infrastructure (and, over time, vice versa), and because the organisation of research and development can influence the manufacturing arrangements of the MNC concerned. The most contentious aspect of the manufacturing arrangements of an MNC arises from the possibility which usually exists, and is commonly taken, to manufacture components separately in each of several countries, assembling them into a finished product in yet another, or others (Michalet, 1976). Though this may not be the main intention, such a policy evidently reduces the leverage of governments and unions in the countries where component manufacture and assembly take place, even more so if all processes are duplicated. As to concern with technological near-monopoly, the obvious, though not the only, example is naturally IBM in the context of whose activities many governments have striven desperately to maintain, with mixed success, some independent national capability.

Apart from these various problems associated with, especially, the high-technology MNCs, there is also the consideration, almost the

The International Political Economy of Technology *The International Political Economy of Technology* 75

paradox, that although MNCs are very efficient instruments of technology transfer across frontiers, this transfer is nearly always under their own tight control. In recent years governments in the developing countries have complained vigorously, though it should perhaps have come as no real surprise to them, that the technologies brought by the MNCs to whose subsidiaries they provide homes are neither appropriate to local circumstances nor capable of acting as nuclei for the evolution of locally developed and locally appropriate technologies.

The multinational company has now generated a large literature and it has been possible here to treat it only in outline and in respect of its contribution to the international political economy of technology. The last, summarising, word on it in the present context may perhaps be left with the OECD code of practice for MNCs drawn up in the mid-1970s (OECD, 1976). This requires MNCs to behave, in specified ways, as good corporate citizens, publishing as much information as possible about themselves, and respecting union and related activity. It looks to them never to seek to reduce competition, to have regard for the balance of payments and credit policies of affected governments, and to act fairly in regard to taxation and transfer pricing. The code also asks MNCs to enhance the local capacity to innovate. The two key points about this code, and other efforts like it, are, first, that they are just codes and statements of principle and not the substance of international law; and second, that in drawing attention to what MNCs should avoid tacitly acknowledgement is being made of what some MNCs at least do or have done. That is some measure of the basic problem which the MNCs pose.

Technology Gaps

From the MNCs one turns to the wide range of capabilities for taking advantage of technology existing among the world's states. Here again, as in the case of MNCs, and for similar reasons, it is the gap between the developed and the developing states which is of greatest moment. Possibly the cruellest current manifestation of the differential in this case occurs in respect of technologies for exploiting the seabed and ocean floor, these being very much vanguard technologies. The fundamental question here is, to whom do the various riches of the ocean floor, most immediately the minerals contained in the ubiquitous manganese nodules and in hot springs, actually belong – to mankind in general, to the maritime states in some kind of proportion to their seaboards, or to those countries and industrial groups best able to exploit them? The developing countries, or some of them, stand to lose in both of two ways in this case. In the first place, many of them are dependent to a greater or lesser extent upon mineral extraction and cannot, therefore, but be threatened by alternative sources of these minerals. And in the second place, most developing countries are excluded from participating in the exploration of the ocean floor in that they lack both access to the requisite technologies and control over the more promising parts of the floor – though there are exceptions, like the involvement of Saudi Arabia and Sudan in the exploration of the hot springs of the Red Sea. The long-drawn-out international conference on the law of the sea has been much exercised by issues of this kind, and has also provided a running illustration of the overwhelming importance, in national decision-making bearing upon international questions, of technological feasibility and economic interest. As it happens, exploitation of the ocean floor is a medium- rather than a short-term proposition, and it is hardly cynical to suggest that it is this consideration, rather than any more altruistic motive, which delayed unilateral national action for so long until, in fact, the United States under President Reagan decided to withhold final approval of the proposed law of the sea convention pending a review of American mining interests, American firms being suspicious of the proposed international authority and of technology loss.

A second example of major political and economic consequences deriving from differential access to new technology arises with earth satellites. Here there are technologies both of launch and of satellite construction, with satellites usable for a multiplicity of purposes, including personal and business communications, radio and television broadcasts and propaganda, navigation, meteorological and agricultural research and, of course, espionage. In this instance developed as well as developing states may find themselves disadvantaged – this, indeed, was one of the principal reasons why France determined to continue with development of a launch vehicle, complete or virtually complete dependence on the United States being regarded as politically unacceptable.

Inadequate access to technology, though a basic shortcoming, remains as is well known far from the only serious problem the developing world faces (Stewart, 1977; Ramesh and Weiss, 1979). Nor is technology by any means the only, or even the main, source of disagreement between the developing and the developed world, as the Brandt Commission report (1980) and the World Bank Study (1978) both demonstrated. There is, in fact, a long tradition of such overviews and associated international conferences, and they almost always attract good media coverage as well as broad statements of approval from the governments of the industrialised countries. Obtaining positive action from these governments is, however, quite a different matter. They usually say they must postpone any increase in their existing, and mostly not impressive, aid commitments until their own economic circumstances are more favourable, and the matter then lapses until the next similar report. Occasionally there is a direct clash between the developed and developing states, as for instance when in 1980 the OECD countries, with only one vote short of unanimity, rejected the demands of the Group of 77 that the rich countries create a fund to finance the industrialisation of the developing world. Ironically there are good grounds – above all, the world's alarming instabilities and the historically demonstrated capacity of technology to produce economic benefits which are not zero-sum – for believing that in their attitude to developing world industrialisation governments in the industrial countries are failing to distinguish between short- and long-term self-interest, more lofty considerations quite apart.

Turning from problems felt most severely in the developing countries, it is clear that whatever may be the optimum conditions and practices for successful technological innovation, even the world's developed states are far from equally good at providing them. Thus, for example, the postwar period has witnessed such markedly different trends as the resumption by West Germany of steady technological development and industrial growth; the genuinely astonishing rise to technological and industrial dominance by Japan; the discovery by France of a technological and industrial route out of its prewar slough; a practically boundless technological and industrial self-confidence on the part of the United States for three decades, giving way to growing self-doubts from the mid-1970s; and a continuation, and even acceleration, of long-run industrial decline by the United Kingdom. These processes must have explanations, but the explanations are complex and the subject of much theoretical discussion and political argument. The really essential point for the purposes of this chapter in any case is that whatever the detailed explanations for the various processes of industrial change, the end-result is the bringing about of major shifts in international economic power and therefore, ultimately, if not automatically and smoothly, in international political power as well.

It is precisely because of the strikingly different facility with technology evidenced by different states that much research has been and is being done on the conditions for successful technological innovation and commercial exploitation. It is apparent that a wide range of factors could possibly be relevant. They might include primarily political variables – for instance, the existence or otherwise of ideological differences within a state in regard to the ownership of industry and the characteristics of national decision-making styles. Or mostly bureaucratic considerations might be important – for example, the scope for individual initiative encouraged in both the public and the private sectors, and the style and professionalism of administrative and managerial practices. There are cultural elements that could have a significant influence, such as national attitudes to pure as opposed to applied science, or to predictable causes offering security as against entrepreneurial ones entailing risk. The distribution of research expenditures as between the more scientific or the more technological, the public and the private sectors, military and non-military technology, old and new industries – all these too are potentially significant determinants of overall national performance. Other weighty considerations might be the existence of definite barriers to technical change, such as (in some instances) regulatory requirements, tax structures, the antipathy of affected groups, or shortages among key manpower categories.

As to the end-result, the actual shifts in international economics and political power deriving in large measures from differential facility with technology, among the principal developments here have been a quarter-century of peerless American superpower, a slow withdrawal by Britain from far-flung international responsibilities acquired, when it was Britain that held the technological and industrial lead among the world's powers, and the sharp contrast which has emerged between Japan's economic and political strengths. The changes in the status of Britain and Japan, together with a somewhat diminished self-assurance on their own part, have in turn led the Americans to look to Japan to play a political and military role in the 1980s more commensurate with its new economic strength (Vogel, 1979). In the same part of the world China's determination, after the Cultural Revolution, to modernise as rapidly as possible by means of Western technology has opened up new prospects, above all for Japan, with whom a symbiosis of very great moment and potential is as a result conceivable (Mendl, 1978). In Western Europe the industrial and technological well-being of West Germany and France has certainly contributed to the forming of the firm political axis which has come to exist between these two countries in recent decades. Examples could be further multiplied, but probably the most significant of all differentials in facility with technology among industrial states is still that between the countries of the Soviet bloc and those of the Western alliance. The imbalance here is so great, and the consequences for consumers in Soviet bloc countries so painful, that it is impossible to imagine these regimes surviving in their present forms were they not in the last analysis buttressed by the coercive power of the Soviet state.

The more enlightened Soviet leaders, among whom it was usual to nominate Kosygin's as the chief influence, having become fully aware of their country's technological weakness, managed (Amann *et al.*, 1977) from the late 1960s to have the Soviet Union become an important customer for Western technology, and the promotion of technology links thereafter also became a principal plank in Kissinger's conception of *détente*. In some respects Yugoslavia, outside the Soviet bloc, acted as a pacemaker, in particular as regards the joint venture – which binds partners together as a simple co-operation or licence agreement does not. Several Comecon countries then followed suit and it is now probable that several thousand co-operative agreements have been signed between Soviet bloc countries and Western governments and companies (Levcik and Stankovsky, 1979). On Wilczynski's figures (1976) more than a quarter of the top Western MNCs have found dealing with the Soviet bloc attractive. The Soviet Union itself is much less dependent on foreign trade than are its Comecon partners, but this did not prevent it shopping for Western technology in the new climate of the 1970s. Among the major Soviet–Western deals of this period were the Togliatti car plant, built largely by Fiat, the sale of Soviet natural gas to Western Europe in exchange for several billion dollars worth of gaspipes and associated equipment, and the 20 billion-dollar arrangement with Occidental involving the supply of Soviet ammonia and urea for American superphosphoric acid. The USSR has also joined in technology agreements with Japan and was throughout the decade looking to Western technology to help exploit its Siberian energy and mineral resources. There were always influential American doubters as regards the wisdom of making Western technology and its products available to the Soviet Union, and others who sought to use the opportunity of doing so for other political purposes, as illustrated *inter alia* by the American Trade Act of 1974 and the Stevenson amendment. Then came the Soviet invasion of Afghanistan in late 1979 and the decision of the Carter administration to halt further provision of technology (Sobeslavsky, 1980). Soviet economic circumstances are likely to make the country's fundamental need for Western technology still more pressing in the 1980s, but the paramountcy of the political in the Soviet Union, and its limited coupling to the economic, will continue to mean that, except symbolically, the 'technology card' is playable by the West only when the USSR does not feel a vital national interest to be at stake. And the Soviet perception of that national interest can be wide, and certainly need not correspond with any Western definition.

International Co-operation

It has been said that 'what could help us most would be to unite our labours, to share them advantageously and to regulate them in an orderly way. But at the present, men barely touch what is difficult and has not yet been attempted; but all run in crowds to what others have already done, where they cease not from copying and even from striving with one another'. Though that is not as true now as it was when Leibniz wrote it, it is still far from having been falsified even in the sphere of science and technology, where considerable international co-operation has taken place in the last two decades (OECD, 1971; Williams, 1973).

Important examples of international scientific co-operation have included the European Science Foundation, the European Centre for Nuclear Research (CERN), the European Molecular Biology Laboratory and the Joint European Torus. These organisations do experience political and administrative difficulties arising from their international nature, but on nothing like the scale typical of international organisations and projects concerned with technology, the industrial and economic dimensions being so much more important in the latter case. Especially well known for the political complications which have attended them are the efforts of the European Communities in the technology field. Originally there was actually a community specifically concerned with a technology (Euratom), but in the 1970s the European Commission in the unified Community tried both to diversify its research and development interests, and to work towards a common science and technology policy among member-governments, with very limited success. It will be appreciated that, to the Commission, co-operation is a means as well as an end, but as Hoffman put it in 1966, 'The nation state is still here, and the new Jerusalem (of European unification) has been postponed'. It is this consideration which has frustrated the ambitious co-operative objectives of the Commission. Indirectly it has also led to the Co-operative Science and Technology projects, of which there were some thirty by 1980, bringing in some twenty European governments, though with all of these projects essentially ancillary to the main thrust of contemporary technological development.

Like the EEC, the OECD and NATO have also sponsored scientific and technological co-operation. Thus OECD has had its co-operative Research Project on Food Production and Preservation, NATO its Committees on Science and on the Challenges of Modern Society. OECD is also the parent, as it were, of the International Energy Agency, an important part of whose work has become the stimulation of international co-operation in technological projects related to energy – there were over fifty of these by 1980, as well as many others wholly independent of the IEA.

Outside these various international bodies there has also been extensive bi- and multilateral technological co-operation between governments. In the nuclear energy field the most significant example of co-operation to date has been that between Britain, the Netherlands and West Germany in the development of the centrifuge method of uranium enrichment: France and Italy are linked in the alternative enrichment route via diffusion. In another part of the nuclear-fuel cycle the OECD European Nuclear Energy Agency built Eurochemic as a fuel-reprocessing facility, and Britain, France and West Germany are joined in United Reprocessors in an effort to keep European reprocessing capacity in line with demand. As regards reactors the most important joint venture until the mid-1970s was the Dragon high-temperature reactor programme involving several West European governments, but this was then curtailed despite earlier promise. The

Liquid-metal fast-breeder reactor has now taken over as the major European project involving international co-operation. West German, Dutch and Belgian firms have been co-operating on one version of this since the 1960s and, in addition, electricity utilities from these countries, and France, Italy and Britain, have arranged to co-operate in operating the commercial version now being built in France, as well as that planned for West Germany.

In aviation international co-operation has now become of pivotal importance. One of the main reasons for this has been the growth to prominence of Airbus Industrie, a *groupement d'intérêt economique* (GIE), established in 1970 to build the A300 wide-bodied airliner (Schumacher, 1979). Backed initially by the French and West German governments, with Britain negotiating a re-entry in 1979 after having pulled out a decade earlier, the project has been carried through by firms in these three countries, with Spanish, Dutch and Belgian companies also contributing. Sales of the airbus and Airbus Industrie's plans between them seem likely to turn this, in the 1980s, into one of the world's leading aircraft manufacturers. Certainly, the airbus stands in marked contrast to the technologically successful but commercially disastrous Anglo-French Concorde. Looking beyond Europe, the American manufacturers Boeing and McDonnell Douglas both wanted European partners in the late 1970s for their new aircraft projects, and Boeing eventually did secure Japanese involvement in one of their new projects.

In military airframes France and West Germany began co-operating in the late 1950s on the Transall transport, France and West Germany co-operated again on the Alphajet trainer, and Britain and France put together a co-operative package in the mid-1960s comprising the Jaguar trainer/support aircraft and three helicopters. Anglo-French co-operation was to have extended to a variable geometry aircraft but France withdrew, a development which eventually precipitated the largest European co-operative development programme to date in military aircraft, between Britain, West Germany and Italy on the Tornado. Co-operation has also taken place in missile development.

The aeroengine sector too has seen many examples of international co-operation, for example, between General Electric of the United States and SNECMA of France on the CFM56 engine, between SNECMA and Rolls-Royce on Concorde's Olympus, and between Rolls-Royce and Turboméca on the Jaguar's engine, and Rolls-Royce and West German and Italian firms on the Tornado engine. In the mid-1970s Rolls-Royce also became involved with a Japanese grouping.

In space technology the European Space Agency, with some ten member-countries, rose like a phoenix from the ashes of Europe's earlier intergovernmental ventures, the European Space Research Organisation (ESRO) and the European Launcher Development Organisation

(ELDO), both of them having had severe organisational and political problems. Among private firms there have been in the space field at least six European manufacturing consortia created for various purposes.

A number of other important examples of international co-operation in technological projects could also be cited, among them the package of projects agreed between Japan and the United States in 1980, for instance, the Franco-American companies which have been set up in the microelectronics field on the initiative of the French government, or the British Leyland–Honda collaboration on automobiles announced in the late 1970s.

Overall it can be said that international co-operation has now become an important mode, or option, in technological development; that intergovernmental agreements have tended to dominate, but that private firms appear increasingly willing to take the lead; and that Europe has been very much the centre of the patchwork of arrangements which have resulted. There is a definite tendency for projects to become international in proportion to the costs, risks and timescales involved, and a distinct possibility that what surfaces at the international level will have passed upwards from the institutional or firm level, first, to the national level, and then upwards again, as too expensive or uncertain to be handled at those lower levels, however, desirable the eventual product.

This last point apart – and it can obviously be a critical weakness – international co-operation in technology has also now taught many other lessons. To begin with, international projects always cost more – the hope being that these additional costs can be offset both by the fact that work is shared and, in appropriate cases, by the possibility – almost the necessity – of an extended market. Next, differences between partners in competence, circumstances, or priorities can cause difficulties, as can the actual organisational arrangements made, these themselves being the monument to possibly unresolved political differences. Almost always there is friction between the pursuit of efficiency and the requirements of equity, partners all looking to share in the work of a project in proportion to their financial contributions, the optimum arrangement from the perspective of the project itself being otherwise. Almost always there are wider interests to be considered than those immediately involved in a project. Maintaining financial and managerial control can prove exceptionally taxing given the general tendency towards cost escalation in technological projects, and the additional factors here that national practices can differ substantially, and that the work is taking place in several geographically and institutionally separate centres. Having the right product at the right time, technologically sound and commercially and operationally competitive, is difficult enough when a firm has to co-ordinate only its own efforts, but here there are other firms and other governments also involved. It is altogether understandable that preferences should have developed among governments for keeping the number of participants to the minimum compatible with objectives, and for operating on an à la carte basis with maximum flexibility; and on the part of firms for keeping politics, and government, at as great a distance as possible. There remains, all in all, a good deal of truth in the words of General Forget of Air France: 'Co-operation', he has said, 'is like a marriage – partly love, partly reason, partly money'.

Regulation

In addition to the international co-operation in technological projects, there is also a long tradition of international co-operation of a programmatic or regulatory kind, intended to accommodate the international dimension of technology's dynamic (Brown *et al.*, 1977). Thus there are such bodies as the International Telecommunications Union (ITU), the International Telecommunications Satellite Organisation (Intelsat), the Intergovernmental Oceanographic Commission (IOC), the World Meteorological Organisation (WMO), the International Civil Aviation Organisation (ICAO) and many others. In recent years the more dysfunctional aspects of technical change have also, and increasingly, attracted attention, that is, the physical risks and hazards which are often the inescapable corollary of technological development. International developments have now begun to reflect this – the United Nations Environment Programme, for example, or the OECD's Chemicals Programme, intended to harmonise national chemical control policies. Some international action in this area long predated the public concern of the 1970s with the hazards of technology – the work of the International Commission on Radiological Protection, for instance. International co-ordination is certainly highly desirable in this context, to eliminate duplication in research, to provide companies with uniform standards, to ensure the early recognition of dangers and to prevent countries being put at a disadvantage. This last is bound to happen, to some extent, in that one is back here to the multinational company and its ability to organise its affairs so as to take maximum advantage of national provisions in regard to occupational health, environmental regulations, and consumer and patient protection.

It is likely that there is much more still which could usefully be done as regards the international regulation of technology, and there are also several other directions in which international project co-operation might advantageously proceed – generic technologies, for example, or filling the gap between basic science and commercially oriented research and development. There is also the case of what might be called socially relevant technologies – there is a much better chance of the military bringing about co-operation to meet their specifications, or of commercial firms doing so to minimise their risks, than there is of, say, municipalities in two different countries recognising a common problem which could be solved by co-operative technical effort.

Security and Defence

Mention of the military should remind one that demand from, and opportunity in, this quarter, and its near relative, the space sector, have constituted probably the main drives behind technological development for the last forty years. The international security consequences of this have no part in this chapter, but there are certain points arising from the economic and commercial aspects of military technology which do need to be touched upon here. Thus it must be noted that, political motivations for weapons supply apart, and viewed simply commercially, the arms trade has grown to become a significant international business (Freedman, 1979; Kolodziej, 1980). Behind the superpowers, for whom political objectives remain decisive in determining the direction, form and terms of weapons supply – though certainly not to the complete exclusion of commercial interests in the American case (Farley *et al.*, 1978) – Britain and France are the major commercial suppliers, leading what is now a large and growing group. And in this as in other industries, export prospects can influence both domestic design and decision-making, and also domestic politics.

Another sense in which the economics of military technology are important occurs in connection with the strategic competition between the United States and the Soviet Union, there being Americans who believe that the American economy and American technology put the US government in a stronger position than the Soviet government to compete in successive spirals of the arms race, and that advantage should be taken of this situation.

A third economic point in connection with military technology is that spinoff certainly occurs from the defence sector to the civil economy, a flow from which the United States has undeniably derived great advantage. On the other hand, the process has its limitations, and these are counter-considerations. Thus spinoff can only be expected in technologies of importance to the military, and countries like Japan, to take the extreme example, which have maintained a low level of defence spending, leave themselves as a result with more freedom to concentrate on civil technologies. It may also be said with confidence that arms purchases, of which those by the countries of the Third World stand out, convey next to no economic benefit. On the one hand in order to make them recipients have to forgo more constructive purchases, and on the other to those recipients they involve technologies only of application, and not technologies of manufacture.

Nuclear Technology

It was said in an introductory paragraph that the technology of nuclear power has such profound political ramifications, and also exemplifies so many facets of the international political economy of technology, that it deserves briefly to be considered in its own right. Here, *par excellence*, is a civil technology developed from a military one (Royal Commission on Environmental Pollution, 1976; Ford Foundation, 1977; Willrich, 1971b). This happened in the 1950s in the initial nuclear states, but the civil technology is no less capable in the 1980s of reversion into its military form where this path is politically willed. One must also conclude that the technology of nuclear power has spread far more rapidly than it need have done, partly because of such political initiatives as the Atoms for Peace Programme, partly because of the efforts to sell abroad of private companies and public corporations in the nuclear field in the United States, France, West Germany, Canada and, lastly (not from choice but rather from incapacity), Britain. The most serious result of the forced dissemination of civil nuclear knowledge has been a much-accelerated threat of nuclear weapon proliferation (SIPRI, 1979; Fischer, 1971; Quester, 1973; Epstein, 1976; Greenwood *et al.*, 1977; Rochlin, 1979). This, in turn, led in the late 1960s to a Non-Proliferation Treaty, in the mid-1970s to a 'trigger list' of sensitive nuclear components drawn up by the so-called 'London Club' of nuclear suppliers and in the late 1970s to the fruitless efforts of the International Nuclear Fuel Cycle Evaluation Programme (IAEA, 1980) – insisted upon by the Carter administration in the hope of finding a less weapons-related nuclear-fuel cycle. Meanwhile concern has steadily grown about the spread of uranium enrichment and spent fuel-reprocessing facilities, the former opening the way to the procurement of uranium 235 and the latter to the procurement of plutonium 239, these being the two fissile materials used for nuclear weapons.

In parallel, opposition to nuclear energy has taken root in the liberal democracies, in response both to the perceived risks of the civil technology itself and in reaction to the bolted horse of weapons proliferation. This opposition has also in a sense been exported with the reactor technology – opposition having expressed itself forcibly in the United States, countries like West Germany, Austria, Switzerland and Sweden which have adopted the American or a closely similar technology have also found themselves with substantial public opposition; though some countries, notably France, despite a huge nuclear programme based on the American reactor, have largely avoided or ignored such public resistance.

Civil nuclear technology also provides an excellent example of the international regimes which technological development can bring into being. In this instance there are in particular the International Commission on Radiological Protection, mentioned above, which is concerned with radiation safety standards, and the International Atomic Energy Agency, concerned especially with safeguards against the diversion of civil nuclear material to military uses.

The history to date of nuclear power shows, incidentally but starkly, the great difficulties countries in the non-communist world face in holding to an independent technological line when the United States has made a major commitment in the same technology. Canada, to be sure, continues with an independent national technology, and Britain still hovers, as it has done for almost two decades, between persisting with the national technological line and switching to the American one; but France made an unequivocal switch to American technology following the departure of President de Gaulle; and the other Western European countries, and Japan, all have readily followed the American strategy. However, the nuclear construction organisation in West Germany, having begun with an American reactor licence, has shown that it is perfectly possible to develop from this an independent domestic version, and France is on the point of underlining this lesson. This is, in fact, a particular instance of a more general rule, namely, that it is not necessary for a country to develop a given technology for itself from scratch, or to make every important 'breakthrough', only to have the overall capability to recognise and exploit developments taking place elsewhere, the basic technology underlying those developments then being obtained on the best licence terms which can be secured. Unfortunately for Britain, and more recently also for the United States it seems, this is easier said than done. Both countries, it would appear, suffer from the 'not invented here' syndrome, which makes them reluctant to adopt and adapt foreign technology. Japan, on the other hand, built its industrial climb in the 1950s squarely upon cheaply obtained foreign licences, happily running a negative technological balance of payments (licence fees received as against those paid) while doing so.

Nuclear power economics as assessed by utilities, the limited indigenous fossil-fuel reserves possessed by most countries and the uncertainties attaching to oil supplies all point in one direction, and only public opposition and government caution in the face of it have checked the further expansion of civil nuclear power in most Western countries. Most certainly, the technology has its risks, and they are not minor – but energy availability presents risks of its own, and bearing in mind conditions in the Middle East, these are not minor either. In the long run, and despite the warnings which were issued in the 1970s, it is unlikely that man will encounter any serious and permanent resource limitation. This is because, in the end, the only critical resource is energy, since given adequate supplies of this all other resources can be obtained albeit at high cost. And in that end, renewable energy resources and conservation apart, it is probable that the human race will face the choice of, in effect, 'burning the rocks' with the fast-breeder fission reactor or 'burning the seas' with the, as yet unbuilt, fusion reactor. But to amend Keynes, we may be dead long before 'the end', and it is difficult presently not to feel but that present Western energy policies, with their twin absurdities of profligacy and dependence upon unstable supplies, are likely to lead to some unpleasant 'end' in the near never mind the long term. Such an 'end', should it come, would have to be attributed to political and not technological shortcomings, not that that would make it easier to bear.

The communication, and perhaps also co-ordination, across frontiers between those who oppose nuclear power which was referred to above is a specific example of a general possibility, essentially that those affected by technological development, whether occupationally, environmentally, or through the products they buy, might exchange information, or even combine, to defend their interests. One might perhaps expect most in this regard of unions, and there has indeed been some transnational activity among some of them, but this has been very peripheral by comparison with the multinational operations they have had to try to monitor (Kujawa, 1976). Consumer associations in various countries appear to have done rather better, jointly testing for instance items internationally available for sale. And environmental groups, even outside the nuclear field, have taken great advantage of the opportunities for mutual support and assistance, being frustrated more by the circumstances of particular political systems and cultures than by their failure to learn from the experience of one another. Unions, consumer groups and environmental bodies perforce remain reactive, holding in most cases neither initiative nor advantages, and having done as yet only enough to suggest that they might ultimately do much more.

So that one may if possible avoid Mill's stricture – 'As often as a study is cultivated by narrow minds, they will draw from it narrow conclusions' – let the last words on the international political economy of technology rest, for the present, with Galbraith and with Bell. Galbraith's is the conception that technology contains or creates its own imperatives (Galbraith, 1969; Skolnikoff, 1972). In essence his thesis is that technological development having become in recent decades high-cost, high-risk and prolonged, the state is as a result drawn in to share the burden, considerations of national security, prestige and economic well-being leading to the selfsame policy. One can certainly question whether an 'imperative' is, well, imperative, but if one accepts that it is, then Bell (1974) has been as categorical as anyone as regards the consequent international political economy of technology. Bell's concept of 'post-industrial society' is as well known as Galbraith's 'imperatives' – a state of affairs in which a major shift has taken place from production to service industry, with knowledge and information taking over from capital and labour as the 'transforming resources' of society. Bell further regards the linking of developments in telecommunications and computers as revolutionary, likely to make what he calls the 'communication network', rather than the networks of transport or energy, the 'central infrastructure tying together a society'. In his view 'in the broadest sense, we have for the first time a genuine international economy in which prices and money values are known in real time in every part of the globe'. This must lead, he argues, to two important consequences: first, a new international division of labour, and secondly, 'more subtle, yet perhaps more important . . . an expansion in the political arenas of the world, the drawing in of new claimants, and the multiplication of actors or of constituencies' (Bell, 1979).

This is a future not without excitement. The main idea to carry away is of technology accelerating change, with the prizes going to those individuals, corporations and states which can best seize the unending stream of opportunities which result. Much is gained, but much also is lost and trampled upon. In embracing technology, an embrace about which there could never have been any real choice, one might perhaps say that the world has accepted new lamps for old: the seeing is obviously far better, but we may find ourselves with more than we bargained for and, of course, the possibility of magic is gone.

References: Chapter 5

Amann, R., Cooper, J., and Davies, R. W. (eds) (1977), *The Technological Level of Soviet Industry* (New Haven, CT: Yale University Press).

Baranson, J. (1978), *Technology and the Multinationals* (Lexington, MA: Lexington Books).

Barnet, R. J., and Müller, E. R. (1975), *Global Reach* (New York: Simon & Schuster).

Basiuk, V. (1977), *Technology, World Politics and American Policy* (New York: Columbia University Press).

Bell, D. (1974), *The Coming of Post-Industrial Society* (London: Heinemann), 2nd edn 1978.

Bell, D. (1979), 'Communications technology – for better or for worse', *Harvard Business Review*, (May–June), pp. 20–42.

Bergsten, F. C., Horst, T., and Moran, T., (1978), *American Multinationals and American Interests* (Washington, DC: Brookings Institution).

Brandt, W. (Brandt Commission) (1980), *North–South: A Programme for Survival* (London: Pan Books).

Brown, S., and Schwartz, B. (1977), *Regimes for the Ocean, Outer Space and Weather* (Washington, DC: Brookings Institution).

Buckley, P. J., and Casson, M. (1976), *The Future of the Multinational Enterprise* (London: Macmillan).

Curzon, G., and Curzon, V., with Franko, L., and Schwamm, H. (eds) (1977), *The Multinational Enterprise in a Hostile World* (London: Macmillan).

The Economist (1977), 'East–West industrial cooperation' (Business Brief), 6 August.

The Economist (1978), 'The Continental challenge' (Business Brief), 4 February.

Epstein, W. (1976), *The Last Chance* (New York: The Free Press).

Farley, P. J., Lewis, W. H., and Kaplan, S. (1978), *Arms across the Sea* (Washington, DC: Brookings Institution).

Fischer, G. (1971), *The Non-Proliferation of Nuclear Weapons*, trans. D. Willey (New York: State Mutual Book & Periodical Service).

Ford Foundation (1977), *Nuclear Power Issues and Choices* (Cambridge, MA: Ballinger).

Freedman, L. (1979), 'The arms trade: a review', *International Affairs*, vol. 55, no. 3 (July), pp. 432–7.

Freeman, C. (1974), *The Economics of Industrial Innovation* (Harmondsworth: Penguin).

Galbraith, J. K. (1969), *The New Industrial State* (Harmondsworth: Penguin), ch. 2.

Granger, J. V. (1979), *Technology and International Relations* (Oxford: W. H. Freeman).

Greenwood, T., Feiveson, H. A., and Taylor, T. B. (1977), *Nuclear Proliferation: Motivations, Capabilities and Strategies for Control* (New York: McGraw-Hill).

Heenan, D. A., and Keegan, W. J. (1979), 'The rise of the Third World multinationals', *Harvard Business Review*, (January–February), pp. 101–9.

Holsti, K. J. (1974), *International Politics: A Framework for Analysis*, 2nd edn (Englewood Cliffs, NJ: Prentice-Hall), p. 76.

IAEA (1980), 'International Nuclear Fuel Cycle Evaluation', *INFCE Summary*.

International Organization (1975), 'International responses to technology', vol. 29, no. 3 (Summer).

Kelly, P., and Kranzberg, M. (eds) (1978), *Technological Innovation: A Critical Review of Current Knowledge* (San Francisco, CA: San Francisco Press).

Kolodziej, E. A. (1980), 'France and the arms trade', *International Affairs*, vol. 56, no. 1 (January).

Kujawa, D. (ed.) (1976), *International Labour and the Multinational Enterprise* (New York: Praeger).

Levcik, F., and Stankovsky, J. (1979), *Industrial Cooperation between East and West* (London: Macmillan).

Madden, C. H. (ed.) (1977), *The Case for the Multinational Corporation* (New York: Praeger).

Mansfield, E., Rapoport, J., Schnee, J., Wagner, S., and Hamburger, M. (1971), *Research and Innovation in the Modern Corporation* (New York: Norton).

Mendl, W. (1978), *Issues in Japan's China Policy* (London: OUP).

Michalet, C.-A. (1976), *Le Capitalisme mondiale*.

Nau, H. R. (1976), *Technology Transfer and US Foreign Policy* (New York: Praeger).

OECD (1971), *International Cooperation in Science and Technology: A Role for OECD* (Paris: OECD).

OECD (1976), *International Investment and Multinational Enterprise* (Paris: OECD).

Quester, G. H. (1973), *The Politics of Nuclear Proliferation* (Baltimore, MD: Johns Hopkins).

Ramesh, J., and Weiss, C. (1979), *Mobilizing Technology for World Development* (New York: Praeger).

Rochlin, G. (1979), *Plutonium, Power and Politics* (Berkeley, CA: University of California Press).

Royal Commission on Environmental Pollution (1976), *Nuclear Power and the Environment*, 6th Report (London: HMSO).

Schumacher, H. H. (1979), 'Europe's airbus programme and the impact of British participation', *World Today*, vol. 35, no. 8 (August), pp. 332–9.

SIPRI (1979), *Nuclear Energy and Nuclear Weapons Proliferation* (London: Taylor & Francis).

Skolnikoff, E. B. (1972), *The International Imperatives of Technology* (Berkeley, CA: University of California, Institute of Industrial Relations).

Sobeslavsky, V. (1980), 'East–West détente and technology transfer', *World Today* (October), pp. 374–81.

Stewart, F. (1977), *Technology and Underdevelopment* (London: Macmillan).

Turner, L. (1978), *Oil Companies in the International System* (London: Allen & Unwin).

Utterback, J. M. (1978), 'Management of technology', in Arnold C. Hax (ed.), *Studies in Operations Management* (Amsterdam: North-Holland Publishing Co).

Vernon, R. (1977), *Storm over the Multinationals: The Real Issues* (Cambridge, MA: Harvard University Press).

Vogel, E. F. (1979), *Japan as Number One* (Cambridge, MA: Harvard University Press).

Wilczynski, J. (1976), *The Multinationals and East–West Relations* (London: Macmillan).

Williams, R. (1973), *European Technology: The Politics of Collaboration* (London: Croom Helm).

Williams, R. (1979), 'The multinational enterprise: a 1977 perspective', in J. E. S. Hayward and R. N. Berki (eds), *State and Society in Contemporary Europe* (Oxford: Martin Robertson), ch. 12.

Willrich, M. (1971a), *Global Politics of Nuclear Energy* (New York: Praeger).

Willrich, M. (ed.) (1971b), *Civil Nuclear Power and International Security* (New York: Praeger).

6

Money and World Politics

DAVID CALLEO and SUSAN STRANGE

No political scientist, no political journalist, certainly no working politician needs to be reminded of the political nature of monetary policy, especially in a predominantly market or mixed economy. In an inflationary age such as this surely no one can be unaware that decisions concerning the management of money substantially affect other matters of great political sensitivity, like the relative prices of different sorts of goods or the balance of risks and opportunities for investors and entre-preneurs. More broadly, the management of money helps determine, in actual fact, the relative priority a particular society gives to order as opposed to freedom, or wealth as opposed to equity.

In today's world the management of money, and hence those basic outcomes strongly affected by it, cannot be confined neatly within the territorial limits of individual national political systems. Even centrally planned economies frequently suffer inflation that is not solely domes-tic in origin, and since they almost invariably need international credit to pursue their plans, they are compelled to bargain with bankers over the supply and cost of that credit (Portes, in Hirsch and Goldthorpe, 1978). For states that live more fully in the world market economy, that is to say, most states, domestic control over money is very seriously constricted. Monetary management in these states is bound up, in large part, with what might be called the 'foreign policy' of money – the relationship of the national currency to the currencies of other states. This relationship of currencies, in turn, is strongly conditioned by a global structure, an international monetary 'system' that has evolved over 200 years. This system is a web of institutions and practices reflect-ing not only the accumulated political decisions of governments, but also countless choices of individual entrepreneurs, investors and enter-prises. To grasp the practical scope of the system the student needs not only a diplomat's map with its familiar coloured patchwork of states, but a banker's map of the world's major money marts. In many respects these form a single unsleeping market that follows the sun from New York and Chicago, to Tokyo, Sydney, Hong Kong and Singapore, to Frankfurt, Zurich and London and back again to New York. Whatever the hour, funds move ceaselessly in and out of currencies in response to all the diverse political events and economic expectations around the world. These monetary movements, or policies undertaken in expectation of them, profoundly affect and shape economic conditions within separate national economies. In short, not only does money go a long way to shape the world in which we live, but the decisions that control money are complex, cosmopolitan and elusive.

Political scientists who try to locate and analyse the power that moves money must thus look not only to the national, but also to the international level and, indeed, to what might be called the global structural level as well. Monetary conditions result from the interaction of forces at all three levels. Analysis has grown more difficult in recent years because of the rapid shift in the relative significance of the three levels. Capital and money markets throughout the world have been integrating so rapidly that national political authorities have lost a considerable part of their ability to intervene effectively in national monetary mechanisms. International banking has seemingly won its independence from national politics. The growing importance of international transactions has, in turn, greatly increased the visible significance of the international organisations set up to oversee the system and of the informal global structure within which these transactions take place. These organisations – the International Bank for Reconstruction and Development (IBRD), the International Monetary Fund (IMF) and the Bank for International Settlements (BIS) – have become household names in recent years. For although the financial resources are relatively small, the absence of a world central bank or any single monetary authority for the global financial system brings them constantly into the limelight.[1] Both the policies of the international monetary organisations and the nature of the informal global structure have increasingly become bones of contention among nation states.

Analysis of how this internationalised monetary mechanism works, and the issues involved, has largely been left to the economists. Political scientists interested in the politics of money are directed to learn monetary economics. This advice, even when followed, is not always helpful. For conventional economics, and international monetary economics above all, achieves its much-envied analytical precision by neglecting not only questions of power, but also other values save for economic 'efficiency' itself. Power is thus ignored as a significant variable in economic systems, while efficiency in the production of wealth is assumed to be the first priority of society. The very questions about power and value that concern the political scientist are, for the economist, only the market's 'imperfections'. To find the things that interest them, political scientists have to sift through the trash of economic analysis.

These philosophical weaknesses in conventional economic analysis are of more than academic concern. Since the struggle over power and other values forms a large part of the real world, and not least the world of international economic relations, practical analysis heavily influenced by economics has had grave empirical deficiencies. While a rather large literature, for example, exists on international monetary reform, much of it, thanks to its economic bias, is excessively mechanistic. Ills of the world's monetary system are treated like oil leaks or blown gaskets, defects to be righted so that the machinery can go on as before. Such analysis thus focuses exclusively on means and ignores ends. Differing diagnoses of the 'system's' defects, or technical prescriptions for its 'reform', are solemnly elaborated without penetrating to the conflicts of national interest and social regime that lie beneath the technical surface.

Economic Analysis and Political Predisposition

Economic analysis does not, of course, do away with political preferences. It merely assumes them silently. Thus when the technicalities and jargon of monetary economics are stripped away, the precepts and prescriptions of the experts turn out to reflect rather familiar philosophical views about the international system as a whole. The distribution of these views among the experts, moreover, tends to correlate rather closely with their respective national interests and domestic preferences.

These various approaches may be usefully grouped into three rough categories: liberal, mercantilist and revolutionary-utopian. Among the more fashionable economists of North America, Western Europe and Japan, a liberal world view is predominant (Kindleberger and Lindert, 1978). The market is seen as the mechanism that most efficiently establishes natural comparative advantage in the world and reconciles private gain with public welfare at home. Their country's wealth merely reflects the natural laws of economics, laws that can be depended upon to produce a maximum of wealth and harmony – so long as governments do not gum up the market's wonderful mechanism with artificially imposed non-economic values.

Less common among economists in Western universities or international agencies, but strongly entrenched in national bureaucracies, is the mercantilist approach (Schmitt, 1979a; Vines, 1979). Historically this is the view that has appealed to powers on the make – Britain in the seventeenth and eighteenth centuries, America and Germany in the nineteenth, Japan in our own time. For the mercantilist, the world appears through Hobbesian or Darwinist glasses. The international economy is seen to reflect the ceaseless competition of organised powers. Some states will flourish and others decline. Order will be produced not by the artless nature of the liberals, but either imposed by a hegemony of wilful power or else sustained by a carefully nurtured balance of power. Preference between hegemony or balance tends to distribute itself differently among analysts from small, medium and large states. Abstract preference also tends to give way before the actual political and economic conditions and possibilities. In periods of expansion and abundance hegemony is easier to support than in periods of contraction and more desperate competition.

Revolutionary-utopians, Marxist and non-Marxist alike, tend to be radical-structuralists (Wallerstein, 1979; Diaz-Alejandro, 1978; Cardoso and Faletto, 1979; Magdoff and Sweezy, 1977). Like the mercantilists, they see the world system reflecting dependency and exploitation based on power. Like the liberals, they tend to project an ideal system where conflict gives way to a natural harmony. But whereas the rich liberals tend to see harmony merely awaiting the reinforcement of the existing market mechanism, the revolutionary-utopians require a revolutionary change of structure leading to a radical redistribution of power and wealth. For understandable reasons, such views have strong appeal among the more aggressive countries of today's Third World, as well as among their academic defenders elsewhere.

To achieve a political analysis of international monetary issues requires perceiving the influence of these broad political predispositions in the supposedly technical questions of how the international system works or ought to work. Only studies sensitive to this interplay can avoid confusion about ends and means and realise some sort of analytical clarity.

The Concept of the Balance of Payments

The need for such analysis can be demonstrated with the very concept basic to almost all international monetary debate, the concept of the balance of payments itself. In its theoretical ambiguities are to be found the roots of many of the 'practical' problems that bedevil the international system. The very phrase 'balance of payments' carries elusive and contentious economic, political and even moral assumptions. To begin with, the notion of balances between countries implies a nationalist definition of the world economy. Each national economy is taken as a discrete entity, a common household whose accounts should be kept in relation to the rest of the world. A more cosmopolitan and liberal view might argue that with the world increasingly a 'global village' of free men and multinational enterprises, the whole concept of national balances is obsolete and an impediment to progress. No one, after all, keeps a formal balance between New York and Texas. Flows do occur, but the adjustments take place through the movement of goods, capital and labour – without anyone reckoning a formal balance that the governments of New York and Texas feel they must somehow act to regulate. Why should the same not be true for flows between the United States and West Germany?

The answer seems obvious. The United States and Germany are sovereign nation-states, whereas New York and Texas are not. Having a balance of payments is an attribute of national sovereignty, for in the present world sovereignty extends to economic as well as political self-determination. Governments of modern nation-states want growth, stability and prosperity and are expected to regulate their domestic economic environments accordingly. They are also expected to do their best to ensure a favourable international context for that domestic prosperity. To meet these expectations governments normally seek to regulate the national money supply and to promote an exchange rate favourable to domestic development. Economic conditions in New York and Texas are not deprived of this governmental solicitude. As parts of a larger monetary unit, the United States, the two states share together the policies set by the US Treasury and the Federal Reserve.

In the world of the 1980s the American policies do, in fact, strongly affect not only New York and Texas, but West Germany as well. Much of the capitalist world does, in some respects, form a highly integrated monetary union with a common money supply. America's special reserve currency role combined with the postwar interdependence of capital markets means that monetary conditions in the United States have a powerful influence upon monetary conditions in West Germany. Some find this monetary integration part of a general world progress towards political integration. In this hegemonic 'federalist' view the Federal Reserve should quite properly play the role of world central bank. In an integrating world monetary system if the American central bank fails to act as world regulator, the system's structural weaknesses will produce instability and inequity to an intolerable degree. The practical problem is to make the policies of the American central bank responsive to the needs of the system as a whole (Streit, 1939).

Mercantilist realism intervenes at this point to suggest that the federalist's hopes will fail. In the mercantilist perspective American monetary policies are understandably directed towards manipulating America's exchange rate in a fashion conducive to its own national growth, stability and prosperity. Its balance-of-payments policy is a weapon in a Hobbesian world political economy where prizes go to those best able to compete or to shift to others the need to adjust to change. American monetary institutions are part of the American political system, and American monetary policies are made mainly with American preferences in mind. They reflect the complex realities of the American economic, social and political scene. A world system managed by the US Federal Reserve will inevitably reflect American national interests and preferences. Germans are, therefore, quite properly unwilling to make over the management of so crucial an aspect of their economic environment to the Americans. In particular, postwar Germans do not care for American inflation rates. Germans thus insist, as best they can, that their monetary policies should be made by institutions that reflect the particular nature of their own economic, political and social community. In so far as 'interdependence' or American 'hegemony' makes some sort of global monetary governance unavoidable, Germans are primarily concerned with manipulating the global system in a fashion conducive to their own national interests. Hence the Germans and Americans each maintain their own institutions and currencies, and thus keep a balance of payments between them.

Not only does the concept of a balance of payments suggest a nationalist international system, but it also traditionally implied a certain balanced relationship among the members of that system. The word 'balance' is itself just as highly ambivalent as it is in discussions of the 'balance of power'. Balance may mean simply a reckoning of pluses and minuses. But it may also mean an equilibrium, as when accounts are 'in balance' (Haas, 1953; Devlin, 1971).

Such a notion of equilibrium applied to the balance of payments suggests that a country ought ideally to have neither a surplus nor a deficit. Behind this prescription is the liberal vision of a system underwritten by a natural law. Equilibrium is to be achieved by a 'hidden hand', the natural result of unspoilt competition. Liberals (quite

Table 6.1   *Eurodollars and the US balance of payments*

	Estimated net size of the Eurodollar market	US reserves	US basic balance ($ billion)
1964	9·0	16·67	−0·100
1965	11·5	15·45	−1·817
1966	14·5	14·88	−1·474
1967	17·5	14·83	−3·303
1968	25·0	15·71	−1·297
1969	44·0	16·96	−3·943
1970	57·0	14·48	−3·989
1971	71·0	12·16	−10·478
1972	91·0	13·15	−11·580
1973	132·0	14·38	0·979
1974	177·0	16·06	−5·586
1975	205·0	15·88	−1·239
1976	247·0	18·32	−10·693
1977	300·0	19·39	−27·612
1978	377·0	19·58	−26·079
1979	475·0	20·20 (Nov.)	−18·967

Sources: Bank of International Settlements, *Annual Report* 47; IMF, *Balance of Payments Yearbook*.

against recent experience) tend to see balance-of-payments disequilibria resolved through shifts in trade, and the problems of the system therefore springing from mercantilist obstacles to the market's 'natural' flow of goods, or its natural 'price' for a particular currency in relation to the others. Liberal analysis thus frequently underestimates the significance of short-term capital movements. This 'hot money', however, often plays a far greater role in the balance of payments than trade flows, and often does not appear to respond to the same classic economic stimuli (Strange, 1976; see Table 6.1). In contrast to liberals, mercantilists tend to see a nation's surplus not as a disequilibrium to be adjusted, but as a superior competitive performance, an advantage to be maintained through active manipulation of trade flows, monetary policy, or the exchange rates directly. 'Adjustment' is more likely to come from political action than from automatic economic process (Schmitt, 1979b). Structuralists meanwhile see the balance of payments mainly as a mirror reflecting the dependencies embodied in the system. From this perspective, poor countries can seldom expect favourable exchange rates or fair terms of trade from rich countries. Those who need to borrow capital for development can anticipate being dominated through a mounting burden of debt (Diaz-Àlejandro, 1978).

Reserve Currencies

These differences over the significance of the balance of payments are further complicated by the asymmetries introduced into monetary relations by the presence of 'reserve currencies'. The issue goes back to the interwar years. In the First World War European countries printed money to cover their enormous expenses and, in the process, soon broke the tie between their currencies and gold. The classic gold standard was thus fatally disrupted. For several years only the dollar remained tied to gold. Dollar credits from the United States, moreover, became increasingly the means by which the Allies financed international transactions outside their own imperial systems. Under these circumstances the international monetary system became a 'gold-exchange standard', with the dollar becoming a reserve currency held by others in place of gold. In due course the dollar was joined by the pound, which had always been a reserve currency for countries within the British imperial orbit, but which was now also held as part of the national reserves of independent countries, like France and Switzerland. Whereas the Americans, at this early stage, showed some diffidence about the dollar's reserve role, the British eagerly embraced the new system as a way of restoring London's financial pre-eminence and worldwide investments. With the pound a reserve currency, Britain could continue to play its old international financial role, even though its net reserves and basic economic strength was greatly diminished.

The whole system was formally acknowledged in the Genoa Agreement of 1922.[2]

The arrangement was ripe with possibilities for mutual misunderstanding. Under the terms of a gold-exchange standard the country issuing the reserve currency has a legal obligation to take it back, if requested, and to pay out a set amount of gold in exchange. The reserve-currency country is supposed to regulate its affairs so as to be able to meet this contractual obligation. As Triffin notes, putting a reserve currency in the hands of foreigners requires the issuing country to run a national balance-of-payments deficit (Triffin, 1960, 1966). And as Rueff notes, running that deficit can easily become habitual for the reserve-currency country. For unlike other countries, when it sends its money abroad, its own domestic money supply is not thereby correspondingly reduced. The economy of the reserve-currency country grows addicted to its apparently costless balance-of-payments deficits, while the foreign recipients of these deficits grow into increasingly reluctant holders. Accordingly both issuer and recipient grow self-righteous and irritable. The reserve-currency country sees itself providing 'liquidity' to a world that needs capital to grow. But neighbouring central banks who increasingly accumulate the reserve currency see themselves making forced loans to cover the profligacy of a country abusing its reserve-currency status – its exorbitant privilege of running regular payments deficits (Kooker, 1978).[3]

Normally reserve currencies are also widely held in the private markets. The reserve-currency country thus has not only a large debt to foreign central banks, but an 'overhang' of redeemable currency in the hands of private foreigners. This results in the situation described in Professor Triffin's paradox. Foreigners, official and private, gradually refuse to hold the reserve currency without larger and larger discounts or special guarantees. As long as exchange rates are fixed, this means they insist on higher and higher interest rates, which means higher and higher domestic interest rates in the issuing country. The tight money needed to please foreign holders meets increasing domestic resistance in the reserve-currency country itself. Hence a growing conflict develops between the reserve-country's domestic demands and external obligations. Government policy oscillates between tight money to please its foreign creditors and easy money to satisfy its domestic constituency. Ultimately a crisis of foreign confidence ensues and confronts the issuing country with demands for gold payments that cannot be met (Triffin, 1960).

According to both Rueff and Triffin, these theoretical problems of the gold-exchange standard have twice in this century led to the breakdown of the international monetary system. For these reasons the British-dominated reserve-currency system is seen to have collapsed in 1931, and the American in 1971. In both cases the gold-exchange standard was caught in a fatal contradiction. Whereas reserve-currency countries did seek to act, in effect, as central banks supplying money for the whole system, the other countries ultimately expected them to act as a nation like any other, that is, to keep their external accounts in balance.

In summary, the very concept of a balance of payments, complicated as it has been by the presence of reserve currencies, is loaded with ambiguous and arguable implications towards which analysts and governments have shifting and ambivalent views. The lack of real agreement on these fundamental questions reflects itself in the inability of states to formulate and sustain any durable international monetary regime.

As political scientists should quickly understand, this lack of agreement does not merely represent á perverse incapacity of economic experts from different countries to resolve technical problems. Mercantilists and structuralists have hold of a fundamental point. In the end an international monetary regime, like domestic monetary institutions, reflects the general world balance of political and economic power. A monetary system with special rules for one power reflects a group of states dominated by that one power. When the hegemony erodes, the monetary system starts to break down or to transform itself radically. By contrast, a system characterised by equal rules equally obeyed, like the gold standard, reflects an integrated group of states with a plural diffusion of power among them. Even the biggest states in such a system cannot break the rules with impunity. A pluralistic liberal system of this sort lasts as long as the political balance and shared perspectives that it reflects. Fear of the consequences of breakdown may keep an integrated system, plural or hegemonic, going for a while, as probably happened in the late 1920s. But eventually integrated monetary regimes will tend to come apart when the constituent states no longer feel constrained to accept hegemony or find themselves without sufficient common interests, perceptions, or institutions to consent to common rules. In this situation, a pluralistic international system without consensus, the world's monetary regime tends towards a series of monetary blocks, separated by floating rates and controls (Strange, 1971; Calleo and Rowland, 1973; Calleo, in Rowland, 1978; Calleo, 1976).

Not only, of course, does an international monetary system reflect the relative power of states, it also reflects the domestic economic, social and political character of its principal members. No integrated international monetary regime is likely to survive unless the domestic economic and social order in each major country is in harmony with the international regime. The classic gold standard, as Rueff imagined it, reflected not only a plural but integrated world system in which all major powers were constrained to follow the same rules, but one in which their domestic societies were dominated by those social classes interested in monetary stability (Rueff, 1932; Maier, 1975).

A final and critical point remains: to say that world monetary order must conform to international and domestic political realities is not to say that money, and economics generally, have no laws of their own, or that politics may flout these laws with impunity. Men may be slaves to money, but the institution of money, after all, is what makes a free society possible. Money permits wealth to be created through a complex division of labour without requiring some central authority to direct people's labour or specify their consumption. In a society that permits relatively free choices of work and consumption money serves as the essential mediator between men's infinite desires and the limited resources of the economic system. When, for one reason or another, money no longer serves as a reliable standard of value, the stability of society itself – international as well as domestic – is gravely undermined. Inflation with its disruptiveness, and slow growth with its frustration, are the obvious consequences of monetary mismanagement in our own time. Inflation is, so to speak, the revenge of natural law on political power (Rueff, 1973).

Measuring the Balance of Payments

An analysis of the political dimension of the balance of payments can be extended to its statistical presentation. Ambiguities in the concept itself are more than matched by the ambiguities in the way that a national balance of payments is measured and presented (Devlin, 1971). Statistics, like maps, are designed to highlight and draw attention to certain aspects of a situation rather than others. In the American balance-of-payments statistic, particularly, shifts in the conventions used to measure and present the accounts reflect changing perceptions of the national interest in the monetary system. Political scientists need to understand the technical shifts in order not to miss their political significance.

A variety of official definitions have been used. Any overall balance must obviously have a number of components each of which is, in effect, a lesser balance. The two basic components are generally current account and capital account. Current account includes the trade balance, net foreign expenditures of the government and the balance for services or 'invisibles' – a figure that encompasses not only freight, insurance and banking fees, but the return on overseas investments. Capital account is subdivided into long-term capital flows – funds earmarked for investment of some duration, including the direct investments of corporations in foreign plant and equipment – and short-term capital flows – liquid funds in search of higher interest rates.

Recent years have seen at least three ways of totting up these components into an overall balance. The most comprehensive is the 'liquidity balance' that includes the current account and all non-bank capital flows. This measures, in effect, the flow of dollars between residents and non-residents of the United States. Since short-term capital is volatile, sometimes building up for several years and then flowing out again in a great rush, it has sometimes been thought useful to compute a 'basic' balance that leaves out short-term capital, and thus presumably gives a more accurate picture of the 'real' economy in a given year. This basic balance, therefore, includes the entire current account (trade, government and services) but only long-term capital flows, presumably because they represent real investment rather than 'hot money'. Finally, a 'reserves transaction' or 'official settlements balance' shows the final change in US monetary reserves. This computation reveals, in effect, only those flows that end up in foreign central banks and leaves out those that remain in private hands. It does not measure the degree to which non-residents may be accumulating dollars as future claims on the American economy.

Approaches to Analysing a Deficit

The complexities of measuring a balance are amply reflected in the explanation for a persistent imbalance. Two broad approaches are common among policy-makers.[4] One is an item-by-item approach, the other a monetarist approach. The item-by-item approach looks at the specific elements in the balance of payments and tries to assign the cause for disequilibrium to some particular item or group of items. Implied is some notion of a normal set of trade, capital and governmental flows. Anything that seems exceptional is suspected. Measures to curb particular outflows or augment particular inflows seem the obvious prescription. Mercantilist countries where the banking system is highly integrated and controlled, like Japan and Italy, often have remarkable success in using such specific measures to regulate their balance of payments. Trade too can often be manipulated with considerable success by such specific mercantilist measures (Allen and Stevenson, 1974; Suzuki, 1980).

The monetarist approach, by contrast, traces a deficit not to any particular items in the balance of payments, but to the general management of the domestic economy, management of the money supply in particular. A balance-of-payments deficit is taken as *prima facie* evidence that the national money supply is expanding too rapidly. Money is being created that cannot be absorbed by growth in real economic activity. Depending on the circumstances, this excessive creation of money will either cause domestic price inflation, as too much money chases too few goods, or else flow outward and cause a balance-of-payments deficit. Some combination of both external deficits and internal rising prices is normal. In the postwar period with some degree of inflation nearly everywhere, and a high degree of freedom for international capital movements, countries that suffer balance-of-payments deficits are, in effect, those that inflate their money supplies more than the norm. In the monetarist view a payments deficit will occur from excess money creation regardless of whether the money is needed for either foreign or domestic expenditures. Hence the item-by-item figures of the basic balance are of no great interest to monetarist analysis. Nor does it matter in what fashion the excess money is created. Central banks may print money to finance government deficits and stimulate the economy, or private banks may pyramid credit in response to demand, at home or abroad.

Public and private analysis of the American payments deficit has in the past used both item-by-item and monetarist approaches. Official American analysis tended to be item-by-item until the later 1960s, when it began to turn monetarist, but often with very different practical conclusions from the European variety. A brief survey of the various analytical approaches will help focus the real issues involved in the payments question.

The Item-by-Item Approach: Empire and Trade

Item-by-item analysis shaped American balance-of-payments policy in the Kennedy, Johnson and even early Nixon administrations. In the 1960s the annual outflow from the real economy – the basic balance as opposed to the ebbs and flows of the short-term market – revealed a striking pattern. Despite a regularly positive balance on services and, until 1971, on trade, two large negative items seemed to push the overall basic balance into deficit. These were government transactions (overseas troops and aid) and long-term capital flows (overseas corporate direct investment) (see Table 6.2) This pattern suggested an imperial explanation for America's disequilibrium. The payments deficit seemed the consequence of America's hegemonic role within the international system. The imperial burdens might be military – like keeping troops overseas – or economic – like providing the public and private capital for reconstruction and development.

As the 1960s progressed this imperial explanation seemed increasingly inconvenient and either irrelevant or unacceptable. It was inconvenient because by pinpointing overseas government expenditures and corporate investments as the causes of a weak dollar, it implied that these ought to be cut. Balance-of-payments arguments could thus become a pretext for neo-isolationism and protectionism. Apprehension grew particularly strong when Nixon's Secretary of the Treasury John Connally, kept noting the rough equivalence, year after year, between the exchange costs of American troops in Europe and the basic Ameri-

Table 6.2   *Elements of the US Basic Balance of Payments, 1970*
($ billion)

Merchandise trade balance	2·3
Exports	42·0
Imports	−40·0
Other services, net	0·6
Travel and transportation	−2·0
Investment income, net	6·2
US direct investments abroad	8·0
Other US investments abroad	3·5
Foreign investments in USA	−5·2
Remittances, pensions and other transfers	−1·4
Military transactions, net	−3·4
US government grants (excluding military)	−1·7
US government capital flows, excluding non-scheduled repayments, net	−1·8
Non-scheduled repayments, of US government assets	0·2
US government non-liquid liabilities to other than foreign official reserve agencies	−0·4
Long-term private capital flows, net	−1·5
US direct investments abroad	−4·4
Foreign direct investments in USA	1·0
Foreign securities	−0·9
US securities other than Treasury Issues	2·2
Other, reported by US banks	0·2
Other, reported by US non-banking concerns	0·6
Balance on current account and long-term capital	−3·0

Source: US Department of Commerce, *Survey of Current Business*, June 1971, table 1.

can balance-of-payments deficit (notably to the American Bankers' Association, 28 May 1971; see Table 6.3). To partisans of the Pax Americana an annual outlay of 2–3 billion dollars in foreign exchange seemed absurdly insignificant compared to the geopolitical, and indeed financial, interest involved in the defence of Europe. But even the less apocalyptic remedies implied by this approach, like controls on foreign investment or increased European contributions to NATO, all met with increasing resistance.

In any event, as offshore dollars built up into an organised capital market, the basic deficits seemed increasingly irrelevant to the dollar's defence, except perhaps as indicators affecting confidence among the holders of the volatile dollar 'overhang'.[5] In technical terms attention shifted from the basic balance to the liquidity balance – the flow of 'hot money'. Ultimately the dollar's fate depended, of course, on the reserve transactions balance, the degree to which non-resident dollar-holders

Table 6.3 *US Basic Balance and Net Military Transactions Compared*
($ million)

	US basic balance	US net military transactions
1960	−1,155	−2,752
1961	20	−2,596
1962	−979	12,449
1963	−1,262	−2,304
1964	28	−2,133
1965	−1,814	−2,122
1966	−1,614	−2,935
1967	−3.196	−3,138
1968	−1,349	−3,140
1969	−2,879	−3,341
1970	−3,038	−3,371

Source: As Table 6.2.

were going to foreign central banks for exchange, as well as the degree
to which the central banks were willing to accept the dollars. Under the
circumstances managing the already existing pool of expatriate dollars
grew far more significant for the dollar's parity than the 'real' flows of
the basic balance. With multinational corporations routinely moving
several billions in response to interest rates, the relatively small basic
deficits, never more than 3–4 billion dollars, were swamped, exacer-
bated or multiplied by short-term capital flows of 10 or 20 billions
(United States Government, 1975, 1981). Abandoning the defence of
Europe in order to save 2–3 billions out of deficits running up to 20
billion seemed preposterous. The inconvenient emphasis on overseas
military costs and corporate investments could thus be pushed aside.

As it happened, the imperial explanation did, in fact, provide a major
insight into the nature of the American predicament. The Vietnam War
undoubtedly cost the country's economy a great deal (Eckstein, 1978).
Enormous defence budgets throughout the postwar era very probably
have sapped American economic growth. Steady overseas investment
may well have slowed the modernisation of domestic industry (see
Tables 6.4 and 6.5). Above all, the determination to pursue simultaneously domestic full employment and world leadership was certainly a
major cause of inflation. Few of these imperial costs, however, were
accurately measured by specific items in the basic balance of payments.
To make sense, the imperial explanation of deficits had first to be recast
into a broader structural analysis of American inflation and of the
Western political economy in general. The burdens of the imperial role,
including the managing of the international monetary system, had to be
related to the American economy's persistent tendency to inflation and

Table 6.4   *Defence Expenditure as Percentage of GNP*

	1958	1965	1970
United States	11·1	8·0	7·8
Federal Republic of Germany	3·8	4·4	3·3
France	8·0	5·6	4·0
United Kingdom	7·8	6·0	4·9
Japan	—	1·3	0·8

Source: International Institute for Strategic Studies, *The Military Balance, 1971–72*, pp. 60–1; *1968–69*, pp. 55–6; *1963–64*, p. 32.

Table 6.5   *Investment Balances, 1961–72* ($ million)

	US direct investment abroad	Foreign direct investment in the USA
1961	2,852	482
1962	2,559	220
1963	3,460	332
1964	3,744	419
1965	4,994	434
1966	5,325	257
1967	4,692	869
1968	5,492	892
1969	6,050	1,003
1970	7,145	1,452
1971	8,020	385
1972	7,833	708

Source: International Economic Report of the President, 1974, p. 103.

its structural shortcomings generally. Analysis had to relate, in effect, the costs of America's world role – security, foreign aid, investment, 'liquidity' – to the troublesome weaknesses of the American domestic economy.

The Structural or Systemic Explanation: the SDR Debate

The official shift away from item-by-item explanation began to take place in the Johnson administration. What replaced it was, in effect, a structural critique of the international monetary system itself (Strange, 1976; Roosa, 1963, 1967; *ERP*, 1967, 1968). Unfortunately the new approach was as incomplete as the old. Preoccupation with the mechanics of the international monetary system, of course, went back to the interwar debate over reserve currencies. Rueff's writing, politicised by de Gaulle, continued the debate into the 1960s. Meanwhile the Belgian-American economist, Robert Triffin, had given a new twist to Rueff's attack on the gold-exchange standard. Triffin assumed that the dollar would ultimately be forced to stop running deficits. At that point, he argued, not enough internationally acceptable money would be available to finance the world's growing trade and transnational investment. In other words, unlike Rueff, Triffin assumed the continuous creation of new money was essential. But like Rueff, he saw that it could not be provided indefinitely by a national currency. Triffin, therefore, proposed empowering some international agency to create new assets that could take over the 'liquidity' function, hitherto supplied by dollar deficits (Triffin, 1966).

Triffin's proposals, along with a number of variations sponsored by others, coincided with the widespread perception of a world shortage of 'liquidity'. National reserves seemed inadequate to cushion growing deficits, particularly as the growing volume of world trade and investment (and inflation of prices) made international currency flows larger and larger in relation to national foreign-exchange reserves. These perceptions were particularly acute not only in the reserve-currency countries, Britain and the United States, but also among developing countries, who were exceptionally prone to deficits, and within those international agencies, like the World Bank or the International Monetary Fund, who were supposed to help reconcile 'development' with world financial order. American policy-makers meanwhile were essentially searching for a new source of credit. By the mid-1960s they began to perceive the utility and convenience of the SDR idea.

Triffin's proposals, despite their wide appeal, suffered from a major practical defect. The logical link between the imaginary problems of what might happen if the United States should end its deficit, and the real problem of actually getting it to do so remained elusive. Seeing the SDR machinery as a solution to the American payments deficit either presupposed that IMF credit could shore up the dollar indefinitely or else genuinely saw the dollar deficits as nothing more than an altruistic American desire to provide liquidity to the world. According to this latter belief, once creation of world money was turned over to the IMF, the United States would no longer be forced to run deficits to service the world economy. The dollar's problems would be over. For Washington, however, the practical problem was not the lack of liquidity in the world at large, but the lack of foreign exchange in American reserves. In reality, the United States had no intention of giving up control of its foreign 'burdens', including the tribulations of monetary hegemony. Overseas troops and investments were expressions of American ambition and power as well as idealism. The United States was not running deficits to provide liquidity to others, but as a by-product of pursuing its domestic and foreign ambitions. As long as the United States held the monetary hegemony involved in its reserve currency role, it could be certain that ample 'liquidity' would be available to finance its foreign positions. While the United States was quite happy to use the IMF as a gloss over its monetary hegemony, it had no intention of ceding its real power over the world's money supply. The United States was all for 'supranational' government in Europe – especially if it would produce a single alliance partner in place of an agglomeration of 'free riders', unsuited either for discipline or for sharing the burden of defence (Kindleberger, 1973; and in Calleo, 1976). But in matters pertaining to their own prerogatives American statesmen kept a firmly nationalist grip on power. The SDR idea was seen simply as a source of new credit to finance America's own deficits, not the start of a new international regime.

By 1968 the Americans had their way and the SDR machinery was put into place.[6] Ironically the first creation came in 1970, just as Nixon was setting an unprecedented explosion of American 'liquidity' loose on the world. To repeat, in no way could the SDR be expected to get at the cause of American deficits. This cause was the creation of money in the United States beyond the capacity of either the domestic or world economies to absorb it. As Cleveland and Brittain pointed out in their study of the Johnson–Nixon period, *The Great Inflation*, American monetary policies meant not only a huge payments deficit, but an explosion of inflation throughout the world (Cleveland and Brittain, 1976).

Systemic Arguments Continued: Benign Neglect and Floating

On the whole American economists have seldom lagged behind their statesmen in displaying a strong patriotic bias. By the late 1960s fashionable American economics had taken up a new systemic cause, 'floating exchange rates'. In effect, the arguments counselling 'benign neglect' and floating were rationalisations for a depreciation of the dollar – a mercantilist remedy the Nixon administration came to believe essential for the rejuvenation of America's faltering domestic economy.

The academic rationale for Nixon and Connally's mercantilist offensive based itself on the supposed deficiencies of the Bretton Woods system of fixed rates (Haberler and Willett, 1971; Krause, 1970). The academic analyses, to be sure, gave a plausible enough view of the American predicament. By the late 1960s the dollar was clearly overvalued, the domestic economic effects deleterious and America's allies reluctant to give up their advantages. Devaluation was certainly much easier than deflation, a painful and doubtful remedy.

As analysis, however, the academic apologies for benign neglect and floating suffered from a fatal deficiency. While they gave an accurate enough description of the American predicament after the dollar had become overvalued, they provided, in themselves, at best only a very partial explanation of why the dollar had become overvalued in the first place. As a result, they could not really provide any policy to keep the dollar from becoming overvalued again. That, however, was the real problem. The 1971 devaluation was not (as they seemed to suggest) a once-for-all cure, but the beginning of chronic depreciation. The basic reason for the dollar's chronic depreciation after 1971 was the same as the reason for its weakness before 1971, namely, accelerating American inflation prompted by relentlessly expansionary fiscal and monetary policies.

By contrast, the reasons assigned in official analyses reflected the endemic tendency among American economists to blame unpleasant facts within the situation under analysis on 'exogenous' disturbances from without. Explanations for the overvalued dollar thus typically ignored general economic factors, like inflation, in favour of more specific political factors, like an overly generous American exchange-rate policy at the outset of Bretton Woods, or the Machiavellian mercantilism of the allies thereafter (*ERP*, 1973). Explanations for inflation typically showed the same tendency. In the late 1960s and early 1970s inflation was blamed on the Vietnam War. A few years later it was oil prices. Similarly, the failure of floating rates to restore the American balance was blamed on the 'dirty floating' of the Europeans and the Japanese (*ERP*, 1975). In short, economic analysis was reduced to a series of catastrophes and conspiracies. Not until the late 1970s was the role of inflationary domestic management so clear in the dollar's problems that even official economists could no longer ignore it. Even then, American ingenuity was ready with the 'locomotive theory', the gist of which blamed the dollar's problems on the failure of Europeans to achieve the high inflation rates of the Americans.[7]

The Strange Blindness of American Economic Analysis

Unwillingness to face the link between the dollar's weakness and the country's long-range domestic and international policies proved the great failing in American policy itself. On the whole American academic analysis gave policy very little assistance or guidance. The lack of interest from the Keynesians in the linkage was not surprising. Their prescription, expansion at home in the interest of domestic equity, was after all in good part responsible for America's domestic inflation. The international inequities and dislocations that resulted were, understandably, not prime topics for Keynesian analysis. When neo-Keynesians did extend their pattern of thinking to the international political economy, they came up with visionary plans for worldwide equity, like the 'Link' – SDRs issued to LDCs to spend on development, or the big-scale World Development Fund proposed in the Brandt Report (Park, 1973; Brandt *et al.*, 1980; Lipton, 1980). Such prescriptions jarred uncomfortably with the growing awareness of the limits to the world's resources. Keynesians began to rediscover what Keynes had concluded by the 1930s: that equity at home required mercantilism abroad (Keynes, 1933). In short, for the Keynesians, the whole question of America's inflation was even more embarrassing internationally than domestically.

More puzzling, however, is why American monetarists were as diffident as the Keynesians about noting the connection between American inflation and the dollar's weakness. As discussed above, the basic monetarist approach to the balance of payments explicitly links a deficit to an inflationary excess of monetary creation. In addition, Friedman's celebrated monetarist attack on the Phillips Curve had presumably aimed to show how Keynesian demand management was inherently and progressively inflationary. The Phillips Curve, by suggesting a stable relationship between moderate inflation and moderate growth, implied that a little more inflation could be traded for a little more growth. Countries pursuing such policies, according to Friedman's critique, should not expect stable real growth, but progressive inflation with social disruption and economic stagnation (Phillips, 1962; Friedman, 1968b; Lehrman, 1976). Presumably countries infected with excessive Keynesian preference for full employment over monetary stability (or in the case of LDCs, for economic growth) should also have been expected to run a balance-of-payments deficit. A monetarist analysing the balance-of-payments problem of a country that had been in deficit for two decades might reasonably be expected to suppose that country more inflationary than the norm for the system as a whole, its balance-of-payments deficit the normal consequence of its higher inflation. That inflation, moreover, might be expected to have some relationship to those analyses of unemployment and inflation that so preoccupied American monetarists in the domestic context.

Most puzzling of all, however, was the prevailing enthusiasm in American monetarist circles for floating exchange rates. For by abandoning the Bretton Woods system of fixed exchange rates, the United States gave up the last remaining major institutional restraint on domestic inflation. In this respect American monetarists were completely at odds with their conservative French counterparts, like Rueff. On the face of it the French monetarists seem to have been more consistent. Rueff's emphasis on the gold standard was in harmony with his aim of restoring monetary stability at home.[8] By contrast, Friedman's advocacy of floating rates appears logically inconsistent with his monetarist prescriptions for domestic policy (Friedman and Roosa, 1967;

Friedman, 1968a). Floating rates might have made sense for a mercantilist Keynesian hoping to insulate an economy from the international consequences of his inflationary domestic prescriptions. But for anyone hoping to stop domestic inflation, abandoning fixed rates was to renounce his most effective weapon. The point is sufficiently crucial to deserve further elaboration.

National Inflation and its Limits

What sets the limits to national inflation? How do these limits work on domestic, international and global levels?

At the domestic level, in most countries at most times, democratically elected governments have very strong reasons for a general tendency towards inflation. Politically inflation can be justified by its apparently stimulating effect on growth and employment and its seemingly easy resolution to demands for redistribution (Maier, in Hirsch and Goldthorpe, 1978; Janowitz, 1976). When labour demands more pay, for example, inflation can allow society to spread the cost rather than take it directly out of businessmen or consumers. When government's ambitions or social responsibilities outrun its resources, inflation facilitates the debt financing that avoids higher taxes or the 'crowding out' of private borrowers from capital markets.

Although inflation serves many domestic interests in the short run, and therefore appeals strongly to vote-seeking politicians, in the long run it not only shows an alarming tendency to get out of control, but is also highly disruptive politically. Rentiers see their assets deteriorate and grow more militantly conscious of inflation's redistributive effects. In general, as people lose their 'money illusion', more and more parts of the society are drawn into a conscious struggle over income shares. Since, as Hicks observes, many of the special arrangements of an economy can be explained more plausibly by custom than by inherent economic logic, this contentiousness grows dangerous for social stability (Hicks, 1974; Inglehart, 1971; Crozier, 1975). As property and social peace seem more and more threatened a coalition for stability can be expected to increase its political weight in counterpoise to the hitherto dominant coalition for growth and inflation. (Giscard de'Estaing presumably was counting on such a shift in the balance of interests in France, in 1979, when he joined Schmidt in pushing for the European Monetary System to achieve a 'zone of stability'.) The shift however is seldom achieved quickly, easily, or completely. In any society dissatisfied interests expecting to profit from growth are always numerous, particularly after a long era in which inflation has become habitual. Renouncing the dream of even illusory growth is slow and bitter.

This is why in most postwar economies inflation has been curbed by limits operating at the second level, the international one, long before the domestic balance of interests has changed sufficiently to bring about the same result. Anti-inflation policies have been adopted in order to defend the currency, for fear of the alternatives, rather than from collective conviction that they were socially desirable. Fixed exchange rates, while they lasted (and managed floating ones too to some extent), therefore provided a sort of political myth which could be enlisted to justify the defence of monetary stability by often painful and unpalatable measures (Lehrman, 1976).

That the advanced industrialised countries had significant differences in their willingness to take such measures is undeniable. National character, past national monetary experiences and differences in the ease or difficulty of adjusting to deflation by losing jobs does undoubtedly explain a great deal about divergent inflation rates in different countries. For example, the German tribal memory heightens political awareness of the long-run penalties attached to inflation and, therefore, substantially assists inflation-resisting policies. But other factors also enter in. Inflation will be easier to check if production of goods is growing fast as a result of high investment rates, up-to-date plant, managerial enterprise, technological research and development. And the share going to labour from the national product will be determined by other variables, such as national bargaining process, education, social mobility and labour organisation. In all this there is one factor, the character of the workforce, which seems particularly important. Countries like West Germany and Switzerland with low inflation rates have unusually homogeneous and generally skilled workforces. Neither has a native *lumpenproletariat*; both employ large numbers of 'guest-workers' who can be paid off and sent home when deflationary policies begin to bite (Kuhn, 1978).

By contrast, countries with relatively high inflation rates like Britain with its class and racial divisions and Italy with its still undeveloped south have to cope with social cleavages and social tensions without such a safety-valve. To sustain full employment in such societies requires relatively more monetary stimulation than in Germany; and they therefore appear to have a higher 'natural' rate of inflation. France, with its submerged pool of illegal immigrants and therefore docile immigrant workers, is in a somewhat intermediate position and its inflation rate has consequently tended to lie somewhere between those of Britain and Italy and Germany and Switzerland. It was not, of course, that the United States was more committed to full employment than low-inflation countries like Germany. Quite the contrary. But considering the domestic differences, achieving a tolerable level of employment in the American economy may well have required more expansive policies than in the Federal Republic.[9]

In any event it is certainly beyond dispute that American fiscal policy carried a far greater proportional burden of foreign expenditure, particularly military expenditure. American inflation became a way of shifting or masking the burden to American taxpayers and, through a balance-of-payments deficit, of shifting it to foreign economies. From a strictly economic point of view, the whole procedure was an 'exorbitant privilege'. But from a political and military perspective, it was 'burden-sharing', made necessary by Europe and Japan's unwillingness either to defend themselves or to pay a reasonable portion of their imperial protector's military budget. Throughout the postwar era, it bears remembering, America's proportional defence expenditure has generally been double or triple that of its major European allies. At least half the annual American defence budget, moreover, has generally been earmarked for NATO (Calleo, 1981; see Table 6.4).

Few countries, of course, have lacked strong inducements for inflationary policies. The principal difference between American inflation and that of other major capitalist countries lies less in the cause than in the consequences. For under both the fixed-exchange rates of Bretton Woods and the subsequent floating regime that prevailed afterwards Americans have been able to run balance-of-payments deficits without external restraint, and hence to 'export' a good part of the consequences of their inflation.

Under fixed rates surplus countries were more or less compelled to augment their domestic money supplies by absorbing America's excess dollars into their reserves. The shift to a global structure of more flexible rates did not make America's deficits any more subject to external restraint. Quite the contrary. Surplus countries could continue as before, and go on supporting the dollar through 'dirty floating'. Otherwise they could either revalue – not a popular course for countries heavily dependent on exports – or else watch the dollar depreciate, with the same generally deleterious trade effects. The logical response to this dilemma would have come from a European bloc protecting itself against American money and goods. But in a divided and dependent Europe this was not a likely option. Not until the late 1970s did a European–Arab coalition finally succeed in forcing the Americans to defend the dollar and hence to control domestic inflation. Thanks to Khomeini, the Americans entered the age of Volcker.

Even then, the situation was highly unsatisfactory for the Europeans. Within a few months they began complaining bitterly at America's excessively tight monetary conditions with consequent high interest rates (Strange, 1976; Calleo, 1982; Tsoukalis, 1977; Ludlow, 1982; *ERP*, 1980). In the short run, at least, this produced a substantial appreciation of the dollar and forced Europeans to maintain correspondingly tight monetary conditions in the midst of a recession. The prospects for relief seemed bleak (*The Economist*, 26 September 1981). With power in the Reagan administration being shared between conservative monetarists and expansive militarists, the chances for a return

Table 6.6   *Volcker's Credit Crunch and the Dollar*

	Prime rate charged by banks (%)	US dollar multilateral trade-weighted average March 1973 = 100
March 1979	$11\frac{3}{4}-11\frac{3}{4}$	88·4
June 1979	$11\frac{3}{4}-11\frac{1}{2}$	89·6
December 1979	$15\frac{1}{2}-15\frac{1}{4}$	86·3
March 1980	$16\frac{3}{4}-19\frac{1}{2}$	90·3

Source: ERP, 1981, pp. 309, 343.

to fiscal equilibrium in the United States, and hence to lower interest rates without inflation, were not promising. In effect, the high American interest rates and consequent disruption of currency markets and monetary conditions in Europe were simply the latest way by which the United States was exporting the effects of its chronic indigestion. Once again, the lack of external restraints on unsound domestic policy, and the concomitant capacity to export many of the effects, gave American policy a licence for indiscipline, which was denied to its allies.

In any event, in the late 1960s and early 1970s, linking America's monetary hegemony, its capacity to run balance-of-payments deficits without international restraints and its propensity for inflation could hardly have been an abstruse or novel connection. The odd thing is that it seems to have eluded so many American economists, even conservatives preoccupied with curbing domestic inflation. Nevertheless, the inflationary proclivities that go with monetary hegemony have never been a popular theme for American economists. Even those preoccupied with curbing domestic inflation have fiercely resisted any external check on America's international hegemony. The Friedmanite analysis, by overplaying domestic differentials and underplaying international and structural ones, turns out to be only a sophisticated version of the 'national character' analysis of behaviour in the international political economy.

Hegemony, National Interest and Monetary Ideology

General de Gaulle once described American policy as the will to power cloaked in idealism. American policy towards the balance of payments might be described as the will to power cloaked in academic economics. The defence of American hegemony does seem to provide the one consistent impulse through the otherwise tortured course of the mainstream of American balance-of-payments theory. The otherwise inexplicable blindspots and obsessions – ignoring the capital market and underplaying the capital account, harping on the liquidity problem, inflating the role of the IMF, seeking to 'demonetise gold', rationalising the resort to floating exchange rates – all have reflected a basic urge to dominate the monetary system so that external constraints may not limit the American political economy's expansive impulses, at home or abroad. Differences among American economists have always seemed to stop at the water's edge. Keynesians and monetarists, liberals and conservatives have fiercely resisted any external check on America's international hegemony. American theorising has thus become an elaborate ideology to resist sharing American monetary power with the Europeans and Japanese, let alone the oil-producing states or the Group of 77. The end has been to keep the world subject to American monetary policy, and that policy in turn free from external constraint, including the discipline of some collectively agreed-upon 'regime'.

Given the numerical predominance of Americans in the economics profession, and the discipline's intrinsic political obtuseness, this American ideology has been eagerly adopted in academic teaching, writing and research far beyond the confines of the United States. Indeed, it may be seen in the work of many (or even most) economists in Britain, France, Germany and other European countries, as well as in Japan and the Third World.

Hegemonic monetary systems are hardly novelties in history, nor are open apologies for them without force or adherents. Indeed, many political economists have unquestioningly accepted Kindleberger's powerful case (developed in *The World in Depression* and much other writing) for international monetary 'governance' imposed by a dominant power (Kindleberger, 1973; Strange, 1971). The role is presumably justified for others by a close and self-evident coincidence between the hegemon's interest and that of the system as a whole. In this respect, however, the United States has grave deficiencies. It differs from most other economies in the system, in being naturally far more autarkic. Intrinsic differences are magnified further by peculiar institutions and attitudes. Its politicians and policies, and its system of financial governance in general, still do not recognise the extent that American multinationals and banks do depend on the world economy. With the Federal Reserve continuing to respond primarily to domestic stimuli, the United States is not very well suited to be a monetary Vatican City.

From the perspective of the other powers, American monetary predominance thus results less in a dutiful management of the collective economic interest than in a nationalist exploitation of power. Under the circumstances a foreign observer might be forgiven for ascribing the insensitivities of American academic analysis less to intellectual deficiency than to mercantilist nationalism – all the more irritating in so far as it is usually quite unselfconscious.

An American, of course, might find national interest no less present in the technical theories of his European colleagues. The French have been the principal, and often the only, intellectual opponents of American policy. The French monetarists have been far more consistent and reliable analysts of the international monetary regime and its link with inflation than their American counterparts. In retrospect Rueff's argument that the use of reserve currencies in the gold-exchange standard was bound to be inflationary was difficult to fault. Since the switch to floating rates, moreover, the theoretical case for some version of a gold standard has certainly not lost its force – as some recent American polemics illustrate (Lehrman, 1976). The vast increase in dollar currencies since the oil crisis, the spread of other reserve currencies, the liberated credit-creating powers of international banking have all relentlessly assaulted monetary stability. The theoretical case for gold – for some standard tied to real values and less subject to manipulation – has grown more and more intellectually compelling.

The failing of French analysis is, therefore, the reverse of the American: American analysis is wrong but predominant; French analysis is correct but impractical. For a modern gold standard can be made to work only in certain circumstances. As argued at the outset, a gold standard is like any truly plural system. It ultimately depends upon there being enough power dispersed throughout the system to force even the biggest state to obey the rules. And it depends further upon there being within the member-states domestic regimes which see their own interests furthered by the external restraint. But a modern gold standard also requires some kind of hegemonic manager to smooth the correction of disequilibria in the world economy, along the lines so well explained by Kindleberger. Someone has to be an ever-open market for other people's surpluses, a lender of last resort in moments of financial crisis and the source of long-term countercyclical lending.

The problem is to have a manager without having a tyrant. In other words, the balance of power must be such that the country exercising the managerial hegemonic role is held to its task of defending the system rather than permitted to exploit it.

In the later nineteenth century such conditions did prevail (Polanyi, 1944; Skidelsky, 1978). European states in general were ruled by a bourgeoisie concerned with the preservation of capital. The gold-standard discipline merely reinforced their position. The British Empire had the resources and experience to manage the system. Britain's hegemony was nevertheless bound within the rules of the gold standard itself. Britain did not run perennial balance-of-payments deficits with the other independent centres, nor did central banks outside the imperial system hold reserves in sterling (Calleo, 1978; Cairncross, 1953; Drummond, 1981). Behind these technical limits on Britain's capacity to exploit the system lay a European balance of power and the growing plurality of financial power and institutions.

Today none of the political conditions that would permit a return to the gold standard exists. The political balance has been insufficient to compel the United States to stay within even the attenuated gold standard of Bretton Woods. It is questionable, moreover, whether the dominant political forces within either Europe or America genuinely prefer monetary stability to inflation. Nor is it clear that the United States, even if it were constrained to remain within the basic rules of the gold standard, has the means or the expertise to play the manager's role in today's turbulent world.

From this perspective, the French monetarists are no less nationalist than the American. Their nationalism is that of a middle power, unable itself to pretend to hegemony, but seeking to escape from the unsympathetic hegemony of another.

The 'impracticality' of French analysis, therefore, is that France lacks the power either to impose its own formula on the system (or itself!), or the will to break the American hegemony. If the American domestic economy exploits Europe as the French maintain, it is because the Americans can get away with it. For Europeans, the French included, a system with American exploitation has seemed better than chaos. Europe's monetary weakness stems from its geopolitical weakness – its disunity and hence dependence upon its American protectors. Under these circumstances American exploitation of the monetary system seems natural. Europeans should blame themselves rather than the Americans.

As de Gaulle noted often enough, the weak generally suffer the fate they deserve. In view of the temptations – the domestic pressure and foreign weakness – the Americans could have been a good deal worse. America's monetary exploitation, moreover, needs to be put in its proper geopolitical context. That Americans have so long carried such a disproportionate defence burden is surely a major cause of their inflation. If the United States has been able to carry its disproportionate military burdens only because of its exploitation of monetary hegemony, it ill-behoves its rich protectorates to complain. Until the affluent allies can combine the will and resources for a political and military equilibrium within the capitalist system they should expect to adjust to policies made for the convenience of others.

But if power has its own rules, economics also has some laws of its own. Key among them is the deleterious effect of bad money. Thus the triumph of American policy has, more and more, become the ruin of American prosperity at home and the erosion of American legitimacy abroad. The problem with American economics has not been its natural concern for the national interest, but its myopic inability to define that interest intelligently and imaginatively over the long term.

Some Academic Conclusions

This lack of objectivity in political–economic analysis does not speak well for the pretentions of our profession. Quite apart from falling short of its own scientific standards, academic analysis, by failing to provide a moral, political and historical critique to bureaucratic policy, has been of little service to national interest or the international community. The great bulk of research and writing has simply been a technical obligato to the themes set by short-sighted government policies. The agenda of international negotiations has essentially been framed by the American government, guided by its own rather narrow view of national interest. Academic studies have, to a great extent, merely reflected the same skewed perspective. Such, for example, is the pervasive character of most textbook treatments of international monetary relations.

A more useful and honourable role might result if scholars resolutely determined to widen the perspectives open to themselves and their students. A more intimate but sceptical view of conventional Western economic analysis would be a good start. While orthodox neo-classical economics represents a dazzling intellectual edifice, it suffers from grave deficiencies in analysing the real world. Even if the contemporary writings of neo-mercantilists, Rueffian liberals, or Marxists should seem less 'rigorous', academic analysis that does not absorb their insights too often remains a priggishly learned apology for the official policies of the moment (a betrayal of academic responsibility that seems particularly shameful). The best antidote to the superficialities of contemporary analysis is probably an open-minded return to the classics of political economy. Direct study of writers like Munn, Smith, Ricardo, Malthus, List, J. S. Mill, Marx, Weber, Lenin, Luxemburg, Schumpeter, or Keynes himself enriches present analysis with the broad accumulated insight of generations of serious speculation about man's economic life.

A certain familiarity with past events and theories, moreover, suggests the mortality of current arrangements and doctrines. Certain historic studies, like Bagehot's immortal *Lombard Street*, give moreover the texture of practices and institutions in other periods (Bagehot, 1922). They provide an indispensable sense of perspective for judging contemporary studies of financial markets and institutions.

Monetary questions in particular and economic questions in general cannot, of course, be separated from larger social, political and historical issues. The genius not only of Marx, but of liberal or conservative writers like Coleridge, Mill, Weber, Schumpeter and Polanyi lies in their sensitivity to the intertwining of politics and economics. Structuralist historians would doubtless contribute a great deal to the education of political scientists and economists alike if they dealt with monetary issues, institutions and relationships in the later twentieth century as Braudel does for the seventeenth. Much may be hoped for from several contemporary historians who are putting monetary questions into a broad political and social context (Skidelsky, 1967; Feldman, 1977; Schuker, 1976; Maier, 1975; Cleveland and Brittain, 1976; Hirsch, 1976).

Expanding the scope of study and analysis by history and philosophy is not meant to proliferate arcane specialisation or ancient error. Rather it is the means to furnish our imaginations with the perspective needed to control those facile theories and institutional contraptions that are the stock-in-trade of most contemporary analysis.

Improving the analysis of policy is not, to be sure, only a matter of academic virtue and self-respect. International monetary issues are a crucial test of whether national states can comprehend and manage the increasing complexities of an interdependent world. Sorting out the monetary issues among states requires, in effect, a working consensus on the limits to competition and the sharing of values. Better academic analysis and education, and a broader public understanding of these matters, will presumably temper excessive claims and will aid the necessary processes of reconciliation. Time, moreover, may well be running out. The increasing storminess of the world economy over the past decade does not reflect merely a series of fortuitous accidents. More plausibly, it signals a disintegration that grows more and more unmanageable.

Notes: Chapter 6

1   The IBRD (also known as the World Bank) and the IMF were both set up after the Second World War under the Bretton Woods Agreement of 1943. Both are loosely attached to the United Nations but are based in Washington, indicating the dominant influence on them of the United States. The World Bank lends foreign exchange for economic development projects. It raises funds for these long-term loans by borrowing at market rates on the world's capital markets. The IMF has not so far borrowed money in this way, though it is thinking it might do so. Its funds consist of the contributions of member-states in gold and their own currency and can be supplemented, if necessary, by further contributions from the richer countries under the General Arrangements to Borrow (GAB) (1962 and 1983). Quota contributions to the Fund and Bank have been successively increased over the years but the proportion of total finance for development (including private bank loans) from both bodies has remained about the same. The Fund's purpose was to provide foreign exchange for member-countries in temporary balance-of-payments difficulty, and members could draw on it in proportion to their quota contributions or arrange stand-by credits in case of need. Small drawings could be made automatically but later 'tranches' of credit could only be drawn on conditions regarding economic policy laid down by the Fund staff. In 1968 members agreed that the Fund could also issue Special Drawing Rights (SDRs) also in proportion to quota contribu-

tions; one issue was made in 1970–3 and another in 1979–82. Decisions in both organisations are made on a weighted voting system which gives the United States (and the European Community if its members can agree) a veto. In recent years as oil deficits and falling commodity prices hit developing countries the distinction between the World Bank as a source of long-term development finance and the Fund as a source of short-term balance-of-payments lending has become blurred. The Fund has eased its terms and added special 'facilities' for its poorer members and actively intervened as a kind of official receiver when debtor countries were unable to renew commercial bank loans. Both organisations urge on members the virtues of economic liberalism and financial conservatism. Both are also useful sources of statistical and other information. So is the Bank for International Settlements located at Basle in Switzerland and technically a Swiss bank not an intergovernmental organisation. But its shareholders are the central banks of the major trading and financial countries of the West, and their representatives meet every month in Basle and are in constant touch with one another by telephone and telex. Whenever financial markets have threatened to disrupt the world's monetary system, the BIS has proved an invaluable means by which the major national monetary authorities could combine forces to restore order. The BIS, having functioned as a bank since 1930, has substantial resources of its own which it could use to intervene in the markets or to help members in distress, but it rarely does so.

2   London, the principal centre of the international system before 1914, was after the First World War increasingly rivalled and constrained by New York. American loans were, for example, the principal source of international liquidity for Germany. The United States had a large proportion of the world's gold (44 per cent in 1923), while the British reserve position (9 per cent in 1923) was precarious in view of the country's economic weakness after the war. The pound's collapse in 1931 brought down the gold-exchange standard. The United States ended dollar convertibility into gold in 1933. American stabilisation in 1934, with the dollar devalued to 59 per cent of its former parity, and the tripartite agreement of the United States, Britain and France in 1936, restored a semblance of the gold-exchange standard, but within the general protectionist climate of the time: see Lewis, 1970; Brown, 1940; Rowland, 1978.

3   Rueff's initial critique of the gold-exchange standard was linked to Anglo-French political and financial rivalry in Eastern Europe during the 1920s. As he wrote in 1932: 'The application of the gold-exchange standard had the considerable advantage for Britain of making its real position for many years. During the entire postwar period, Britain was able to loan to Central European countries funds that kept flowing back to Britain, since the moment they had entered the economy of the borrowing countries, they were deposited again in London. Thus, like soldiers marching across the stage in a musical comedy, they could re-emerge indefinitely and enable their owners to continue making loans abroad, while, in fact, the inflow of foreign exchange, which in the past had made such loans possible, had dried up': Rueff, 1932, trans. 1964, p. 30.

4   Among economists themselves, three broad analytical approaches can be found to explain the balance of payments: the relative prices, absorption and monetary approaches. The first approach focuses on relative prices and

ignores the influence of important macrovariables such as income flows and stocks of assets. To cure an inbalance this approach recommends relative price adjustment through exchange-rate changes or demand-management policies. The absorption approach sees payments inbalances characterised if not caused by differences, *ex ante*, between an economy's aggregate income and its aggregate domestic spending (absorption). Income not spent at home tends to be exported. In effect, the approach extends to an open economy the Keynesian model for a closed economy. Income and expenditure flows are emphasised and monetary variables and relative prices ignored. While the model's explanatory power is weak, linking the balance of payments to domestic income and expenditure is at least suggestive to policy makers. The third, monetary approach, is described in the text. The 'item-by-item' approach also described in the text seems more an accounting mechanism than an analytical approach. It lacks an inherent central model to link the balance of payments to the overall economy. Since its explanations and prescriptions are, therefore, essentially arbitrary, it is particularly conducive to the political manipulation of trade and capital flows: see Pierce and Shaw, 1976; Corden, 1977; Whitman, 1975; Johnson, 1972.

5   This 'Eurodollar market' developed, in the 1960s and 1970s, into a highly organised financial system by which dollar accounts, building up in European or 'offshore' banks, can be reloaned abroad without being converted into some currency other than dollars. Most loans are short term. Considerable technical controversy exists over the market's actual size and relation to United States balance-of-payments deficits. With the Eurodollar market unregulated by reserve requirements, credit pyramiding is controlled only by bankers' notions of prudent reserves and margins. Thus while the initial credit base presumably consisted of dollar outflows for the United States, the unregulated system has permitted rapid expansion of credit beyond those outflows. Money has 'leaded out' of the system only when actually spent in the United States or converted into foreign currency. The scale of 'creation' and 'leakage' are both disputed among experts.

6   Under final arrangements at the IMF Rio de Janeiro conference in 1967, from each $1 billion of SDRs created, the United States was to receive about $250 million, the Common Market countries as a group about $180 million, the United Kingdom $116 million, Canada and Japan about $35 million each, other developed countries $280 million altogether and the less developed countries $280 million. Creation required an 85 per cent majority. Distribution of voting power in the IMF gave veto power both to the United States and the Common Market countries as a group: see *ERP*, 1968; International Monetary Fund, *Summary Proceedings, Annual Meeting 1967*, pp. 271–9; Cohen, 1970; Solomon, 1977; Strange, 1976; Williamson, 1974.

7   OECD economists, for example, counselled governments to react to the oil crisis by stimulating consumption further, lest higher fuel prices suck away buying power, and by lowering consumer demand, result in unemployment and eventual worldwide recession. The United States, adopting such a policy, claimed to be running a trade and payments deficit not because its economy was too expansive, but because other economies were not expansive enough. The consequent United States trade deficit and declining dollar were badges of American virtue. General world equilibrium was to be

restored not by dragging everyone down through a misguided preoccupation with restoring trade balances, but by everyone's joining the United States in expansion: see McCracken, 1977; *ERP*, 1977.

8 Rueff consistently argued that balance-of-payments deficits 'exploit' inflation. These deficits have essentially the same effect on the inflation 'importing' countries (that is, those maintaining their balance of payments in surplus) as would excessive monetary growth within their own economies. Rueff, of course, defined inflation as excessive monetary growth, with rising domestic prices an epiphenomenon. Such a definition made irrelevant the frequent American rejoinder to Rueff in the 1960s that the United States could not be exporting inflation since its rate of domestic price increases was lower than in most countries in Europe, France included: see Rueff, 1967, 1972.

9 This whole line of argument combines Friedman's notion of a natural rate of unemployment with a monetarist view of the balance of payments. To understand the causes for balance-of-payments deficits the domestic relationship between the natural rate of unemployment and monetary stimulation must be compared among individual nations in the open system. For the American Phillips curve's 'shifting to the left' and the inflationary consequences, see Perry, 1970, and Schultze, 1971.

References: Chapter 6

Allen, K., and Stevenson, A. (1974), *An Introduction to the Italian Economy* Oxford: Martin Robertson).

Bagehot, W. (1922), *Lombard Street: A Description of the Money Market* (New York: Arno Press).

Brandt, W. (Brandt Commission) (1980), *North–South: A Programme for Survival* (London: Pan Books).

Brown, W. A. (1940), *The International Gold Standard Reinterpreted, 1914–34* (New York: AMS Press).

Cairncross, A. K. (1953), *Home and Foreign Investment, 1870–1913* (Brighton: Harvester Press).

Calleo, D. P. (1978), 'The historiography of the inter-war period: reconsiderations', in B. M. Rowland (ed.), *The Balance of Power or Hegemony: The Interwar Monetary System* (New York: New York University Press).

Calleo, D. P. (1976), 'The decline and rebuilding of an international economic system: some general considerations', in D. P. Calleo (ed.), *Money and the Coming World Order* (New York: New York University Press).

Calleo, D. P. (1981), 'Inflation and American power', *Foreign Affairs*, vol. 59, no. 4 (Spring).

Calleo, D. P. (ed.) (1982), *The Imperious Economy* (Cambridge, MA: Harvard University Press).

Calleo, D. P., and Rowland, B. (1973), *America in the World Political Economy: Atlantic Dreams and National Realities* (Bloomington, IN: Indiana University Press), esp. chs 5 and 10.

Cardoso, F. H., and Faletto, E. (1979), *Dependency and Development in Latin America* (Berkeley, CA: University of California Press).

Cleveland, H. van B., and Brittain, W. H. Bruce (1976), *The Great Inflation*.

Cohen, S. (1970), *International Monetary Reform, 1964–69: The Political Dimension* (New York: Praeger).

Corden, W. M. (1977), *Inflation, Exchange Rates in the World Economy* (London: OUP).

Crozier, M., Huntington, S., and Watanuki, J. (1975), *The Crisis of Democracy: Report on the Governability of Democracies to the Trilateral Commission* (New York: New York University Press).

Devlin, D. (1971), 'The United States balance of payments: revised presentation', *Survey of Current Business* (June).

Diaz-Alejandro, C. (1978), 'Delinking North and South: unshackled or unhinged', in A. Fishlow *et al.* (eds), *Rich and Poor Nations in the World Economy* (New York: McGraw-Hill).

Drummond, I. M. (1981), *The Floating Pound and the Sterling Area, 1931–39* (Cambridge: CUP).

Duffy, G., and Giddy, I. H. (1978), *The International Money Market* (Englewood Cliffs, NJ: Prentice-Hall).

Eckstein, O. (1978), *The Great Recession* (Amsterdam: North-Holland Publishing Co.).

Feldman, G. D. (1977), *Iron and Steel in the German Inflation, 1916–23* (Princeton, NJ: Princeton University Press).

Fishlow, A., *et al.* (eds) (1978), *Rich and Poor Nations in the World Economy* New York: McGraw-Hill).

Friedman, M. (1968a), *Dollars and Deficits* (Englewood Cliffs, NJ: Prentice-Hall).

Friedman, M. (1968b), 'The role of monetary policy', *American Economic Review*, vol. 1.

Friedman, M. (1969), 'The Euro-dollar market: some first principles', *Morgan Guarantee Survey* (October).

Friedman, M., and Roosa, R. (1967), *The Balance of Payments: Free versus Fixed Exchange Rates* (Washington, DC: American Enterprise Institute for Public Policy Research).

Haas, E. (1953), 'The balance of power: prescription, concept or propaganda?', *World Politics*, vol. 5.

Haberler, G., and Willett, T. (1971), *Strategy for US Balance of Payment Policies*.

Hicks, J. (1974), *The Crisis in Keynesian Economics* (Oxford: Blackwell).

Hirsch, E. (1976), *Social Limits to Growth* (London: Routledge & Kegan Paul).

Hirsch, F., and Goldthorpe, J. (1978), *The Political Economy of Inflation* (Oxford: Martin Robertson).

Inglehart, R. (1971), 'The silent revolution in Europe: inter-governmental change in post-industrial society', *American Political Science Review* (December).

Janowitz, M. (1976), *Social Control of the Welfare State* (Amsterdam: Elsevier).

Johnson, H. G. (1972), 'The monetary approach to balance of payments theory', *Journal of Financial and Quantitative Analysis* (March).

Keynes, J. M. (1933), 'National self-sufficiency', *Yale Review* (June).

Kindleberger, C. (1973), *The World in Depression, 1929–39* (Berkeley, CA: University of California Press).

Kindleberger, C. (1976), 'Systems of international organization', in D. P.

Calleo (ed.), *Money and the Coming World Order* (New York: New York University Press).

Kindleberger, C., and Lindert, P. (1978), *International Economics*, 6th edn (Homewood, IL: Richard D. Irwin Inc.).

Kooker, J. (1978), 'French financial diplomacy: the inter-war years', in B. M. Rowland (ed.), *The Balance of Power or Hegemony: The Interwar Monetary System* (New York: New York University Press).

Krause, L. (1970), 'A passive balance of payments strategy', *Brookings Papers on Economic Activity*.

Kuhn, W. E. (1978), 'Guest-workers as an automatic stabiliser of cyclical unemployment in Switzerland and Germany', *International Migration Review* (Summer).

Lehrman, L. (1976), 'Creation of an international monetary order', in D. P. Calleo (ed.), *Money and the Coming World Order* (New York: New York University Press).

Lewis, W. A. (1970), *Economic Survey, 1919–39* (London: Allen & Unwin).

Lipton, M. (1980), 'Brandt: whose common interest?', *International Affairs* (Spring).

Ludlow, P. (1982), *The Making of the European Monetary System* (London: Butterworth).

McCracken, P. (McCracken Committee) (1977), *The Current and Future Role of the Dollar: How Much Symmetry?* (Paris: OECD).

Machlup, F. (1971), 'Euro-dollar creation: a mystery story', *Banco Nazionale del Lavoro Quarterly Review* (September).

Magdoff, H., and Sweezy, P. M. (1977), *The End of Prosperity: The American Economy in the 1970s* (New York: Monthly Review Press).

Maier, C. (1975), *Recasting Bourgeois Europe: Stabilisation in France, Germany and Italy in the Decade after World War One* (Princeton, NJ: Princeton University Press).

Mendelsohn, S. (1980), *Money on the Move* (New York: McGraw-Hill).

Park, Y. S. (1973), *The Link between Special Drawing Rights and Development Finance* (Princeton, NJ: Princeton University Press).

Perry, G. (1970), 'Changing labor markets and inflation', *Brookings Papers on Economic Activity*.

Phillips, A. W. (1962), 'Employment, inflation and growth', *Economica* (February).

Pierce, D. G., and Shaw, D. M. (1976), *Monetary Economics: Theories, Evidence and Policy* (New York: Crane, Russak & Co.).

Polanyi, K. (1944), *The Great Transformation* (London: Octagon).

Roosa, R. (1963), 'Reforming the international monetary system', *Foreign Affairs* (October).

Roosa, R. (1967), *The Dollar and World Liquidity* (Random House).

Rowland, B. M. (ed.) (1978), *The Balance of Power or Hegemony: The Interwar Monetary System* (New York: New York University Press).

Rueff, J. (1932), *Les Doctrines monétaires a l'épreuve des faits*: English translation in *The Age of Inflation* (1964).

Rueff, J. (1967), *Balance of Payments*, trans. J. Clements (New York: Macmillan).

Rueff, J. (1972), *Monetary Sin of the West* (London: Macmillan).

124   *Paths to International Political Economy*

Rueff, J. (1973), *The Gods and the Kings: A Glance at Creative Power* (London: Macmillan).

Schmitt, H. O. (1979a), 'Mercantilism: a modern argument', *The Manchester School* (June).

Schmitt, H. O. (1979b), 'Rejoinder on mercantilism', *The Manchester School* (June).

Schuker, S. (1976), *The End of French Predominance in Europe: The Final Crisis of 1924 on the Adoption of the Dawes Plan* (Chapel Hill, NC: University of North Carolina Press).

Schultze, C. (1971), 'Has the Phillips curve shifted? Some additional evidence', *Brookings Papers on Economic Activity*.

Skidelsky, R. (1967), *Politicians and the Slump: The Labour Government of 1929–1931* (London: Macmillan).

Skidelsky, R. (1978), 'Retreat from leadership: the evolution of British economic foreign policy, 1870–1939', in B. M. Rowland (ed.), *The Balance of Power or Hegemony: The Interwar Monetary System* (New York: New York University Press).

Solomon, R. (1977), *The International Monetary System, 1949–1976: An Insider's View* (New York: Harper & Row).

Stem, C. H., Makin, J. H., and Logue, D. E. (eds) (1976), *Euro-Currencies in the International Monetary System* (Washington, DC: American Enterprise Institute for Public Policy Research).

Strange, S. (1971), *Sterling and British Policy: A Political Study of an International Currency in Decline* (London: OUP).

Strange, S. (1976), *International Monetary Relations. Vol. 2, International Economic Relations of the Western World, 1959–71*, ed. A. Shonfield (London: OUP).

Strange, S. (1982), *The International Monetary System, 1945–1981*.

Streit, C. (1939), *Union Now: A Proposal for a Federal Union of the Democracies of the North Atlantic* (London: Cape).

Suzuki, Y. (1980), *Money and Banking in Contemporary Japan* (New Haven, CT: Yale University Press).

Tew, B. (1982), *Evolution of the International Monetary System, 1945–76* (London: Hutchinson).

Triffin, R. (1960), *Gold and the Dollar Crisis* (New Haven, CT: Yale University Press).

Triffin, R. (1966), *The World Money Maze: National Currencies in International Payments* (New Haven, CT: Yale University Press).

Tsoukalis, L. (1977), *The Politics and Economics of European Monetary Integration* (London: Allen & Unwin).

United States Government, *Economic Report of the President* (Washington, DC: United States Government Printing Office), various years.

Versluysen, E. (1981), *The Political Economy of International Finance* (Aldershot: Gower Publishing Co.).

Vines, D. (1979), 'Competitiveness, technical progress and balance of payments surpluses', *The Manchester School*.

Wallerstein, I. (1979), *The Capitalist World Economy* (Cambridge: Cambridge University Press).

Whitman, M. von N. (1975), Global Monetarism and the Monetary Approach to

the Balance of Payments, *Brookings Papers on Economic Activity*, No. 3 (Washington, DC: Brookings Institution).
Williamson, J. (1974), *The Failure of World Monetary Reform, 1971–1974* (Walton-on-Thames: Thomas Nelson & Sons).

7

The Politics of International Trade

L. RANGARAJAN

> Then the Goddess, flashing eyed Athene, ans-
> wered him: 'There fore of a truth, will I frankly
> tell thee all . . . I put in here, as thou seest,
> with ship and crew, while sailing over the wine
> dark sea to men of strange speech, on my way to
> Tamese for copper: and I bear with me shining
> iron'.
>
> The *Odyssey*, Bk I

The aim of this chapter is to identify the main economic and political factors necessary to any understanding of the problems relating to international trade in the modern world. There is, indeed, a vast difference between trade in Homeric times and international trade in the difficult economic environment of our time. Even so, the quotation from the *Odyssey* illustrates a number of points which can help us to understand why people and governments behave in the way they do when trading with one another.

We notice, first, that the goddess Athene did not have copper on her own ground and had to go to Tamese for it, bartering it for iron. Since the natural resources of this world are more unevenly distributed than human wants, people as well as gods need to trade. Secondly, perceived need brings about dependence. If the need is sufficiently acute, the user of a commodity or product may travel long distances or may be willing to pay increasingly higher prices; if his need is too great and dependence on foreign sources too high, he may even be tempted to bring the source under control by force. A third essential characteristic of international trade is the existence of a boundary between buyer and seller. Where there is a boundary, a barrier can be erected by one side or the other. A large part of the politics of international trade is thus concerned with the erection and dismantling of the barriers to free trade.

Three conclusions follow from these observations. Because trade helps to redress the uneven distribution of resources and goods, it adds to welfare by a more effective division of labour and more efficient use of resources. In primitive societies barter was a means of increasing total welfare by division of labour. If an efficient potter could earn all the grain he needed by selling his pots, there was no need for him to be a farmer as well; the community as a whole benefited by each member doing efficiently what he could. The principle that the most efficient producer must be free to make and sell his wares (the principle of comparative advantage) is still relevant to international trade today.

The second conclusion is that trade besides increasing wealth and efficiency, offers a greater freedom of choice to consumers. In the Odyssean example Athene's people could choose to drink out of copper chalices instead of more fragile earthenware; and the Tamesians could have sharper and more durable iron tools instead of bronze ones. In the twentieth century trade enlarges the range of choice available to consumers in two ways. They can buy goods normally not produced in their own countries (coffee, tea, or bananas in Europe), and they also have a wider range of choice among similar goods (for example, cars) produced both at home and abroad.

Thirdly, the increasing dependence brought about by trade adds to the possible sources of insecurity for both the state and the individual. The sense of insecurity created by the oil price rise produced, in most developed countries, a panicky reaction that similar powerful groups might emerge in other raw materials, particularly minerals. Dependence, and the consequent feeling of insecurity, are not only confined to import dependence; there can also be excessive dependence on the export of just one or two commodities. This is particularly important in the case of developing countries, many of whom do not have a diversified export pattern.

Where benefits and disadvantages lie is perceived differently by people and governments at different times and in different circumstances – and even for different kinds of trade. Sometimes, as in a cold war, or for a strategic sector like arms or energy, security of the state is most highly rated. At times the protection of employment in an industry takes precedence. At other times efficiency and the freedom to choose for the consumer comes first. The choice between these conflicting values is inherently political and will be influenced by subjective ideologies, as well as objective political and economic considerations. States, in short, are obliged to choose policies towards trade which reflect the importance they attach in their perceived self-interest to the different opportunities and benefits, the risks and the costs which trade opens to them.

In order to acquire some grasp of the main outlines of the modern trade system we have to look closely at four aspects. In the first place, we need to know, at least in broad outline, who trades in what with whom. This is a good starting-point that keeps our feet on the ground of reality. Secondly, we have to understand the origins of the postwar international trading system and the changes in the environment that have affected its efficient functioning. Next, we need to know something about the 'rules of the game' which have been agreed to, since these rules are devised by negotiation between governments to find a balance between conflicting principles. Lastly, we have to understand the different values of different nations, the choices made by them and the extent to which these choices lead them to diverge from the agreed rules. Conflicts ensue when these policies clash.

The brief introduction to the political economy of international trade offered in this chapter ends with an attempt to look at the possible trends in international trade in the years ahead.

For reasons of space, the outline will deal principally with trade within the world market economy – that is, it will exclude trade between centrally planned economy countries which anyway make up only 10 per cent of the total picture. Nor will it deal with the special issues of trade within regional groupings like the European Community. The focus will also be on visible trade in primary commodities and industrial products and not with trade in services with invisibles which are often subject to rather different politics of the world's economic system. Even so, brevity will enforce a measure of generalisation. Let me, however, register the point that the politics of trade in different sectors often differ quite sharply. The policies are not always consistent; the same government can, and often does, adopt different attitudes between trade in minerals and trade in agricultural products or between temperate and tropical crops.

The Pattern of International Trade

World trade has grown remarkably fast since the end of the Second World War, particularly in the 1970s. The figures in Table 7.1 show that world exports nearly doubled in value between 1948 and 1958, and more than doubled between 1958 and 1968. It is harder to assess the real increase in international trade in the next ten years. Between 1968 and 1978 trade increased five and a half times in dollar terms; but these figures have to be treated with some caution. A large part of the increase in the value of world exports, especially since 1973, reflects the quadrupling of oil prices and the effect of higher worldwide inflation.

Table 7.1 also shows the share of world exports of different classes of participating countries, including the centrally planned economy countries. Other tables give the facts only for market economy countries. Of these, the share of the developed countries increased steadily between 1948 and 1972 (64·2 per cent to 71·8 per cent). Thereafter their share

Table 7.1 Growth of World Trade: Exports of Different Economic Classes

	Value of exports ($ thousand million)					Percentage shares				
	1938	1948	1958	1968	1978	1938	1948	1958	1968	1978
World	23·5	57·0	108	239	1297	100	100	100	100	100
Developed countries	15·2	36·6	71	168	872	65	64	66	70	67
OPEC	} 5·9	3·1	7	14	145	} 25	5	7	6	11
Non-oil developing		13·6	17	29	156		24	16	12	12
Centrally planned	2·4	3·7	12	27	124	10	6	11	12	10

Table 7.2 Trade in the Market Economy, World: Unit Value and Quantum Indices – 1970, 100

	Quantum index					Unit value index				
	1948	1958	1968	1973	1978	1948	1958	1968	1973	1978
All commodities	22	38	82	131	158	90	90	92	142	264
Food, raw materials	36	55	88	125		102	91	93	147	
Fuel	18	39	85	126	125	104	111	95	177	620
Manufactured goods	16	32	81	131		84	86	91	138	

declined mainly because the oil price rise doubled the share of OPEC countries, from 6·6 per cent in 1972 to 13·2 per cent in 1976. Conversely, the share of the non-oil-exporting developing countries was halved between 1948 and 1978. This is relevant to the perception of the poor countries of being pushed to the periphery of the international economic system.

Table 7.2 shows, for selected years, the change in the volume (quantum) and unit value of different types of commodities. The growth was fastest in manufactured goods; over ten times the quantity of manufacture was exported in 1978 compared to 1948. By contrast, the quantities of food and raw materials exported grew only by about four times. The increase in the unit price of manufactures was also much higher than in the case of food and raw materials. The engine for the growth of world trade, both in quantity and in unit value, has been the growth in trade in industrial products.

Terms of trade (the ratio of unit value of exports to unit value of imports) measures the concept of how much a country has to pay by way of its own exports for the imports it needs. It is a very contentious point in North–South relations, particularly in measuring how much raw material has to be exported by developing countries to import machinery from the developed. Table 7.3 shows that developed countries have, on the whole, managed to maintain their terms of trade around 100 up to 1973; thereafter the high price of imported energy required them to export more for their imports. The terms of trade of developing countries, as a whole, appears to have improved dramatically between 1973 and 1978; this is an illusion in so far as non-oil-exporting developing countries are concerned. When we disregard the effect of the oil price rise, we see that terms of trade of developing countries, excluding fuel exported to developed countries, has steadily declined from 117 in 1950 to 90 in 1976. Developing countries without oil have been able to buy less and less with their exports.

Table 7.3 also shows two interesting facts about the trade of developing countries. Their share in the exports of primary commodities has been steadily declining between 1958 and 1978 (from 40 per cent to 28 per cent). The industrialised countries have as important a stake in the export of primary commodities as they have in exporting manufactured goods. The rich countries are preponderant exporters of wheat, maize, wood and pulp, meat, wool, wine, butter and lard, bauxite, lead and zinc. Half the world exports of copper, iron ore, rice, tobacco, edible oils and oilseedcake also originate in the developed countries. The poor countries have lost ground rapidly in the non-ferrous metals trade. There has, however, been some industrial development in the poor countries enabling them to diversify their export pattern by exporting more manufactured goods. Industrial products earned just over one-tenth of their foreign exchange earnings in 1950 but nearly one-quarter

Table 7.3   *Trade between Developed and Developing Areas*

	1950	1958	1968	1973	1978
1 Terms of trade					
Developed areas	97	98	100	98	92
Developing areas	109	105	98	107	135
Developing areas less oil- producing areas	117	104	97	97	93
2 Food and raw materials, excluding fuels					
Quantum 1970, 100					
Developed	50	88	125	148	
Developing	66	88	117	115	
Share of developing countries as a percentage	40	33	32	28	

3 Percentage share of manufactured goods in total exports of developing
   countries
   1950 11·7
   1958 11·3
   1973 25·5
   1978 23·7

4 Exports of manufactures of developing countries share of				
Non-ferrous metals	62	45	29	18
Textiles, clothing	18	24	27	27

in 1973. The growth in manufactured exports was achieved by the development of simpler industries, like textiles and clothing.

Who trades with whom is also important. Tables 7.4 and 7.5 show the direction of trade, separately for food and raw materials and for manufactures. The diagram shows the exports of each of the four economic classes for the years 1948, 1958, 1968 and 1978.

The following conclusions can be drawn from all this data:

(1) Trade is mainly between the rich countries, which account for 80 per cent of total world import market.
(2) The share of the developing countries in exports of manufactured goods is still less than 10 per cent; over 90 per cent of all industrial goods originate in rich countries.
(3) Both developed and developing countries are important markets for industrial goods, the latter accounting for as much as one-third of the total.
(4) The sharp increase in the import of manufactures by developing countries between 1973 and 1978 indicates the increase in the purchasing power of the oil-exporting countries.

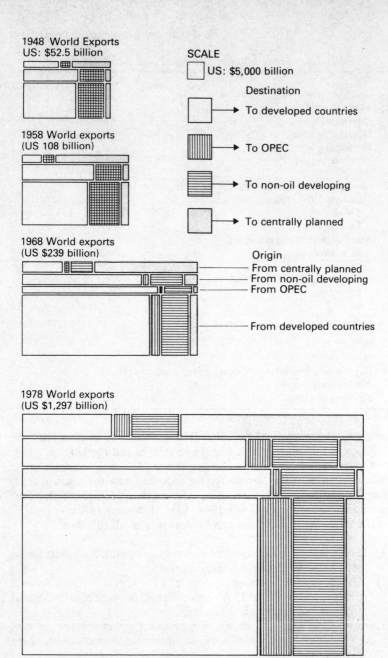

Figure 7.1 *World trade: volume and direction, 1958–78.*
Source: *UN Statistical Year Books.*

Table 7.4 Market Economy Exports of Food and Raw Materials

	Value ($ thousand million)				Percentage share			
	1958	1968	1973	1978	1958	1968	1973	1978
Total market economy	31·96	50·93	113·11	199·58	100	100	100	100
From developed countries	18·37	33·54	79·10	137·77	57·5	65·9	70·0	69·0
From developing countries	13·59	17·39	34·00	61·81	42·5	34·1	30·0	31·0
Exports of developed countries								
To other developed	15·10	28·11	66·65	110·65	82·2	83·8	84·3	80·3
To developing	3·27	5·43	12·46	27·13	17·8	16·2	15·7	19·7
Exports of developing countries								
To developed countries	11·22	14·17	27·07	47·33	82·5	81·5	79·6	76·6
To other developing	2·37	3·22	6·93	14·49	17·5	18·5	20·4	23·4

Table 7.5 Market Economy Exports of Manufactured Goods

	Value ($ thousand million)				Percentage share			
	1958	1968	1973	1978	1958	1968	1973	1978
Total market economy	46·45	127·91	314·04	701·42	100	100	100	100
From developed countries	43·70	119·10	287·55	633·66	94·1	93·1	91·6	90·3
From developing countries	2·75	8·81	26·49	67·66	5·9	6·9	8·4	9·6
Exports of developed countries								
To other developed	28·29	92·22	228·86	462·91	64·7	77·4	79·6	73·0
To developing	15·41	26·88	58·68	17·75	35·3	22·6	20·4	26·9
Exports of developing countries								
To developed countries	1·80	6·47	19·11	44·60	65·5	73·4	72·1	65·9
To other developing	0·95	2·34	7·22	23·07	34·5	26·6	27·2	34·1

Note: To know where to look for and how to interpret data relating to trade, students have to become familiar with the available statistical series. These make use of a universally used classification system – the Standard International Trade Classification (SITC). This system (revised from time to time as SITC-Rev.1, SITC-Rev.2, etc.) assigns numbers to categories of traded goods. Thus sections 0, 1, 2 and 4 cover primary commodities; section 3 is fuels; and sections 5, 6, 7 and 8 cover industrial products. Within each section further numbers indicate sub-classifications (for example, 112.1 – wine, 421.2 – soya bean oil, 684.1 – aluminium). The main source of international trade statistics is the *United Nations Statistical Yearbook* (annual); there is also a section on international trade in the *UN Monthly Bulletin of Statistics*, which also contains useful summary tables. Many organisations publish their own statistics – EUROSTAT (on the Community), FAO (on food, fisheries and forestry), GATT, UNCTAD and the Commodity Councils (tin, wheat, sugar, etc.) are among the more important ones. Individual countries, of course, publish their own foreign trade statistics, with varying degrees of accuracy and promptitude.

The pattern of international trade is, however, influenced by many factors. Among these, we must not forget geography (Cole, 1963). The uneven distribution of minerals or energy resources, the variations in soil and climate, and the distance between production and consuming centres are physical facts which have political repercussions. For example, the fact that a large part of the oil imported by industrialised countries comes from the Middle East affects the politics of that area. Equally politics affects the oil trade; the two have become inseparable. The importance of South Africa as a producer of gold, diamonds, uranium and chrome accounts for the condoning attitude of some industrialised countries towards apartheid. Climate not only determines what can be grown but often decides how much is grown in a particular season. Geography divides the world's agricultural trade into two – the growers of temperate-zone products (generally the rich countries), and the producers of tropical products such as tea, coffee, cocoa, bananas, oilpalm and rubber. When a product like sugar can be got from temperate beet as well as tropical cane, conflicts arise. The impact of floods, drought, or frost on the availability of agricultural produce for domestic consumption and exports needs no elaboration. When food grains are traded between countries in different economic or political groups, the trade becomes political. The most well-known example is the trade in grain between the United States and the Soviet Union.

Another important factor determining the pattern of world trade is the distribution of purchasing power. Exports gravitate to those best able to pay and their needs, translated into demands, prevail over those of others. Coarse grains like millet, the staple food in many African countries, are in demand in the rich countries as animal feed because the rising standards of living in these countries lead to greater demand for meat. The rise in standards of living has also led to an increasing exchange of similar consumer products between the rich countries. While the Japanese as well as the Americans take to Scotch whisky, the Europeans develop a taste for bourbon and hamburgers. The rich exchange jeans for *haute couture*, trade in similar perfumes and cosmetics, and sell cars to one another. To someone from a country where there are few cars the availability of choice between more or less mechanically identical vehicles, different only in shape, appearance, trim and optional extras can only seem a superfluous luxury. But it is not so to the people who buy them. The truth about consumerism is that when a choice between products is available, the consumer welcomes such a choice. This is as true of the Russian who is willing to pay black-market prices for imported jeans as it is of the more prosperous sections in the poor countries. There is now a world market of the affluent, whatever their race, colour, or geographical location.

Yet another factor determining patterns of trade is the astounding development of technology after the Second World War. Technology has spanned whole new industries and new markets – electronic calculators, video recorders, instant cameras, jumbo jets and nuclear power plants, not to speak of ever-more sophisticated armaments. Technology also determines the range of goods produced and their costs. For example, when technology allows the development of substitutes and synthetics, this reduces the export possibilities of the competing natural products and also diminishes the prices which poor countries are able to get for them. Another consequence of technological advance is that geographical distance has decreasing effects on international trade. Mammoth tankers for transporting oil, bulk carriers for grain and ore, more efficient methods of cargo handling like containerisation – all these developments have made proximity between sources and markets less important than it was in past periods. Technology has also given even poor countries greater possibilities of protection from weather or pests and this has had an impact on the trade in food and agricultural raw materials.

To summarise, the pattern of international trade is largely determined by the economic power of countries, though constrained to some extent by geography and climate. Some limitations can be overcome by the application of modern technology, the source of which is the rich countries, particularly the United States. No wonder that most of the growth in world trade is accounted for by trade generated by the developed countries, both as exporters and as importers. They are powerful because four-fifths of market economy trade is in their hands in all products. They have a predominant share in the export of capital goods, food, many agricultural raw materials, many minerals and even coal. The only product whose marketing they cannot control is oil. They are important as markets for the exports of developing countries. Equally the developing countries provide increasingly valuable markets for the products of the rich. Each needs the other.

Because the rich countries operate and control such a large part of international trade, they have a vital stake in preserving the postwar international economic system. We must now ask, therefore, how this system was created and how it has operated in the last thirty-five years.

Stability, Order and Change

To understand the politics of international trade it is necessary to know something of its recent history. Though some events before the Second World War (such as the Great Depression of the 1930s or German hyperinflation in the 1920s) influence the thinking of people and of governments today, it is nevertheless the post-1945 history which is most directly relevant to trade in the 1980s (Shonfield, 1976).

In 1945 the United States was the most powerful state in the world not merely as the sole possessor of the atom bomb, but also because of its industrial might, agricultural plenty, technological leadership and minimal destruction during the war. Britain, though weakened by the war, still had a far-flung empire. Most European nations and Japan were in ruins and the Soviet Union, under Stalin, had embarked on autarkic economic policies, confined only to the region under its influence. It is, therefore, not surprising that the philosophy which guided the thinking on the shape of the economy of the postwar world was an Anglo-American one. The aim was to create a set of interlinked institutions which would so regulate the international economy as to avoid recurrent bouts of instability, depression and unemployment. There were to be three international organisations – one to regulate international trade, a fund to oversee a regime of stable exchange rates and a bank to provide loans for reconstruction and development. Of the three, only two were actually established – the International Monetary Fund (IMF) and the World Bank (International Bank for Reconstruction and Development – IBRD).

The third institution, which would have been known as the International Trade Organisation (ITO) never came into being. The principles for regulating all international trade were agreed upon at the United Nations Conference on Trade and Employment held in Havana in 1948 and embodied in the Havana Charter. The Charter ran into fierce opposition from the Republicans in the United States Congress on the ostensible grounds that it interfered with so-called 'market forces'. President Truman, fearing defeat, declined to submit the treaty to the Senate for ratification.

Something was salvaged from the wreckage. The countries which held the preponderance of economic power recognised the benefits of free trade – only in industrial goods; they could not agree on free trade in agricultural products and raw materials. The salvage operation was, therefore, restricted to separating out manufactures from the rest of the Charter and negotiating a separate instrument – an executive agreement that did not need Senate ratification – called the General Agreement on Tariffs and Trade (GATT).

The search for some agreement on the regulation of trade in primary commodities was entrusted to an Interim Co-ordination Committee on International Commodity Agreements. ICCICA survived till 1964, working desultorily and to little avail; its disappearance into UNCTAD (United Nations Conference on Trade and Development) was hardly noticed.

When one of the three legs of the open economy tripod was sawn off into half a leg, the resulting system became inherently unstable. The deliberate preference of the rich countries for free trade in manufactures but protectionism in primary commodities is one of the main causes of the great divide between the industrialised temperate-zone North and the poor tropical South.

The remaining half-leg, the General Agreement part of the Havana Charter, became effective on 1 January 1948 and was to have been suspended if ever the full Charter came into force. Since the ITO was scuttled by the United States, GATT has continued its existence as a multilateral treaty. The term GATT is used ambiguously to denote the agreement as such, the contracting parties acting together under it and the organisation set up by them in Geneva.

The original membership of GATT was just twenty-three – the United States, the then independent countries of the British Commonwealth, Western European countries and a few others like Brazil and Chile. Currently it has eighty-five full contracting parties; two provisional members; and thirty other independent countries to whom it is applied *de facto*. The membership covers almost the whole world and includes five East European countries. The most notable absentees are the Soviet Union and China.

The main objectives of GATT were to get a substantial reduction of tariffs and other barriers to trade and the elimination of discriminatory treatment in international trade. Indeed, non-discrimination is the most important principle of GATT. Each contracting party is entitled to receive from every other party the lowest tariff or any other concession that is applied to any one of them. In other words, no member-country should be treated less favourably than any other member. The application of the most favoured nation (MFN) principle has been the key to the multilateral dismantling of barriers; without it barriers could be dismantled between two countries, leaving the rest out in the cold.

Four permitted exceptions to the GATT principles of non-discrimination have to be noted. Some prewar preferential arrangements (for instance, Commonwealth Preference) were initially allowed to continue but the value of these preferences has been whittled down over the years.

Secondly, GATT reductions have primarily been made on trade in manufactures; agricultural products and raw materials are covered only to a very limited extent, though access for American agricultural products into Europe was a contentious point in the early stages of the Kennedy Round.

The third exception was the addition of a Part IV to GATT in 1966, which made it possible for the industrialised countries to give tariff preferences to developing countries without demanding equivalent concessions from them in return and without granting such preferences to other developed countries.

And the last exception is the 'waiver' given to countries in the process of integrating their economies into larger units. The EEC, which provides for total free trade among the member-countries but with a common tariff against the rest of the world is the best example.

While it emphasises tariff reduction as a means of liberalising trade, the General Agreement deals with many other activities concerning barriers to trade. A major principle is that once a product has been imported inside a country, it must then be treated like domestic products and not subjected to any special discrimination (Article II). The Agreement is firmly against export subsidies and dumping (Articles VI and XVI), imposition of quantitative restrictions on imports or exports (Article XI) and selective application of quotas (Article XIII). It also deals with monopolies (Article II), state trading (Article XVII), the maintenance of import restrictions in the special case of promoting economic development (Article XVIII) and the relationship between free trade and economic integration (Article XXIV). In all these cases the theme of the Agreement is that any actions taken should be in accordance with the basic principles of non-discrimination and non-distortion.

The main method used for trade liberalisation is mutually agreed tariff reductions, negotiated in periodic 'rounds'. There have been seven such rounds up to now; in the first six tariff reductions were negotiated over some years, each time in a simultaneous set of bilateral negotiations. Each country made offers of tariff reduction which were then reconciled with the offers of other parties to ensure that there was a mutuality of benefits and sacrifices. The set of bilateral agreements were then multilateralised, that is, made applicable to all contracting parties. The latest round – the Tokyo Round (1973–9) – was a round of multilateral trade negotiation (MTN); this resulted in tariff reductions, to be made over a period of seven years, by many of the ninety-nine countries which participated in it.

The trading system developed under GATT remained reasonably stable so long as the American economy was head and shoulders above that of any other country and so long as the dollar was supreme. From 1945 until the late 1960s the system could be made to operate under the rules of the game as the United States saw them. But throughout this period changes were taking place which gradually undermined the stability.

A major change was the emergence of other centres of trading power, particularly Japan and Western Europe. The emergence of Japan as a major trading nation is all too well known. Briefly, in the early 1960s, Japan became the largest shipbuilding nation, acquired a reputation for high-quality cameras and electronic consumer goods and laid the foundations for an export assault in many other industries. By the early 1970s Japan was producing over a 100 million tons of steel, was a major exporter of cars and had established a high-technology electronic industry. All this was achieved with high efficiency and increasing productivity based on automatisation, computerisation and robotisation. Japan is a clear beneficiary of the system of industrial free trade.

Another change was the economic integration in Western Europe which started as early as 1951 with the European Coal and Steel Community. But it was only with the signing of the Treaty of Rome in 1957 that the foundations for a powerful economic grouping were laid. The motivation for integration was primarily political, economic conflicts being subordinated to the will for unity. An important point to note about the Community is that it did not attempt to follow the dichotomy in the international system between industrial goods and primary products. A corner-stone of the Community is its Common Agricultural Policy (CAP) having as its basic objectives free trade in agriculture within the Community and protection against imports from outside it. The initial British reaction to the concept of free trade agriculture was, in fact, to attempt to preserve the dichotomy by organising a competing European Free Trade Association in which free trade applied only to manufactures. The evolution of the Community within a few years into a major trading and economic group forced Britain to reconsider. Today's Community of Ten has power (if it chooses to exercise it) commensurate with that of the United States and Japan and with its enlargement to twelve could play an even more powerful role in world trade.

Not the least important change was the rapid increase in the number of independent countries and their perception that the system was loaded against them. Starting with the independence of India and Pakistan in 1947, most of the erstwhile colonies attained political sovereignty during the next fifteen years. They became members of the United Nations; from only 51 members at the time of signing of the UN Charter in 1945, the membership has swelled to 152 by 1980. Together with the Latin American countries, the newly independent ones brought into focus the widening gap between the rich North and the poor South. Their collective dissatisfaction led to the holding of the first UNCTAD conference in 1964. By 1974 they had become numerous enough (and strong enough with the increasing power of the OPEC countries) to pass through the UN General Assembly a Charter of the Economic Rights and Duties of States and to assert their common objective of creating a New International Economic Order (NIEO) which would be more equitable in its operation than the present system. An important element of the NIEO was reform of the international trading system.

In the eyes of the developing countries an international economic system which promotes free trade in industrial products while considering protectionism in primary commodities is one which fundamentally discriminates against raw material producers by denying them much-needed access to markets. The available market is further restricted when economically powerful countries subsidise exports (for example, sugar dumping by the Community), or when synthetics and substitutes displace natural products, as in the cases of synthetic fibre replacing cotton, jute, or sisal and synthetic rubber taking nearly two-thirds of the total market for rubber.

The export earnings of developing countries are not only reduced by ever-diminishing size of markets, but also suffer from a steady decline in real prices. Commodity prices not only do not keep pace with the rise in price of manufactured goods, they are also subjected to violent fluctuations. The poor countries have been arguing, since 1949, that they were the victims of a secular decline in their terms of trade – an argument vehemently denied by the rich countries. In this unresolved dispute both sides quote extensive statistics and adduce eminent economists in support. Fluctuations in the price of their export commodities are almost always outside the control of poor countries, being determined in far-off commodity markets; futures markets, meant to stabilise prices, often exacerbate fluctuations by speculation (the well-publicised attempt of the Hunts to corner silver is only one among many such instances). In many products, particularly minerals and metals, prices are determined by a handful of powerful multinationals whose pricing policies are based on considerations of global return and minimum taxation, rather than on a remunerative price to the producer.

To developing countries trying to escape the servitude of being only raw materials exporters by increasing their industrial exports it looks as though they are thwarted at every stage. Import duties in the rich countries, which are usually zero for unprocessed material, rapidly escalate when they are exported in semi-processed, processed, or finished form. Schemes (such as the General System of Preferences, negotiated under UNCTAD and intended to make industrial exports from the developing countries duty-free in the developed countries) bristle with quota restrictions and safeguard clauses. Bilateral agreement on so-called 'voluntary' restraints on exports are forced on them. Sometimes these are institutionalised and multilateralised as in the case of the GATT Multi-Fibre Agreement on exports of textiles from less developed countries. While in theory the MFA was intended to provide for orderly growth of such exports, in practice it has been used by the rich as a highly protectionist device.

The developing countries see the rich, industrialised countries as hypocrites. While proclaiming the virtues of free trade and the principle of comparative advantage, the rich ignore them in practice. On top of this the poor are also used as whipping-boys; there is a barrage of propaganda against 'low-cost' competition when, in reality, it is the competition among the rich that creates problems. When American cheap artificial fibre exports threaten European industry, the Community takes it out on the poor's cotton textiles; when Italian shoes flood the American market, Brazil is blamed; and when Japanese electronic goods make sizeable inroads, Taiwan or Korea is victimised.

It is the developing countries which always suffer most in any storm in the system. When powerful OPEC confronts equally powerful OECD countries over the price of oil, the worst-hit victims are the non-oil-producing developing countries. Instability in exchange rates affects their trade more; inflation in developed countries reduces still further their capacity to import developmental goods. They have no influence over any of these vicissitudes. No wonder the poor countries feel that they are being pushed more and more into the periphery of the international economic system. The demand for a wholesale change in the structure of the system is thus born out of frustration that their pleas for change have fallen for so long on deaf ears (Johnson, 1967; Rangarajan, 1978; Mikdashi, 1976).

While this catalogue of woes of the poor countries is by and large justified, it underestimates the industrial development that has taken place in many of the developing countries. India today is the tenth largest industrial nation in the world with nuclear power industry and space research in the vanguard. The emergence of countries like Brazil, Korea, Mexico, Taiwan and Singapore (called, in the jargon, NICs, or newly industrialised countries) is a factor subjecting the international trading system to greater strains. It was inevitable that the newly independent countries should embark on a programme of industrialisation, beginning with those industries that the technologically less advanced were capable of handling – textile and garments, processing of agricultural products, leather goods and, later, labour-intensive asembly of electronic equipment. It was just as natural for them to attempt to export these products to the richer countries in order to be able to buy more capital goods for further development. When textiles or leather goods, necessarily cheaper, attacked the already declining similar industries in the rich countries, the latter were faced with a conflict between adherence to the principles of industrial free trade and a demand for protection from domestic industry.

The emergence of new centres of economic power in competition with the United States and the perception of the North–South divide are the main changes affecting the stability of the postwar international economic system. Earlier we also noted the impact of technology on world trade and the impetus provided to it by the rapid rise in standards of living, particularly in the rich countries. The consumer explosion was, unfortunately, built on the back of cheap energy. For example, immediately after the war, Italy invented the motor scooter, an appropriate mode of transport for that society at that time; then came tiny cars like the Fiat 500. Today the Italian car industry is no different from those of other industrialised countries. Without cheap oil, the car industry would not have developed as it did, there would have been no mammoth tankers, the shipbuilding industry would have been smaller. Without millions of cars and supertankers, the steel industry would not have grown so big and now be faced with problems of contraction. It is astonishing that so few people in the world thought of the consequences of economic development anchored to a convenient, if precarious, fuel. It is only when the few suppliers of this unevenly distributed, non-renewable asset realised their strength and cashed in, that everyone awoke to the consequences of excessive dependence on it.

Among all the factors imposing strains on the system, we should also note that the system itself has become much more complex. More and more countries have become involved in producing an ever-widening range of goods and in competition for the best world market.

Institutions created with a particular set of circumstances in mind cannot cope as effectively when the environment itself changes fundamentally. I am not implying that the international economic system remained ossified throughout the last thirty-five years. Some adaptations were made as, for instance, when GATT added a Part IV to tackle the problems of developing countries. Some problems such as the instability in the trade in primary commodities were not tackled seriously. Some changes, like excessive dependence on imported oil, went unnoticed. In some other areas (for instance, the adjustment of high-cost declining industries in the developed countries) the modifications were too little and too late. Haphazard *ad hoc* tinkering has not proved adequate to cope with all the changes. The cumulative impact is seen in such events as the collapse of fixed exchange-rate system, the massive transfer of funds to oil-producing countries, the impoverishment of the non-oil-producing developing countries, the brake on growth and high inflation in the rich countries, and a widespread belief that the system itself is no longer working.

The Politics of Market Regulation

In the free-traders' ideal world the pattern of international trade would be determined entirely by comparative costs; the most efficient producers would supply the world's requirements and the price would be determined, and adjusted from time to time, by the operation of the market mechanism.

The real world is very different; the distortions in the pattern are created and maintained by governments for reasons which they consider more valid than the criterion of efficiency that would govern entirely free trade. Moreover, the distortions are many and various. Governments hold widely differing views on the extent to which the system needs regulation. They also differ on the techniques of regulation and on the freedom they allow large corporations or producers' (and more rarely consumers') organisations to interfere with market forces.

Political scientists should understand the difference between the major forms of distortion practised by governments and the economic consequences likely to follow them. Distortions occur either because governments erect barriers to prevent imports or because they manipulate prices, export credit terms and exchange rates to make their own exports cheaper.

The commonest barrier is the imposition of a duty on imports, a device used to make imported goods more expensive and thus protect domestic industry. While there are very few countries without an external tariff barrier (totally free trading areas like Hong Kong being a rarity), tariff levels not only vary widely from country to country, but also from product to product within each country's tariff schedule. By and large, duties are very low or zero on industrial raw materials, rising progressively with semi-manufactures and highest for fully manufactured goods. The relationship between tariff level and degree of protection is a complex one and the subject of much economic research; in general, the higher the tariff barrier, the greater the protection.

A whole range of devices, designed to prevent or reduce imports is covered by the term 'non-tariff barriers' (Nowzad, 1978). The easiest method is to impose a quantitative limit on imports, usually called a quota. In theory, quotas are the grossest form of violation of the principle of free trade and, as such, are prohibited under GATT except when export quotas are agreed upon multilaterally under a Commodity Agreement in order to stabilise the market or imposed temporarily and non-discriminatorily for acute balance-of-payments difficulties. In practice, however, GATT rules are regularly and increasingly circumvented by 'voluntary export restraints' and so-called safeguard mechanisms.

There is a range of non-tariff barriers which are more opaque than quantitative restrictions but also have distorting effects. Use of technical standards and health regulations as a means of preventing imports is one of them. For example, whether the regulations preventing the import of fresh liquid milk into the United Kingdom are really essential for health reasons is debatable. Bureaucratic and rigid application of technical standards have kept import of cars into Japan at only 60,000 a year, when Japan herself exported 4·5 million cars. Other methods include (1) use of cumbersome licensing procedures designed to distort free flow of trade; (2) using peculiar methods of valuation of goods for calculating the customs duty payable so as to make imports more expensive (for example, the American Selling Price system for chemicals); and (3) giving a special preference to domestic suppliers in purchase by government irrespective of the availability of cheaper goods from foreign sources.

There are also mechanisms which make exports artificially cheaper. Many governments offer export subsidies and bounties in one sector or another, sometimes openly, often in camouflaged ways. The enormous subsidies given to shipbuilding and steel by almost every industrialised country are well known. Some subsidies (such as promoting development of backward regions, assisting the modernisation of declining industries, relocation of industry, retaining of redundant workers, research and development) have social and economic objectives; how much these distort free trade is a difficult question. Is the availability of cheaper natural gas in the United States a deliberate subsidy to exporters of synthetic fibre? An equally difficult question is how much developing countries should be permitted to subsidise exports of their nascent industries. Open export subsidies are, of course, most prevalent in agricultural products, particularly in the European Community. Dumping is the extreme form of subsidy. Often loosely used, the term is defined in Article VI of GATT as the selling by one country to another of a product at 'less than the normal value'. The explanation of 'normal value' is that the export price should not be (*a*) less than the domestic selling price of the product, excluding taxes paid domestically on it; (*b*) less than the cost of production plus a reasonable margin for selling cost and profit; and (*c*) given a hidden subsidy by operating a different exchange rate for the exported product.

Distortions also occur when countries use artificial exchange rates. If two sets of rates, one for imports and one for exports, are used, imports could be made more expensive and exports cheaper. The best-known example is the use of the 'green' currency for agricultural trade within the EEC. In its practical effect the use of green rates acts as an import duty on some countries and as an export subsidy for some others.

The commercial practices of firms also distort trade. Wherever competition is limited, prices are set arbitrarily. A monopoly is total control over supply in a market by a single entity. State monopolies are quite common. Cartels like OPEC or the uranium producers of the United Kingdom, Australia and Canada divide up market shares and set prices to maximise profit for all members. Monopsony is the converse: total control over demand in a market. Thus a monopsonistic buying cartel, such as that practised by Japanese steelmills buying iron ore, can also distort the market. Control by one, or a few, firms over production, distribution, or marketing also produces distortions. The case of the power exercised by the erstwhile United Fruit Co. over small countries growing bananas is well known. Today one company controls the world market in diamonds, four firms in London control a large part of the tea market, six companies control world trade in bauxite and aluminium, and four American broking concerns dominate the transactions in the world grain market. And now that so much of the world trade is conducted between branches of the same firm, the distortions resulting from corporate control of production, processing, marketing and distribution in many sectors of world economy must be counted as equal in importance to the distortions practised by governments.

The extent to which states decide to intervene in the operation of markets is partly a matter of political or economic ideology. More often, it is the result of perceived national interest.

For example, the United States, the most consistent opponent of attempts to regulate markets or control prices, has had no difficulty in accepting the need for a degree of regulation in wheat trade. The United States has always been an active promoter of international wheat agreements because of national interest as the largest exporter of wheat and because of the need to protect the incomes of the powerful farming community. But as a country which grows no coffee or cocoa, the United States has little interest in price stabilisation or market regulation for these commodities. The intermittent and half-hearted American support for ICAs in these is due to her perceived role in international politics. This schizophrenic attitude to commodity market regulation is nothing new. American opposition to the regulation of primary commodity markets in the Havana Charter was only partly ideological. It was also prompted by fear and envy of Britain which then had an abundance of raw materials produced in its colonies (tin and rubber from the Malay States, copper from Central African colonies, sugar from a number of colonies in the Caribbean and the Pacific, tea and tobacco from others). The United States, though rich in many commodities, lacked some essential raw materials (notably tin, rubber and chrome) and could not grow tropical products (like tea, coffee, cocoa and bananas). It was in the American national interest to oppose any organisation of markets that might prevent it from buying freely at the best possible price, without interference from other governments.

Of the other rich countries, Japan adopts a policy similar to the United States because (i) it is the main beneficiary of the free trade system in industrial products; (ii) it runs a highly protected farming sector; and (iii) it is heavily dependent on imports for almost all raw materials (oil, iron ore, coal, and bauxite) and, therefore, has an aversion to regulation which might push up prices or lead to control of supplies. Further, as the latest recruit to the top table among the rich countries and because of dependence on the United States for markets as well as the security umbrella, it cannot afford to displace America.

The countries of the European Community hold a variety of views based on their respective national interests. Germany, while generally supporting free trade, has accepted an extraordinary degree of regulation within the Community on agricultural products, mainly because protecting German farmers is a political necessity. France has always been dirigiste, believing in market regulation and market guidance; this is due to state ownership of banking and many leading sectors of industry and the close relationship with the private sector. Italy too has large sectors of industry state-controlled and a symbiotic relationship between the leading political party, business, banking and industry. The British attitude, at least until recently, was more pragmatic and less doctrinaire. With such a spectrum of opinions, the collective view of the Community is usually a compromise, reflecting the opinions of the country with the most economic interest. For example, the national interests of France and Germany coincide in protecting agriculture. The Community's attitude to the International Sugar Agreement is, therefore, totally negative; in this case dumping of sugar is preferred to market regulation and market stability, concepts which are promoted assiduously within the Community.

The attitude of the developing countries to the international trading system is based on their perception of its inherent inequity and the feeling that, unless they stay united, they will not be able to extract the necessary changes from the rich countries. In spite of this apparent unity, there is a wide variation in their attitudes. Barring a few island countries in the Caribbean and the Pacific, all the newly independent countries are in Asia and Africa. While quite a few have adopted socialistic economic policies internally, almost all of them have chosen to remain within the market economy system internationally. They had little real choice in this, since the economic ties forged during colonial times with the metropolitan countries continued to persist. The countries of Central and South America, though long independent of European masters, had not joined the ranks of the rich. Because of their relative underdevelopment, comparatively lower standards of living and the feeling of subservience, particularly to multinational companies, they felt an affinity with the newly independent countries of Asia and Africa. Thus the unity of the Group of 77 (as the developing countries are known in UNCTAD, though now there are many more than the original number) is based more on emotional identity born of a common perception of exploitation than on shared economic interests. With the emergence of the oil-producing countries as a separate group of countries, financially rich but still underdeveloped in other spheres, the unity of the 77 has also been subjected to strains.

Though the examples quoted in explaining the attitude of the rich countries to regulation were all taken from primary commodities, we should not assume that governments of developed countries practise what they preach in industrial products, notwithstanding their more ardent commitment to free trade in manufactures. When there is a conflict between domestic pressure groups and international principles, the latter is usually the casualty. The most glaring example of this is the devising of the so-called 'voluntary export restraint'. The articles of GATT strictly prohibit any kind of a quota limitation on imports from particular countries; any restriction imposed for a specific reason, such as balance-of-payments difficulties, must be applied non-discriminatorily to all members of GATT. So when the United States brings pressure on Japan to reduce 'voluntarily' its exports of cars, steel, or colour television sets, it is a clear breach of the spirit of GATT. It was equally so when President Nixon banned the export of soya beans as a weapon to get the kind of monetary reform which the United States wanted.

After OPEC's actions in increasing oil prices, cartels are presented as a bad thing; but only the United States practises a determined anti-cartel policy both at home and abroad. Other economically powerful countries prohibit such practices domestically but make use of them in their external trade. An example is the international trade cartel set up by the uranium producers of Britain, Australia and Canada. This ran undetected for many years until hauled up before American courts by a power company. At this point the supplier countries promptly passed laws which backed up the refusal of their companies to produce documents before the United States courts. The vilification of OPEC as an energy cartel but support for a uranium cartel is one of the many instances of double standards practised by countries. When the European Community dumps high-cost sugar on world markets, when it undercuts New Zealand by subsidising butter exports to the Soviet Union, when Britain taxes wine and beer differentially or France does the same between Scotch whisky and brandy – these are but a few examples of a persistent fact of life, the gap between professions of philosophy and the practice of politics.

Given the pressures that are exerted on governments to erect barriers, what is the case for international regulation? It is simply that unilateral barriers invite retaliation and the more unilateral barriers there are, the less world trade there will be. If we accept the thesis that freer international trade promotes efficiency, reduces the ultimate cost to the consumer and increases the freedom of choice, then a reduction in world trade must imply a reduction in the collective good. The Keynesian conception of stabilising fluctuations in world trade and providing for growth by reducing barriers rested on the assumption that 'beggar-my-neighbour' policies benefited nobody. In this context what the contracting parties to GATT set out to do and how much they have achieved is important.

The operation of the General Agreement has succeeded in bringing down tariffs on industrial goods to very low levels, as a result of repeated tariff-cutting rounds. When the latest Tokyo Round cuts are fully implemented, the tariff level on manufactures traded mainly among the developed countries would be reduced to an average of only 5 per cent. A great deal of progress has also been made in harmonising tariffs, that is, in making the import duties in different countries on similar products approximately the same. Though the question of non-tariff barriers had been raised off and on in the earlier rounds, it was only in the

Tokyo Round that a serious attempt was made to tackle them. A number of Agreements, or Codes of Behaviour, were negotiated covering technical barriers to trade, government procurement, subsidies and countervailing duties, Customs Valuation, dumping and import-licensing procedures.

The failure of GATT is in three areas. First, it is fundamentally flawed in that it confines itself mainly to industrial goods and excludes primary commodities where the trade is least liberal. Secondly, developing countries generally come off worse, compared to developed countries trading among themselves. Thirdly, industrial products of interest to developing countries, such as textiles, are the ones subjected to quotas and other gross forms of distortion.

A recurring theme in this chapter is the distinction between trade in manufactures and trade in primary commodities. Before the Second World War, the emphasis was the other way round. Attempts to regulate international trade were more concerned with organising raw material markets and reducing the violent fluctuations in price. The earliest attempt was a conference of European sugar producers in 1863, convened with the intention of creating some order out of a market then characterised by cut-throat competition, dumping and 'bounties' (export subsidies). The Bandoeng Pool of tin stocks, created in 1921 between Britain (for the Federated Malay States) and Holland (for the Dutch East Indies), was an early attempt to regulate a market by using buffer stocks. The history of the many attempts made since then to negotiate workable international commodity agreements (ICAs) for different commodities (wheat, sugar, tin, rubber, coffee, tea, cocoa, copper, fibres, etc.) is a long and dismal saga. To put it in a nutshell: (i) there are very few commodities for which it has been possible to conclude formal agreements including both producers and consumers, (ii) these take a long time to negotiate, (iii) once negotiated, they frequently break down in their operation and (iv) the essential objectives of reducing violent fluctuations in price and providing an equitable price to the producers have not been achieved.

There are a number of reasons for the failure to bring about some order in commodity markets, the most important being the antipathy of the industrialised countries. They refuse to begin worthwhile negotiations for many commodities, and in the few that do start the negotiations are prolonged on one pretext or another. When at last an agreement is concluded, they fail to join it or implement it. Equally, there is very little unity among the producer countries, particularly the developing ones. National interest in maintaining or increasing market shares or disposing of available surplus at almost any price often overrides the need for collective action. The commodities themselves vary widely in their characteristics such as storability, marketing structures and end-use; a variety of mechanisms for regulation have been tried but no single one can be used successfully for all commodities at all times. For the last five years negotiations have been going on under UNCTAD for the creation of a Common Fund, which would provide funds for holding buffer stocks of commodities with a view to stabilising prices. At last agreement has been reached on creating a Fund but this will be very much smaller than what is needed. There is no agreement on how the Fund will operate. The Fund is supposed to assist ICAs in holding stocks; the past history of such negotiations shows that the number of ICAs will be very few and that their useful life will be short and intermittent.

This section will not be complete without a reference to the politics of selective dismantling of barriers. Just as it is possible for a country to erect selective barriers, it can also give selective preferential treatment. The earlier examples of this kind were those arising from the relationship between a metropolitan power and its colonies (for example, Britain charging a lower rate of import duty on imports from the Empire – the Imperial and, later, the Commonwealth Preference). The similar preferential system between France and her colonies has now been institutionalised in the European Community by means of agreements (the Yaoundé Convention and the two Lomé Conventions) giving special treatment and preferential access to the erstwhile French, Belgian and British colonies in Africa, the Caribbean and the Pacific (the ACP countries). We must note that the former British colonies of South and South-east Asia (India, Pakistan, Bangladesh, Sri Lanka, Malaysia and Singapore) are excluded from these special preferential arrangements. The reason is purely political. Every country gives its preferences according to its political priorities; the bulk of United States aid flows to its allies and the bulk of OPEC aid is given first to Arab and then to Islamic countries. In the case of the Community its political priorities are, in descending order: the Mediterranean countries which are likely to become members, other countries around the Mediterranean in the Levant and North Africa with whom the Community has special Association Agreements and then the former colonies in Africa. The only scheme applicable to all developing countries is the Generalised Special Preference (GSP). This is not a uniform scheme; separate ones are operated by the United States, the Community and several European countries, providing for duty-free access in industrial products, with significant exceptions, originating in the developing countries. The exceptions, as one would expect, are precisely in those sectors where the developing countries are most efficient – textiles, clothing and leather goods.

The politics of market regulation is simply this. However vociferous countries may be in proclaiming the virtues of free trade, they rarely hesitate to distort it in the light of their perceived national interest. All countries protect agriculture, their farmers and their fishermen. They do make rules for orderly conduct of international trade; but they also break the rules when it suits them.

The Rules of the Game

The importance of GATT, as an instrument regulating international trade, lies in its comprehensive coverage of trade in one sector – industrial products. Here GATT has clearly defined objectives and principles, a set of rules for achieving them, a set of criteria allowing for suspension of the rules and a procedure for resolving any conflicts that may arise during its implementation. The exceptional circumstances when divergence from the principles of liberalisation is permitted include times of acute balance-of-payments crisis. But distortions such as import controls have to be temporary and applied equally to all contracting parties. Moreover, when a state contemplates a departure from the objectives, it must obtain a 'waiver' conferring the acceptance of the other parties. When any country takes an action that is seen as likely to have an adverse effect on another, the party likely to be injured can register a complaint. The Agreement provides for an elaborate process for dealing with complaints – how to investigate, what is the extent of the injury, the procedures for consultation and the methods of settling the dispute by conciliation or judgement by a panel. Not only the General Agreement itself, but every Code negotiated at the Tokyo Round has similar sets of detailed rules. The Agreement also provides for a range of solutions to disputes from the removal of the injury-causing action to permitting the injured party to take countervailing action. An example is permitting a party to impose a countervailing duty on imports from another country which is proved to have deliberately made its products cheaper by granting export subsidies (Curzon, 1965: Curzon and Curzon, 1976).

In contrast to GATT, the experience of ICAs on rule-making and rule obedience is quite unsatisfactory. Commodity Agreements depend for their success on compliance with some specific provisions such as export quotas and maintenance of the price within the specified range. The degree of compliance in ICAs is poor. Exporting countries finding themselves with a surplus above their authorised quota, tend to export them all the same, thus undermining the objective of the ICA. In times of shortage there is less self-discipline in maintaining the price below or at the agreed ceiling. In most ICAs compliance is almost voluntary since no effective monitoring arrangements are inscribed in them. In most ICAs the dispute-settlement procedure is sketchy in contrast to the very detailed rules in GATT. There are usually no clearly defined procedures for consultation, conciliation, or arbitration. The set of sanctions and punishments is seldom well enough graded to ensure that the punishment is appropriate to the transgression. Disputes, therefore, either tend to become entangled with larger issues or are elevated to the political level to be settled by exercise of voting power. On top of all this the history of ICAs shows that countries tend to join or leave them as it suits them. In short, there is a much more cavalier attitude to rule-making and compliance.

Though GATT succeeds better in enforcing discipline while other international regulatory mechanisms fail, its record is not unblemished. For example, the MFA negotiated under GATT has not attempted seriously to achieve the objective of an orderly growth of exports of textiles from the poor countries to the rich. On the contrary, the rich have used the MFA as a means of bringing in more restrictions and erecting more barriers. It is true that the MFA has rule-obedience and dispute-settlement procedures; it even has a Textile Supervisory Body. The reason for the failure of the ICAs and the MFA is the same; the economically powerful parties in these Agreements do not, from the beginning, want them to succeed. Not for nothing has GATT gained a reputation as a rich man's club; the contracting parties with economic muscle, that is, the developed countries, share a common belief in free trade in manufactures. They, therefore, have the will to make it succeed. They do not have a faith in Commodity Agreements, nor are they sincere when professing a belief in running down their declining industries in favour of transferring them to the developing countries. The question is: why do countries negotiate and sign agreements which they have no intention of implementing? The answer can only be that they perceive the political cost of appearing intransigent and not signing such agreements costlier than being subsequently accused of bad faith in their implementation. In other words, developing countries can usually be bought off with pieces of paper which are nothing more than expressions of false piety.

At this point we encounter the part played by power in the international trading system, a part which no analysis can afford to ignore. Some basic points are worth noting albeit briefly: (1) economic power cannot be divorced from political power; (2) power is not static, as shown by the decline in American power due to the emergence of new centres; (3) the power of countries is not universally exercisable; with the exception of the United States, which is still powerful in almost every sector of international trade, most countries have power only in some sectors; (4) power is cumulative; sellers and buyers can increase their power by joining together; the countries of the EEC have collectively greater power than the sum of their individual strengths; when economic integration is not possible, countries increase their power by forming coalitions and alliances (for instance, the countries of the OECD presenting a united front against the developing countries); and (5) the power of firms, particularly multinational and transnational companies, is increasingly more important in international trade; it is not an accident most the multinationals are from the rich countries; they derive their power from the economically powerful motherlands and they, in turn, add to these countries' power. While the literature is extensive, I specially recommend Vernon (1971). Lastly, one must also mention a peculiar power which countries, companies, or organisations like trade unions, possess – the power to disrupt, which is sometimes useful in obtaining better terms in negotiations. Thus political and economic power can be used by countries either to promote order or to have their own way irrespective of rules. The willingness of governments to circumvent the spirit of the rules which they had voluntarily negotiated is one of the most disquieting features to emerge in recent years. There is nothing to choose between the economically powerful and the economically weak in their readiness to sacrifice adherence to rule of law for short-term domestic political gains. A number of examples have already been quoted in describing how governments often adopt policies which make nonsense of their professions. More recently a spate of such instances have occurred within the European Community. Since the politics of the Community is a vast subject and is not strictly covered by the theme of this chapter, I will quote only two examples. First, the French refusal to allow imports of British lamb was not only a contravention of free trade principles but was also a clear breach of the Treaty of Rome. Secondly, the Community, as a whole, has stood aside and not joined the International Sugar Agreement 1977, because it wants to dump on the world markets all the high-cost sugar it continues to produce by paying its farmers to produce 135 per cent of the sugar it actually needs for its own consumption. This is economic anarchy and bears no relation to economic principles, free trade policies, or belief in rule and order.

Changing the rules of the game is also a tactic often employed. We have mentioned the case of Britain, Australia and Canada rushing to pass laws to prevent disclosure by their companies of their violation of American anti-cartelisation laws. The powerful London Metal Exchange recently changed the rules of trading overnight – to protect speculators who had only themselves to blame for selling short on the futures market in tin. This is a clear case of a small, powerful group acting against the legitimate interests of producers of tin, almost all of whom are developing countries.

Another disquieting aspect in the deterioration of the rule of law is the repeated inability of the United States to ratify and implement the Agreements, having played a major role in negotiating them. The example of America scuttling the ITO in the early 1950s was mentioned earlier. In the Kennedy Round in GATT the United States, as part of a complex set of reciprocal concessions, agreed to modify the American Selling Price system, a non-tariff barrier making imported chemicals artificially costlier. It failed to do so. In the negotiations for the International Coffee Agreement 1962 the United States insisted on introducing a system of stamps for monitoring exports, an essential prerequisite being the co-operation of the importing countries in sending back the stamps for verification. The United States did not do so for many years, thus removing a keystone of a rule-obedience structure. The United States has always been an active participant in international sugar negotiations because it is not only a major producer of beet and cane, but is also a major importer. It had a powerful voice in the shaping of the International Sugar Agreement 1977 but failed to ratify it for years. In the absence of full participation by an important country the Agreement had to limp along, thereby failing to achieve its objectives.

The usual reason given for all the failures of the United States to implement the Agreements it has negotiated is that Congress did not approve. For example, in the case of the Sugar Agreement the US Congress was more involved in the domestic controversy about the price paid to American beet and sugarcane farmers and paid scant regard to a treaty solemnly negotiated by its Executive. But the difficulties with Congress are not phenomena which suddenly emerged as a total surprise. In the case of tariff-cutting rounds in GATT Congress authorises the Executive to do so under a Trade Act *before* the negotiations even begin. Since the Executive negotiates under the parameters laid down in the Trade Acts, failure to implement the resulting multilateral agreement cannot be blamed on unexpected difficulties raised by Congress. The rest of the world can only negotiate with the United States government; whether that government can persuade its own legislature is an internal problem and cannot legitimately be a matter for other governments. One sometimes wonders whether the so-called Executive–Congress conflict is not just an excuse that enables the United States to get out of agreements which it was reluctant to sign but did so only as a tactic. On the other hand, we should note that voices have begun to be raised in the United States about the functioning of Congress; especially in domestic matters, it is now argued that Congress functions not as a national legislative body, but as a collection of representatives susceptible to influence from a wide range of power, pressure and interest groups.

One conflict highlighted by any study of the rules of the game is that between the desire of people and governments for order and stability and the pressure to break rules which have become irksome. The causes of rule disobedience vary widely – from the marginality of fishing constituencies in Britain and the power of the winegrowers in France to dissatisfaction with quotas in the Coffee Agreement. There is no miraculous solution to this type of conflict.

One last conflict is impossible to categorise. This is the reluctance of people to change the existing order of things. A large number of international trade conflicts arise because people are used to their way of life and any change is resisted. While dependence on foreign sources for oil imports is seen as dangerous, the rich countries, particularly the United States, find it well-nigh impossible to reduce this dependence. A substantial reduction is politically unfeasible because this involves a drastic change in the way of life. Agriculture in the Community cannot be made more realistic without changing the patterns of production of large numbers of farmers, who alone can reduce butter mountains, wine lakes and sugar glaciers. Other examples, adduced earlier on problems of adjustment, equally illustrate the difficulty in getting people to change. We can only conclude that the 'haves' will always be reluctant to renounce something in favour of the 'have-nots' until the change is forced on them by unforeseen events in the environment.

This chapter was written before the conflict between European countries and the United States over the supply of equipment to the Soviet gas pipeline escalated into open confrontation. I refer to the dispute briefly, since it provides a clear illustration of the politics of international trade. It is well known that the United States was eager to ban the export of European-made equipment to the Soviet Union but not anxious to cut down her own exports of wheat. In this case the economic interest in maintaining grain exports was reinforced by the domestic political necessity of preserving the income of American farmers. In the case of Europe the need to protect employment in manufacturing industry especially at a time of recession and high unemployment was more important than any perception of excessive dependence on the Soviet Union for energy. The United States then tried to impose her own national laws extraterritorially and this was promptly countered by European countries passing laws against American encroachment of their sovereignty. In the dilemma over conflicting priorities, even Mrs Thatcher's Britain, whose perceptions of the Soviet threat were closest to that of President Reagan's America, chose to protect employment and national sovereignty than alliance solidarity. This example shows that countries resort to using international trade as a weapon when they have no political solutions to political problems (for instance, making the Soviet Union and Poland act in the way they want). It must be said that use of trade as a weapon is likely to be no more effective than refusing to participate in the Olympics; both are gestures intended to protect one's political image.

In order to be effective in creating order in the international trading system any instrument has to provide some *essential elements for rule obedience and dispute settlement*. These are:

(a) *transparency* – actions of governments likely to injure others should not be clandestine but open, and must be notified to an appropriate body; there should be provisions against refusal to disclose information except in strictly limited circumstances;

(*b*) *investigation* – any complaint or dispute must be investigated, the procedure for which should be an integral part of the rules of the instrument; these could include examination of documents, taking of evidence and physical verification where necessary;

(*c*) *determination* – there should be provision for determining definitively whether injury is likely to be or has been suffered, the extent of such potential or present injury and the nature of the appropriate remedial measures;

(*d*) *surveillance* – the actions of all members of an instrument must be subjected to scrutiny, surveillance and supervision to ensure that the actions are in accordance with the objectives of the instrument;

(*e*) *dispute settlement* – there should be provisions for conciliation and arbitration;

(*f*) *sanctions* – in the last resort the instrument ought to have a graded set of sanctions and punishments, including countervailing measures which will have a perceptible deterrent effect on would-be transgressors.

I am not claiming that all these provisions will make all governments automatically law-abiding. The fact that we know what ought to be done does not mean that it will be done. The best that one can hope for is that such detailed rules would make transgressions fewer. When an economically powerful country chooses to disobey rules which it has been a party to framing, there is little that anyone can do, short of going to war over it. When even the mighty transgress, it is but a symptom of a deeper malaise for which different solutions have to be sought. Whether governments agree to make rules and then to obey them are crucial elements in the politics of international trade.

Conflicts in International Trade

The purpose of the previous sections of this chapter has been to probe why people and governments behave in the way they do in relation to international trade problems. However representative or unrepresentative governments may be, they all have to be eventually responsive to pressures from those whom they govern. The people may collectively desire national security and national survival, may be motivated by rising expectations and greater freedom to choose and may want to preserve and improve standards of living and quality of life. It is in response to these often conflicting pressures that governments act.

Conflicts of sovereignty – that is, the distinction between one nation and another, separated by a boundary – arise because of nationalistic feeling, fear of threats to national security and a desire to preserve national survival. The following have been identified in earlier sections. (1) There is a conflict between nationalistic feeling and the desire for wider choice; a 'Buy Britain' campaign appeals directly to nationalism and pleads with the people to exercise their choice ('buy Leyland and not Japanese cars') in a patriotic way. (2) The fear of threat to national security is at the root of all agricultural protectionism; no country wants to be dependent on foreign sources for food or energy supplies, for fear that in times of tension or hostilities defence would become impossible. This is also the reason for all modern states wanting to maintain adequate steel, armament, transport and shipbuilding capabilities. (3) The desire for preservation of national identity and patterns of living leads to trade conflicts on grounds of deterioration in the quality of life ('French Golden Delicious apples are tasteless'). The conflict over fishing is very similar. The number of British or French fishermen whose livelihood will be affected by free fishing in Community waters is a miniscule part of the total working population; the problem generates far more emotion than numbers warrant. (4) The conflict between the smaller of the developing countries and transnational companies arises from the threat to sovereignty and national independence posed by the much greater economic power of the companies.

Conflicts of ideology and perception have also been explained earlier with a number of examples. These consist of (*a*) the conflict between rich industrialised countries and poor developing countries on whether the international trading system is equitable in its operation or not; and (*b*) the conflict between countries on how much to regulate trade, the attitudes varying in accordance with their own national interests which, in turn, colours their ideological bias. To these two we must add the effect on international trade of purely political conflicts. The ban on the sale of wheat to the Soviet Union by the United States after the Russian intervention in Afghanistan, and the United States cutting off all trade with Cuba, are cases in point. More recently, the United States has attempted to use Western trade with the Soviet Union as a means of securing the kind of internal changes in Poland that it wants. That trade can be used as a weapon in furtherance of objectives which are wider goes without saying. If the developing countries seek to use similar weapons to bring about a change in the detestable system of apartheid in South Africa, that aspiration is as legitimate as the use of trade in East–West conflict; when the rich countries oppose sanctions against South Africa, that is a clear indication of their perception of their own national interest. It is not unfair to say that to the Western countries communism is a worse evil than racialism, whereas to the developing countries it is the other way round; this ideological bias is reflected in their respective trade policies.

The problem of conflicts between equally valid principles is the most interesting in that there are no clear-cut answers. The invidious choices facing governments are such that decisions are necessarily made on the basis of the lesser of two evils. Invariably these are conflicts involving domestic political pressure and power groups. The most important of these conflicts, mainly for rich countries, is the degree of protection to be given at any time to domestic producers. Two major trade-distorting aspects of such conflicts have been analysed – one concerned with preventing imports, and the other with making exports cheaper. The first is the conflict between access to imports and employment protection, that is, how to provide increasing access to simpler manufactures from developing countries, while at the same time minimising the problems of adjustment in the affected industries. Industrial adjustment is a complex sociopolitical question and has been the subject of much research. In practice, the rich countries have taken decisions in favour of protection, sacrificing the principles of free trade and the development of poor countries. The second aspect is how much subsidy a country should give to domestic industry in order to preserve it, even in the face of a self-evident need for its contraction. This is a conflict born out of the emergence of new centres of economic power and is the result of competition between the industrialised countries. Steel is a classic example, chemicals and shipbuilding are others. Closely related to this is the conflict between rich countries on export credit terms; giving export credits for extended periods at low interest rates is also a form of subsidy.

World Trade in the 1980s

The 1970s have now come to be regarded as a watershed in the international economic system. It could pessimistically be seen as the time when all the chickens came home to roost – the burden of excessive dependence on imported oil, the sharpening of the North–South conflict and the realisation of there being limits to growth. Optimistically we can see the period as one where all the benefits of the postwar international economic system have been realised, leaving it to the 1980s to devise a system more appropriate to a world which has changed vastly since 1945.

In guessing what world trade will be like in the 1980s some things seem reasonably certain. For example, the United States, barring wholly unforeseeable accidents, will continue to be the granary of the world, providing much-needed food security. While some countries like India have attained levels of output capable of avoiding famine without having to import grain, there are bound to be areas where there is a food crisis either due to natural causes (for example, Sahel) or manmade (for example, Kampuchea). American grain will, luckily, continue to be available; but American grain sales, whether to Russia or China, will also continue to be affected by broader political considerations. As for the Community, the CAP has helped it to achieve a very large measure of self-sufficiency, its very success creating insuperable problems of surpluses. The Community, however, has the economic strength to surmount the looming cash crisis and could, perhaps, be persuaded to become more liberal and less protectionist. At least one country will emerge as a large exporter of food: Brazil, which has natural resources and shown remarkable success in diversifying her agricultural exports from traditional coffee and sugar to soya beans and frozen chicken, can become a massive exporter. The oil sector will continue to be volatile and subject to ever-increasing political strains; dependence on import may, however, decrease because (1) there is bound to be a slowing down of at least the rate of growth of oil consumption if not actual quantity of consumption; and (2) the large investments in oil exploration by developed and developing countries will, at least in some cases (for instance, the Sudan and India), yield greater production from domestic wells. In the ores and minerals sector developed countries will continue to be dependent on a wide variety of sources for some essential ones. Political instability in one or the other of the major producing countries will, in all likelihood, affect supplies from time to time; a violent conflict in South Africa will have far-reaching implications.

Whether the volume of world trade will continue its rapid growth in the 1980s depends on a number of factors. I doubt whether trade in manufactures between the rich countries can continue to grow as much as it has done in the past; recessions, unemployment, demands for protection and problems of contraction will all take their toll. Growth in world trade will, to a large extent, depend on increasing the developing countries' ability to buy. There are now over a hundred of them, at least one-fifth of which have reached fairly advanced levels of industrial development. Their main constraint is inadequate foreign-exchange resources. To the extent that the rich countries liberalise access to imports of manufactures from the poor, the industrialised countries will be creating extra markets for themselves. The ever-increasing financial reserves of the OPEC countries need not necessarily lead to greater increases in their imports, since many of the less populous OPEC nations have already reached the limits of their capacity to absorb. A direct effect of politics on the trade of OPEC countries will, of course, be the efforts of major arms-selling countries (the United States, Soviet Union, France, Britain and China) to unload more expensive and more sophisticated armaments. The contribution of China to growth in world trade is problematical; the original euphoric estimates of billions of dollars' worth of import market just waiting to be tapped have all been scaled down. Like any other country in the process of development, China's ability to import does depend on her capacity to export.

The big question mark that hangs over the future of world trade is the shape of the international economic system in the 1980s. The restriction of free trade to industrial goods and the activities of GATT have produced significant results, at least for the rich countries. Tariffs, which were the easiest barrier to identify, have now been reduced to low levels; a considerable degree of harmonisation has been achieved and non-tariff barriers are beginning to be tackled. High levels of protection in agriculture have helped the rich countries to provide adequate income levies to their farming communities, comparable to urban standards. The consequence of this success has been the widening of the gap between the rich and poor nations, the resulting frustration of the latter and the rising crescendo of demands for a New International Economic Order.

Just to avoid the suspicion that the above criticism stems from the author's developing country origin I quote from the Supplementary Report on the Tokyo Round of multilateral trade negotiations by the Director-General of GATT. I quote from GATT, and not from the Brandt Commission report or McNamara's address to the World Bank, because the latter two are assumed to have a bias in favour of the developing countries. So the following is from one who does not suffer from this stigma, the Director-General of GATT:

The sensitivities and deeply entrenched problems and attitudes – political and social as well as economic – that invariably bedevil the negotiation of international commitments on agriculture, stood in the way of reaching agreement on the establishment of a formal mechanism.

As for tariffs facing developing countries, the average m.f.n. reductions on industrial products were less deep than the overall cut . . . This reflects the fact that the products to which the tariff cutting formula was not applied are relatively more important in exports from developing countries.

The major industrial sectors of export interest to developing countries were textiles, metals, electric machinery, footwear and travel goods and wood. Taken together these five sectors accounted for over two thirds of imports of processed goods from developing countries . . . the post-MTN tariffs remain quite high for textiles, clothing, footwear and travel goods.

Throughout this chapter I have never suggested that the sharp distinction between industrial goods and raw materials was made by the rich countries with the deliberate *a priori* malicious motive of doing down the poor countries. It is, nevertheless, true that the distinction has inevitably led to the further impoverishment of the poor countries, and by the time the rich countries' attention had been drawn to it, they had gone so far down the road of industrial free trade and agricultural protectionism that they were unwilling to change it. I have always maintained that where self-interest coupled with insensitivity to others can provide an explanation, attribution of premeditation is a superfluous luxury.

An expression often used in writing about political economy is 'political will'; usually the lack of it is blamed for failure to achieve some desirable objective. This shorthand expression only means that governments do not match their deeds to the principles they preach; they do not put their money where their mouths are. It is easy to make resounding speeches about the ever-contracting world and its growing interdependence. When such speeches are made by politicians (for example, Kissinger's many perorations), it is often a signal that the country concerned is about to do something precisely contradictory to the principles loudly enunciated. Recently Mrs Thatcher was quoted as saying: 'I believe in free trade; but it must also be fair trade both ways.' The trouble with this kind of politician's dictum is that it is illogical; it attempts to compare something objective and quantifiable like the existence or absence of barriers to trade with something wholly subjective like 'fairness'. Such elliptic references hide a variety of conflicts which could more usefully be brought into the open. I have tried in this chapter to identify the major ones and to analyse the pressures which lie behind them.

A grave doubt about the future stability of the international economic system is the increasing deterioration in the rule of law. I have drawn special attention to the growing tendency in all governments towards rule disobedience because, in any analysis of the international economic system, this aspect is ignored. Perceived national interest, which itself is an amalgam of psychological attitudes and economic realities, frequently overrides international responsibility. In understanding the politics of international trade, as in solving murder mysteries, the first question to ask is 'who gains?' The second is 'what are they afraid of?' So long as there is a threat of war, apprehension about national survival, or fear of erosion of standards of living, there will be politics in international economy, particularly trade. This should not be taken to mean that I am somehow advocating the abolition of nationalism or preaching the virtues of a world federal solution. These things will not come about just because I or anyone else says so. One cannot change human nature by fist, exhortation, or even by appeals to people's own self-interest. An implicit theme, running through this chapter, is that the developed countries have the greater responsibility for bringing about the changes. They control 80 per cent of the world market economy trade and have the power to promote changes or to thwart them. If I am asked whether I expect a higher standard of behaviour from the rich, my answer must, unequivocally, be 'yes'.

Increasing prosperity has been the main achievement of the postwar world. More and more people all over the world have enjoyed higher standards of living which, after a time, they take for granted. This is true not only of America, Europe, Japan and wealthier countries like Australia, but also of the affluent segments in the poor countries. One may complain about the distribution of wealth within the developing countries, but one cannot say that no wealth has been created. Also the fact that disillusionment with simple material growth has now set in does not nullify the fact that at least a quarter of the world's population has been released from the extremes of poverty, disease and drudgery. The political problem is how to enlarge the proportion of such fortunate people. Reform of the international trading system has a crucial role to play in this.

I do not believe that in a world which no longer has a single centre of economic power a whole new order can be created by agreement among governments. Apart from the natural reluctance of the haves to sacrifice in favour of the have-nots, the idea of revolutionary change frightens many. This does not preclude the possibility of evolutionary changes which can encompass many of the desirable elements of the New Order. The elements which need most urgent attention are those which have been repeatedly stressed in this chapter – a dismantling of agricultural protectionism or at least a reduction of its rigours, more stability and order in international commodity markets, greater access for the exports of poor countries and more stimulation of their economies, thereby creating bigger import markets, and more practical steps for industrial relocation between countries, based on the principle of comparative advantage.

References: Chapter 7

Blackhurst, R. (1977), *Trade Liberalisation, Protectionism and Interdependence* (New York: Unipub).

Blackhurst, R., Marian, N., and Tumlir, J. (1978), *Adjustment, Trade and Growth in Developed and Developing Countries* (New York: Unipub).

Cline, W. R. (1978), *Trade Negotiations in the Tokyo Round: A Quantitative Assessment* (Washington, DC: Brookings Institution).

Cole, J. P. (1963), *Geography of World Affairs* (Sharon Hill, PA: Quest Editions).

Curzon, G. (1965), *Multilateral Commercial Diplomacy* (New York: Praeger).

Curzon, G., and Curzon, V. (1976), 'The management of trade relations in the GATT', in A. Shonfield (ed.), *International Economic Relations of the Western World, 1959–1971* (London: OUP), Vol. 1.

Dam, K. W. (1970), *The GATT: Law and International Economic Organization* (Chicago, IL: University of Chicago Press).

Destler, I. M., Fukui, H., and Sato, H. (1979), *The Textile Wrangle: Conflict in US–Japanese Relations, 1969–71* (Ithaca, NY: Cornell University Press).

Evans, J. W. (1971), *The Kennedy Round in American Trade Policy: The Twilight of the GATT?* (Cambridge, MA: Harvard University Press).

GATT (1952), *Basic Instruments and Selected Documents* (New York: Unipub).

GATT (1952–83), *Annual Reports, International Trade.*

GATT (1958), *Trends in International Trade* (Haberler Report).

GATT (1968), *The Developing Countries and the GATT.*

GATT (1979), *Agreement on Interpretation and Application of Articles VI, XVI and XXIII.*

Golt, S. (1978), *The GATT Negotiations, 1973–79: The Closing Stage.*

Johnson, H. G. (1967), *Economic Policies towards Less Developed Countries* (London: Allen & Unwin).

Keesing, D. B., and Wolf, M. (1981), *Textile Quotas against Developing Countries* (Trade Policy Research Centre).

Kenen, P., and Lubitz, R. (1971), *International Economics* (Englewood Cliffs, NJ: Prentice-Hall).

Krauss, M. (1978), *The New Protectionism: The Welfare State and International Trade* (New York: New York University Press).

Lloyd, P. J. (1977), *Antidumping Actions and the GATT System.*

Mikdashi, Z. (1976), *The International Politics of Natural Resources* (Ithaca, NY: Cornell University Press).

Nowzad, B. (1978), *The Rise in Protectionism*, IMF Pamphlet Series, no. 24 (Washington DC: International Monetary Fund).

Rangarajan, L. (1978), *Commodity Conflict: The Political Economy of International Commodity Negotiations* (Ithaca, NY: Cornell University Press).

Shonfield, A. (ed.) (1976), *International Economic Relations of the Western World, 1959–1971*, 2 vols (London: OUP).

Vernon, R. (1977), *Sovereignty at Bay* (New York: Basic Books).

Vernon, R. (1977), *Storm over the Multinationals* (New York: Basic Books).

8

Political Economy and International Law

SOL PICCIOTTO

Commonly views about international law seem to divide into the sceptical and the idealistic. This divergence is apparent at the very mention of international law whether it is in public discussion of international affairs or in classroom debate. Whatever the forum or context, the mention of international law seems to imply the invocation of a well-meaning set of rules which, according to whether one is a pessimist or an optimist, are either a mere cloak for the pursuit of real political and economic interests or, alternatively, a potential foundation for that more harmonious and settled world order which could be achieved if only baser motives and suspicions could be eliminated from world affairs.

On closer examination this central ambivalence in relation to international law can be seen to reflect some of the general preoccupations of all those concerned with international affairs about the changes that have been taking place in the global system and preferred directions for its future development. In its origins and subsequent development, international law has been characterised as a system of public law governing the relations between states. Indeed, it was in no small measure as a result of the theory and activity of international lawyers that this formalisation of the global system as made up of sovereign independent state units was established. It is this notion of an 'international community' of states that underlies the traditional formulations of international law, in which states are the subjects of that law, but also peculiarly its objects. This fetishisation of the state, whereby it is used as a symbol to represent all social power relations within the global system as relations between states, has made it difficult to analyse the very great changes that have taken place in the role and function of the state, as well as in the nature and form of the international system and international law.

The fetishisation of the nation-state underlies a second major dichotomy in views about contemporary international law, that be-

tween the 'interstate' and the 'transnational' perspectives. Richard Falk
has argued that this divergence involved 'a false dichotomy between
Machiavellian geopolitics (the realm of Henry Kissinger) and the
globaloney of schemes for instant world government' (Falk, 1975,
p. 996). In Falk's eyes both of these are unrealistic, since they both 'fail to
perceive the dominant integrationist thrust of contemporary issues'. He
argues that the role of international lawyers is to help formulate a new
paradigm which can play a positive role in shaping the current reorganisation of the world system. In common with some other writers on
international relations he sees this reorganisation as resulting from a
breakdown of the state-centred system under the pressure of growing
interdependence of which the main features are increased 'central guidance' and an increasing role for 'nonterritorial actors'. Hence, for him,
'We need an interim period of Kissingerian geopolitics as a "minor
premise", to avoid a breakdown of the state system prior to the forma-
tion of a widely shared understanding of the prospects for nonterritorial
central guidance and of the array of plausible options'.

For the student of international relations, this sort of talk is familiar
enough; what is perhaps less clear is the nature of the relationship
between the changes in the character and content of international law
advocated by writers such as Falk and the changes which they see as
taking place in international political economy. Indeed, just as is the
case with international relations theory, there is a variety of different
currents of international legal thought within the 'transnational' perspective (and Falk, 1975, is a useful guide to these different currents).
Whatever their particular emphasis, they raise the issue of how far
international law and lawyers can help to generate a normative basis
transcending the nation-state around which transnational tendencies in
the world political economy can coalesce. To the sceptic such efforts,
especially by radical-populist exponents such as Falk, merely provide a
smokescreen (either well-meaning or malevolent) for the real power-
political processes that lurk behind the rhetoric of 'world order needs'.

This issue goes beyond mere academic debate. There has been continuing controversy about the relationship of international law to the
political and diplomatic processes of negotiation of issues of global
political economy. One noted feature has been the multiplication of
instruments – declarations, codes of conduct, guidelines – whose legal
status appears ambiguous. This development has been considered
either as a bold attempt to adapt traditional international law to the
needs of the modern world community (Hossain, 1980) or as merely the
development of an international economic 'soft law', implying a lack of
the 'hardness' of binding interstate obligations (Seidl-Hohenveldern,
1979).

Ever since the postwar decolonisation process began to produce a
dramatic increase in the number of constitutionally independent states,

there has been debate about the implications for international law of this transformation of the size if not the character of the international community. On the one hand, publicists arguing for the point of view of the new nations put the case for a re-evaluation of the substantive principles of international law which were established during a period when many peoples were denied statehood. From this perspective great importance is placed, in terms of the procedures for such a reformulation of international law, on the United Nations as a universal organisation, and on the power of the General Assembly to contribute to the progressive development of international law. While it is conceded that the General Assembly's routine resolutions cannot be legally binding directly (since they are clearly stated and intended to have the force only of recommendations to states, although they may bind the Organisation internally), it is argued that in various indirect ways they can become, or help to generate, customary international law. In his often-cited dissenting opinion in the 1966 International Court of Justice case on South-west Africa/Namibia, Judge Tanaka stated that, while individual resolutions cannot have the force of law, the mode of generation of principles of customary international law has been greatly facilitated and accelerated by the ease of communication and the institutionalisation of diplomacy through the UN system, so that 'the accumulation of authoritative pronouncements . . . by the competent organs of the international community can be characterised as evidence of . . . international custom'. This may be considered to be the case particularly in relation to major General Assembly resolutions embodying solemn declarations, which may have been approved without a vote being taken, or without dissenting votes, or perhaps even if passed by an overwhelming majority. Such a view has been argued to be based on 'the emerging concept of consensus rather than the traditional concept of consent as the basis of obligation in the international community' (Bulajic, 1980, p. 60, citing Falk, 1966). On the other hand, from the point of view of older or more powerful states it has been argued that new international law cannot be created by majority voting, however great the number of states in the majority, although, admittedly, solemn resolutions can be declaratory of existing law based on actual state practice.

In a sense the new nations have learned too well to use the procedures established originally by the great powers with the aim of generating a normative framework for international relations which might help to avoid the interimperialist conflicts which dominated the first half of this century. The United Nations Charter itself (which is not only binding on members as a treaty, but also explicitly stated, in Article 103, to override all other obligations) set the tone by establishing both explicit obligations as well as general aims for the international community, ranging from the renunciation of the use of force between states to equal rights and self-determination of peoples, economic and social progress, and universal respect for human rights and fundamental freedoms for all without distinction as to race, sex, language, or religion. Such provisions in the Charter were quite quickly followed up by the adoption in 1948 by the General Assembly of the Universal Declaration of Human Rights. It is hard not to see a certain logical pattern in its being followed by other declarations, on the Granting of Independence to Colonial Countries and Peoples (1960), on Friendly Relations and Co-operation among States (1970) and, finally, the Declaration of the Establishment of a New International Economic Order of 1974 and the Charter of Economic Rights and Duties of States (1974). Nevertheless, dispute as to the legal status and role of these declarations increased, which may be linked to their progression from general humanitarian concerns to harder questions of political economy. It is notable that, while the 1948, 1960 and 1970 Declarations were approved without a vote or passed *nem. con.*, the 1974 Charter received six votes against (including Germany, the United Kingdom and United States) and ten abstentions (including the main remaining developed capitalist states). One might also compare the 1960 Declaration on decolonisation with the 1962 Resolution on Permanent Sovereignty over Natural Resources. Although the latter left a delicate ambiguity around the key issue of whether the 'appropriate compensation' for nationalisation of economic resources is subject to an international minimum standard, it also was not adopted unanimously (France and South Africa voted — against, and a dozen states, including the Soviet Union, abstained).

Nevertheless, the effort to develop international law as a means of establishing a new basis for international political economy has continued. While this is commonly argued to involve a transformation of traditional international law (Bulajic, 1980), it is by no means confined to new procedures such as General Assembly declarations. The 1973 NIEO Declaration and the 1974 Charter of Economic Rights and Duties of States were used to establish a general ideological theme around which many specific negotiations have been pursued. Certainly, where definite and specific changes were intended to be brought about, the aim has been to do so by multilateral treaty if possible. For instance, as part of the general campaign on the terms of transfer of technology, a major effort has been put into attempting the revision of the Paris Convention for the Protection of Industrial Property, which was originally concluded in 1883. The basic principle established in that convention of national treatment for holders of industrial property rights (Article 2), requires member-states to give a twelve-month right of priority to any such holder who has filed a patent application in any member-state, and imposes restrictions on the power of states to restrict or withdraw a patent on the grounds that it is not being worked within the country. After considerable background work had shown the disad-

vantages of these arrangements from the point of view of underdeveloped countries (UNCTAD, 1975; Vaitsos, 1976), a diplomatic conference was established in 1980 for the revision of the Paris Convention.
Despite the prospects for this revision being greeted with 'some optimism' (Helleiner, 1979), two negotiation sessions in Geneva and one in
Nairobi seem to have produced little progress so far. Still, these things
take time: fifteen years separate the passing of General Assembly
Resolution 2340 of 18 December 1967 on the peaceful uses of the
seabed and the ocean floor beyond the limits of natural jurisdiction,
which led to the launching of the Third United Nations Conference on
the Law of the Sea in 1973, from the eventual signature on 10
December 1982 of the Final Act and Convention on the Law of the Sea.

However, it is only partly due to the slowness of the processes
involved in negotiating a multilateral treaty that much of the effort
through UNCTAD, and more recently the Commission and Centre on
Transnational Corporations (set up by the UN's Economic and Social
Committee in November 1974), in developing new rules regulating
international business seems to be resulting in codes of conduct
approved by resolution, rather than formal treaties. As Table 8.1
shows, apart from United Nations bodies, the formulation of
guidelines and codes for international business has also been taken up
by other intergovernmental and non-governmental organisations, notably OECD and the International Chamber of Commerce. To some
extent this has been due to a concern on the part of those with a
generally protective attitude towards international business to pre-empt
the Codes being drafted by UN bodies, which they regard as likely to be
dominated by critical perspectives from developing countries.

Nevertheless, despite the political manoeuvrings over the form and
content of these codes, it seems that their emergence stems from an
underlying need to develop an adequate international regulatory
framework for international business. Looking, for instance, at the
regulation of 'restrictive business practices' (RBPs), this issue did not
first arise with the interest shown in it by UNCTAD from 1972 or so. It
should be recalled (see Davidow, 1981) that Article V of the Havana
Charter for an International Trade Organisation contained a list of
prohibited RBPs, and abortive attempts were made in 1951–2 to draft
RBP rules and an implementing procedure, through the Economic and
Social Council (ECOSOC). The origin of these efforts lies more clearly
in the concerns of American policy-makers to ensure an open and
decartelised postwar trading system. Already, as part of this, United
States anti-trust law had begun to be applied to international cartels in
1937–8 by Roosevelt appointees to the Department of Justice, and this
process continued as part of the wartime planning for the postwar
international economic order. Subsequently American lawyers played a
part in the adoption of the anti-cartel laws of Germany and Japan and of

Table 8.1 *Some Codes of Conduct and Guidelines for International Business*

A *General codes for multinational enterprises (MNEs)*
1 UN Code of Conduct for Transnational Corporations, drawn up by the UN Commission on TNCs. Draft Text in *CTC Reporter*, no. 12 (1982). Legal status not yet decided, likely to be GA Resolution.
2 ILO Tripartite Declaration of Principles Concerning MNEs and Social Policy. Adopted by ILO Governing Body, 16 November 1977. Reprinted in *International Legal Materials*, vol. 17 (1978), p. 422.
3 OECD Declaration on International Investment and MNEs, and Annex, Guidelines for MNEs, adopted 21 June 1976, doc. C (76) 20; revised 1979, doc. C (79) 102.
4 European Parliament–US Congress, Draft Code of Principles for MNEs and Government (Lange–Gibbons Code), 16 May 1977, *EC Official Journal*, C.118/15.
5 International Chamber of Commerce, MNEs and their Role in Economic Development, doc. 191/83, 1974.

B *Restrictive business practices and transfer of technology*
1 UNCTAD, Set of Mutually Agreed Equitable Principles and Rules for the Control of Restrictive Business Practices Having Effects on International Trade. Recommendations of UN Conference on Restrictive Business Practices, adopted in UN General Assembly Resolution 3563, 16 December 1980.
2 UNCTAD, International Code of Conduct on the Transfer of Technology. Draft as at close of 4th session of Conference on an International Code of Conduct on the Transfer of Technology, 10 April 1981, UN doc. TD/CODE/TOT/33. Interim committee set up by General Assembly to accelerate conclusion of Code last met September 1982.
3 OECD Recommendation of the Council Concerning Action against Restrictive Business Practices Affecting International Trade including those Involving MNEs, doc. C (78) 133, 9 August 1978. Reprinted in *International Legal Materials*, vol. 17 (1978), p. 1527.
4 OECD Recommendation of the Council Concerning Co-operation between Member Countries on Restrictive Business Practices Affecting International Trade, doc. C (67) 53 of 1967. See report on the operation of the recommendation reprinted in *Antitrust Bulletin*, vol. 22 (1977), pp. 459–85.

C *Social and moral aspects of business*
1 UN Draft International Agreement on Illicit Payments in International Commercial Transactions. Drawn up by committee of ECOSOC and transmitted to General Assembly, UN doc. E/1979/104, 25 May 1979. General Assembly decided to take no action at that time: see doc. A/34/635/Add.3.
2 International Chamber of Commerce, Rules of Conduct to Combat Extortion and Bribery in Business Transactions. Report adopted by ICC Council, 29 November 1977, ICC publication no. 315. Reprinted in *International Legal Materials*, vol. 17 (1978), p. 417.
3 European Communities, Code of Conduct for Companies Having

Table 8.1   (cont.)

Subsidiaries, Branches or Representation in South Africa. Adopted by
Foreign Ministers, 20 September 1977.
4   European Communities, Draft Council Directive on procedures for
informing and consulting the employees of undertakings with complex
structures, in particular, transnational undertakings (Vredeling Directive).
OJ, No. C. 297, 15.11.80, p. 3.
5   World Health Organisation, International Code of Marketing of Breast-
Milk Substitutes. Resolution 34.22, 21 May 1981. Reprinted in *CTC
Reporter*, no. 11 (1982).

D   *Specific sectors and topics*
1   Convention on a Code of Conduct for Liner Conferences, signed at Geneva,
6 April 1974. TD/CODE 11/REV.1.
2   OECD, Recommendation of Council and Guidelines Concerning the
Protection of Privacy and Transborder Flows of Personal Data, doc. C (80)
58, 1 October 1980. Reprinted in *International Legal Materials*, vol. 20
(1981), p. 422.
3   Council of Europe, Convention for the Protection of Individuals with
Regard to Automatic Processing of Personal Data, 28 January 1981,
European Treaty Series, no. 108. Reprinted in *International Legal Materials*,
vol. 20 (1981), p. 317.
4   UN, Proposed Code of Conduct on International Standards of Accounting
and Reporting, submitted by *ad hoc* group of experts appointed by the
Centre on TNCs, September 1982, doc. E/C.10/1982/8.
5   Supervisory Authorities and Central Banks of Group of Ten and
Switzerland and Luxembourg, Basle Concordat on the Supervision of
Banks' Foreign Establishments, agreed by the Committee on Banking
Regulations and Supervisory Practices, 9 September 1974. (Revision
expected June 1983.)

---

the European Coal and Steel Community. There was an awareness
already in the early postwar period both of the need to try to achieve
co-ordination or harmonisation of national regulation of cartels and
restrictive agreements between firms affecting international trade, as
well as of the great difficulties posed by the lack of any political consensus on the form this should take. In the light of this it was no mean
achievement for UNCTAD to achieve broad agreement on the RBP
Code in 1980, although this was somewhat facilitated by separating
some of the more contentious issues to be dealt with in the Transfer of
Technology Code, whose progress has been more problematic.

Indeed, in one sense the relatively well-known codes and guidelines
listed in Table 8.1 are but the tip of an iceberg of international
economic regulatory arrangements made by or through a wide variety
of different organisations and bodies, and which attempt to adapt

national state regulations to an increasingly internationally integrated world political economy. In this context the ambiguities and contradictions of international legality are a manifestation at the international level of the more general problem of legal regulation of economic affairs, caused by the dilemmas of state intervention in economic activities. As the limitations and inadequacies of legal forms of regulation have been increasingly revealed, more direct forms of regulation or state intervention have been attempted. This process poses special problems for the international legal system.

First, it has become clear that there is not a simple choice between 'binding' and 'non-binding' forms of international regulation of business. Reports and studies of the question of the legal form of international economic regulatory provisions have been forced to conclude that the line between binding and non-binding forms is a shady one (Centre on Transnational Corporations, 1976, pp. 12–13, 35–6; Seidl-Hohenveldern, 1979, pp. 194–213). The underlying reason for this is the formal separation of the public-law obligations concluded between states from the private-law obligations which states alone can impose on their subjects. In that sense the 'binding' nature of the international obligation must be distinguished from the question of its actual implementation by the state and from the enforcement of the obligation to implement.

As was pointed out in the 1976 study by the UN Centre on Transnational Corporations, if it were to be decided to give formal binding legal force to a code on multinational business, it would take the form of a treaty under international law binding all state parties to it. This places a state which accedes to it under a duty to implement the treaty's provisions, by translating them into obligations legally binding on companies and individuals as part of its national law. This usually involves a special legislative act, although some legal systems accept under certain conditions that an international treaty duly approved by the state's required constitutional processes might be *self-executing*, that is, become legally binding as part of that state's internal law automatically. Under the United States Constitution, for instance, a treaty made under the authority of the United States is part of the law of the land. However, this bold provision has been much reduced in effect both by practices developed by the Executive branch and by court interpretations. The development of the anomalous category of 'executive agreements', largely in order to avoid the necessity of obtaining the advice and consent of the Senate, has given the Executive extensive prerogative powers to undertake international obligations, which have been increasingly used. Between 1946 and 1972 the United States became party to 368 treaties, while 5,590 executive agreements were concluded (Steiner and Vagts, 1976, p. 589); nor have the latter been confined to minor matters, as the well-known examples of the Yalta Agreement and the GATT agreement show. Although executive agreements may in principle be self-executing, in practice they will usually be implemented under presidential power, or by submitting legislation to Congress (although in the latter case Congress may well feel its hand is being forced). A greater limitation on the automatic transformation of public international law into private domestic law has been the court interpretations, which have confined self-executing effect only to specific and unconditional obligations clearly intended by the parties to have direct effect as law. Thus in *Sei Fuji* v. *California* (1952) the Supreme Court of California held that the provisions on human rights in the UN Charter merely stated general purposes and objectives, and neither imposed legal obligations on member-states nor created rights in private persons; they could therefore not be held to invalidate provisions of the California Alien Land Law. English law does not provide for any direct effect for treaties. However, the European Court of Justice has recently held that a treaty concluded by the Community can include provisions which may have a direct effect as law within member states. The case, *Hauptzollamt Mainz* v. *Kupferberg & Cie KG* [1983] 1, *Common Market Law Reports*, p. 1, concerned a free trade agreement with a non-member state, and the Court held that an undertaking of non-discrimination against imports was sufficiently precise and unconditional to have direct effect (although in the instant case it held that no discrimination had in fact taken place). In contrast, it has held that Article 11 of the GATT, being more flexible and indeterminate, does not have direct effect (*International Fruit Co.* [1972] ECR 1219), and this has been confirmed by recent cases.

The fact that treaties in order to become legally binding on companies and individuals require conversion into the domestic laws of each state party creates extensive divergencies in interpretation and implementation. We may take as an example the Code of Conduct for Liner Conferences, initiated through UNCTAD but finalised by a full diplomatic conference, in the form of a binding Convention (in which respect it is exceptional among such codes of conduct). The convention format was suitable in this case for two reasons: first, it provides basically for self-regulation by shipping conferences, subject to the principles established in the Code; and secondly, universal application is not vital, so it is feasible for the Code to apply only to the trade between contracting states. Although the Convention is now in force (since accession by the European Community states in 1983 brought the number of signatories up to the necessary minimum of twenty-four states covering 25 per cent of world tonnage), the effect of reservations and divergent interpretations is to reduce the Code to a patchwork-quilt being pulled in different directions by states, rather than a single all-enveloping regulatory coverlet. Reservations by the Soviet bloc have excluded shipping lines set up bilaterally between states, and the European reservation excludes trade with reciprocating OECD countries. Furthermore, some divergent interpretations have arisen which involve fundamental policy differences: notably whether the basic principle that cargoes should in general be divided 40–40–20 (that is, 40 per cent to lines of countries at each end of the trade and 20 per cent to cross-traders) applies to conference cargoes only or to the whole trade between countries (Department of Trade, 1980). Although the Convention provides for international mandatory conciliation between shipping lines and conferences (i.e. on the request of anyone), recommendations of the conciliators are to be binding only on parties which accept them. There are no provisions for judicial resolution of disputes between state parties, so the disagreements about the scope of the Code will be a matter for continuing negotiation.

In general, the procedures for the implementation of multilateral treaties tend to result in such treaties taking effect in this sort of fragmented way, rather than as a single comprehensive Code universally applicable. It was soon after the foundation of the UN that the International Court of Justice was faced with the dilemma between universal participation and divergent modification of multilateral treaties, when it was asked by the General Assembly to rule on the admissibility of reservations to the Genocide Convention. By a majority of seven judges to five the Court held that the absence of any provision for reservations does not preclude the possibility of a state acceding to a convention subject to reservations, but that states may not by virtue of their sovereignty make any reservation they choose: the validity of the reservation depends on its compatibility with the object and purpose of the Convention. This rule, subsequently embodied in the Vienna Convention on Treaties (1969), is intended to promote the more universal acceptance by states of conventions, which a state may accept in general, despite one or another specific objection. However, it clearly does so at a cost; the scope of such treaties becomes more indeterminate. What is more, in the absence of any provision in the treaty defining permissible reservations, significant difficulties arise in relation to a reservation which is accepted by some states but denounced as incompatible with the treaty by others.

We see, therefore, that multilateral treaty-making is not a matter of the creation of a unified international legal framework based on a consensus between sovereign states. It has increasingly become, rather, a continuous process of attempts to co-ordinate state regulation, involving a variety of acts with different legal effects and implications: from declarations by individual states or groups, to the formulation of drafts and negotiating texts, to the conclusion and signature of a final text which is open for ratification, followed by the attempt to obtain sufficient ratification to bring the instrument into force, and the manoeuvring about reservations and divergences in interpretation, which increasingly frequently takes place as part of a process of review and renegotiation which is built into the treaty.

This process is clearly illustrated by the past forty years of attempts to regulate the increasingly intensive use of the world's oceans. This opened with the Truman proclamations of 1945 on the continental shelf and on coastal fisheries (Whiteman, 1963–70, Vol. 4, pp. 756, 945), to be followed by the International Law Commission's draft articles on the law of the sea of 1956, and the first and second Geneva Conferences of 1958 and 1960 which produced the basic Conventions on the territorial sea, high seas, the continental shelf and on fishing but left undecided the contentious question of the limits of state sovereignty, which was then the subject of unilateral and collective claims by states. The 1958 and 1960 Conventions have been acceded to by forty-five to fifty-five states, but their status has been complicated by the fact that some of their provisions have been considered to be declaratory of customary international law, but others binding only on parties. A great many issues in relation to the use of the seas have since been subjected to a variety of forms of adjudication, agreement and control, from a series of International Court opinions (for example, *Corfu Channel* case 1949, the *UK* v. *Iceland* fisheries case 1974, the *North Sea Continental Shelf* cases 1969) to bilateral arrangements and agreements between states, and many multilateral agreements both by states and by non-state bodies (for example, the TOVALOP scheme set up by the oil companies to cover the costs of clearing up oil spillages). In this context the new Law of the Sea Convention merely provides a very general framework, whose usefulness derives as much from the intensive negotiations that have gone on around it as on the specific formulations in the final text, especially in view of the opposition of the mining companies and the Reagan administration to the provisions on the seabed. Even if the necessary sixty ratifications can be found so that it will enter into force, the opposition of the United States is bound to limit the authority of the agreed rules. More particularly, the agreed arrangement for an International Seabed Authority (ISA) is likely to be a dead letter. However, the treaty does attempt to set up a universal regime, by restricting reservations to those expressly permitted (although interpretative 'declarations' are allowed). It also sets up a considerable permanent machinery both in respect of the controversial specific provisions for seabed mining in 'the Area' (the ocean floor beyond the limits of national jurisdiction) and for the convention as a whole, including arbitration and conciliation procedures and an International Tribunal for the Law of the Sea, and states are required, with some exceptions, to opt for one of the available forms of dispute settlement.

As can be seen from this brief survey of treaty-making, this apparently most 'binding' form of international obligation can be seen in many respects as an arena in which issues of legitimacy and coercion are subject to negotiation in relation to the interpretation of the specific principles and formulas embodied in the texts. It can, therefore, be readily understood why in many cases internationally agreed regulations are not formalised as a treaty. This is sometimes explained by saying that, regardless of the formal legal nature of the instrument, its effectiveness in any particular case is governed by the willingness of national governments to implement it (Centre on Transnational Corporations, 1976, p. 12). More broadly, one can say that effectiveness depends on the extent to which effective power can be mobilised behind a particular set of provisions. Of course, much effective enforcement power is monopolised by state mechanisms, but the mere fact that certain provisions are embodied in law does not necessarily mean that effective enforcement of those provisions will take place.

One has only to take the well-known example of the UN Security Council sanctions against Rhodesia, which took the most stringent legal form of mandatory action under Chapter 7 of the UN Charter. As was subsequently revealed (Bailey, 1979), the British government's unwillingness to interfere with the operation of oil companies in Southern Africa meant that infringements both of the letter and of the spirit of its oil sanctions legislation were ignored. Thus in that case undoubtedly legally binding international legal provisions, which were apparently being strictly enforced by warship patrols in the Indian Ocean, were in a sense a smokescreen for a tacit acceptance that normal trade would not be interfered with even if it was obviously providing a cloak for breaches of the sanctions.

Like all law, international law does no more than establish a structure or arena within which political and economic power processes of negotiation and coercion, ideological manipulation and popular mobilisation can take place.

As regards the prospects for the effective regulation of international business and multinational corporations (MNCs) those who feel that MNCs must be subjected to stringent controls are naturally suspicious when what they see proposed are codes that are explicitly designated to be 'voluntary'. They should, nevertheless, not allow themselves to confuse effectiveness with legality. Effectiveness depends relatively little on the letter of the law, or even on the action of law-enforcement officials, but generally depends far more on the degree of public awareness and concern. Probably the most effective attempts to establish regulatory controls on international business in recent years have been in the field of health, in particular, the international campaign to promulgate and enforce an International Code of Marketing of Breast-Milk Substitutes. The adoption of this Code by the WHO Assembly in May 1981 owed a great deal to a very effective campaign by pressure groups, internationally co-ordinated by the International Baby Food Action

Network in Geneva. More important, this campaign of mobilisation is continuing to try and get effective enforcement and compliance. For the effectiveness of international regulation depends a great deal on the extent to which adequate international and national mechanisms for supervision, monitoring and enforcement are developed. This, in turn, depends to a great extent on the amount of pressure that is exerted on the formal interstate bodies and national governments by internationally organised popular pressure groups or other organisations such as trade unions.

Nevertheless, not all international enforcement machinery is effective, and there are likely to be many difficulties in relation to powerful organisations such as MNCs. One of the surprises of the OECD Guidelines, for instance, has been the extent to which OECD committees have been pushed, mainly by trade union pressures, into an adjudicatory role in relation to alleged breaches, in publicised cases such as the Badger case (1977) and the Hertz case (1977). However, the unsurprising degree of timidity they have shown in adopting this role (through fear of a business backlash) does not augur well for effective enforcement (Vogelaar, in Horn, 1980; OECD, 1979).

The increasing proliferation of different forms of international or transnational regulation of social and economic matters, albeit in fragmented and very partially effective ways, certainly testifies to the increasing need for regulation to transcend the nation-state. However, this is far from meaning an abandonment of the state – on the contrary, there is an increasing dependence on state intervention in order to achieve both efficiency and equity, in most fields of social activity. It is this dual process, of increasing involvement of the state in social and economic processes, at the same time that they increasingly transcend the state, that has placed the international state system, and international law, under increasing pressures.

I have indicated some of the ways in which the traditional mechanisms of international law were derived from the liberal international state system, in which the interaction of autonomous sovereign units was regulated by *voluntaristic* and *reciprocal* obligations. This system of apparently free and equal state units emerged as part of a process of creation of a single global political economy which, however, entailed very great inequalities, exploitation and dominance, both within and between states. Although it had a real basis in national economic and social differences, the notion of national 'sovereignty' has always been a fetish, the product of the autonomisation of the state and its development as the rule of public authorities over a defined territory (Poggi, 1978). The classic writers on international law played an important role in formulating the ideas and principles which facilitated the transition from the personal sovereign to the state with abstract sovereignty exclusively over its own territory. In its origins this system was strongly influenced by ideas that certain basic principles of law not only should but did have universal validity. Grotius, in particular, saw state sovereignty as defined and limited by natural law, divine law and the *jus gentium* (law of peoples). This perspective was subsequently eclipsed by positivistic views. In its naïve version a positivist like Bentham held that since there is no sovereign above the state, there can be no international law. Later, more pragmatic versions accepted that reciprocity and mutual agreement could provide a basis for international law. However, this was still open to the extreme voluntarist interpretation which found expression in the famous international court judgement in the Lotus case (1927). Judge Huber's famous opinion in this case argued that the rules of international law emanate from the free will of independent states; hence state sovereignty could not be restricted by denying a claim of jurisdiction (even over acts taking place outside the territory) unless such a restriction was based on explicit agreement or a universally accepted general rule.

The main advantage of this international state system was that it permitted a relatively open circulation of people, commodities and capital. Grotius was no mere academic scholar, but an advocate for the Dutch East India Company, whose interest in the freedom of the seas was a very real and material one. (*De Jure Praedae* (*Commentaries on the Laws of Prize and Booty*) was originally written as a defence of the Dutch East India Company, which he had represented in Prize Court proceedings.) The international system which he advocated was one in which states performed the necessary public functions while permitting individuals and companies free access for the economic purposes of trade and investment. This access was, however, somewhat limited thanks to the prevailing mercantilism of his day which ensured a highly regulated system.

An important feature of the emergent international state system was the separation of public and private international law, although they remained joined at the hip through the law of jurisdiction. The emergence of private international law or conflicts of law came from the abandonment of the system of personal law (by which each person was governed by the law of their ethnic group) or the paramountcy of the law of the land developed by feudal absolutism. Instead principles were developed under which the appropriate private law system was applied according to the nature of the transaction and its particular circumstances. This facilitated private commercial transactions, especially where state legal systems were prepared to accept and enforce the specific customs of the international *lex mercatoria*. This was linked to public international law through the development of the principle of territoriality in jurisdiction, which meant that the state had the exclusive jurisdiction to adjudicate and enforce the law within its own territory over all persons found in that territory, even foreigners. However, in order to prevent conflicts of law, each state could give effect to foreign law, either in the adjudication of private transactions with an international or foreign character, or even in enforcing foreign judgements. The implication of the Grotian view that international society was subject to an overarching law was that there was actually an international obligation of *comity*, to give effect to foreign law in appropriate cases provided no prejudice to the interests of the state or its citizens is entailed. The contrary view, which has been maintained in continuing debates among legal scholars, has been that the solution of conflicts of private law is only at the will and discretion of sovereign states, so that foreign law need only be applied and enforced so long as it serves the expediency of sovereign interests (Yntema, 1966).

Although this system laid a basis for the possibility of free movements of persons and resources internationally, the vast intensification of international commerce, especially in this century, has required great and increased efforts, first, to co-ordinate the different national rules of conflicts of law; secondly, to find and develop mechanisms of enforcement of foreign judgements; and thirdly, to harmonise the substantive rules of law applicable to certain appropriate transactions such as international sales.

None of these endeavours have been easy and great difficulty has been caused by the increasing impossibility of maintaining the separation of public and private law, and separating procedure from the substance of regulation. The willingness of states to enforce foreign law in 'appropriate' cases have traditionally been subject to the firm exception that foreign laws of a penal character will not be given effect in any way – and this includes tax and exchange control laws as well as the main corpus of criminal law. In the field of criminal law reciprocal provisions for extradition of fugitive offenders were developed, which firmly reinforce the territoriality of jurisdiction, since extradition is very rarely available for an offence committed outside the requesting state.

The increasingly direct intervention by the state in many aspects of social and economic life, together with the increasing internationalisation of many of them, lie behind the difficulties of conflicts of jurisdiction and attempts to co-ordinate national jurisdiction that have become a feature of international relations (Picciotto, 1983). These began with the application of American antitrust laws to international cartels, but have spread to many areas of economic life, including international banking, securities regulation, trade embargoes, corrupt practices, and so on (Lowenfeld, 1979; Maier, 1982). In keeping with the increasingly protectionist temper of the times recent developments have seen increasingly conflictual stances being taken even by political allies, notably over the application of the United States embargo on supplies for the Soviet pipeline against European companies. Meanwhile international lawyers have been attempting to refine and develop the principles determining and rationalising the allocation of jurisdiction between states in order to cope with the increased strains caused by the intensified internationalisation of economic life. On closer examination of the problem of jurisdiction it becomes clear that the world is not made up of an aggregation of compartmentalised units, but is rather a single system in which state power is allocated between different territorial entities. In reality, exclusive jurisdiction is impossible to define, so that there is in practice a network of interlocking and overlapping jurisdictions. Increased internationalisation of social and economic relations leads to an increase in the areas of overlap of jurisdiction, since territoriality becomes hard to maintain, as it can become impossible to define an act as taking place in a particular territory, or the territory in which it takes place may be arbitrarily chosen by the participants. This factor justifies the assertion of jurisdiction on the basis that the primary 'effects' of an act are felt by the state. This was originally put forward by American authorities and jurists, but is now occasionally propounded by other regulatory agencies, such as the European Commission. Undoubtedly, however, the 'effects' doctrine creates a greater potential for conflicts of regulation. This issue, once again, goes to the basis of the traditional system of international law. One commentator has said that its solution requires

> a refinement of the concept of sovereignty in international law, so that it can accommodate both notions of independence of states and of the increasing interdependence of states, without losing its coherence as a legal principle. (Lowe, 1981, p. 218).

To this, an even bolder response has been that the concept of sovereignty is the wrong starting-point, since it 'seems likely to lead to vertical concepts where horizontal thinking is required' (Lowenfeld, 1981).

At the same time a more radical solution to the problem of conflicts between national states in their attempts to regulate international or transnational affairs is to develop more direct forms of co-ordination between state administrations. From some of the examples we have discussed, it should be clear that this is one of the main motivations behind many of the attempts to formulate codes of conduct and guidelines that we considered in the first part of this chapter. Indeed, some of these codes address provisions not only to companies and individuals, but also to state authorities: on the insistence of the developed capitalist countries the draft UN Code of Conduct for Transnational Corporations (TNCs) contains provisions on the jurisdiction of states. Although the need to co-ordinate national jurisdictions is among the more potent motivations for attempts at international regulation, it cannot be said to have led to any effective or close co-operation between national authorities. There has been a proliferation of provisions for notification and consultation between the national authorities of states, for instance, in relation to the taxation of TNCs. There is a longstanding OECD arrangement for co-ordination of antitrust investigations, which was an attempt to prevent jurisdictional conflicts (see *B*4 in Table 8.1). But so far national authorities have rarely taken these mechanisms beyond mere formal notification. Even in areas where contacts between national officials are fairly close, as with central banks, the degree of international co-ordination has seemed fairly rudimentary. Despite the rapid growth and great importance of 'offshore' banking, the Basle Concordat of 1974 established only a minimal allocation of supervisory functions over foreign subsidiaries and franchises, and the problem of lender-of-last-resort responsibility, strikingly raised by the Banca d'Italia's refusal to accept responsibility in the Banco Ambrosiano affair, remains unresolved (Blunden, 1977).

In the light of this brief survey it is clear that the changing patterns of internationalisation of social and economic life have involved also quite substantial changes in the processes and principles of international law. Undoubtedly these have been strongly influenced by great changes in the role and functions of the state and the relationship of the state to economic activity, symbolised by the emergence of dominating multinational enterprises. In this perspective the view, sometimes labelled 'neo-Grotian', that a growing interdependence of states could lay the basis for a strengthened overarching international legality seems misplaced. The increasing need for public regulation of economic relations, in directly interventionist forms, has meant that social conflict over the organisation of economic life focuses more than ever on the state. At the same time, the growing internationalisation of social and economic relations has created a great need for more effective and direct co-ordination of states' economic regulation. The dominant trend seems to be not towards a strengthening of democratic controls through international legality, but towards forms of international state corporatism, in which disputes are settled and issues managed by direct contacts among corporate and state managers. In this context the propagation of a legal code often seems to be merely an attempt to reassure public opinion that solutions according to rational and equitable principles are being imposed. The search for more effective regulation, and a legality that is more than a decorative veil, depends on a vigorous mobilisation that will give expression to the very real needs of the world's peoples.

References: Chapter 8

Bailey, M. (1979), *Oilgate* (London: Coronet).
Blunden, G. (1977), 'International co-operation in banking supervision', *Bank of England Quarterly Bulletin*, vol. 17, pp. 325–9.

Bulajic, Milan (1980), 'Legal aspects of a new international economic order', in Kamal Hossain (ed.), *Legal Aspects of the New International Economic Order* (London: Francis Pinter).

Centre on Transnational Corporations (1976), *Transnational Corporations: Issues Involved in the Formulation of a Code of Conduct*, Doc. E/C.10/17 of 20 July 1976 (New York: United Nations Organisation).

Davidow, Joel (1981), 'The seeking of a world competition code', in O. Schachter and R. Hellawell (eds), *Competition in International Business* (New York: Columbia University Press), p. 361.

Department of Trade (1980), *United Kingdom Implementation of the United Nations Convention on a Code of Conduct for Liner Conferences*, consultative paper (London: Department of Trade).

Falk, Richard (1966), 'On the quasi-legislative competence of the General Assembly', *American Journal of International Law*, vol. 60, pp. 782–91.

Falk, Richard (1975), 'A new paradigm for international legal studies: prospects and proposals', *Yale Law Journal*, vol. 84, pp. 969–1021.

Helleiner, G. K. (1979), 'International technology issues: southern needs and northern responses', in J. Ramesh and C. Weiss (eds), *Mobilizing Technology for World Development* (New York: Praeger).

Horn, N. (1980), *Legal Problems of Codes of Conduct for Multinational Enterprises* (Deventer, Netherlands: Kluwer).

Hossain, Kamal (1980), *Legal Aspects of the New International Economic Order* (London: Francis Pinter).

Lowe, A. V. (1981), 'Blocking extraterritorial jurisdiction: the British Protection of Trading Interests Act, 1980', *American Journal of International Law*, vol.75, pp. 257–82.

Lowenfeld, A. F. (1979), 'Public law in the international arena', *Hague Academy of International Law*, vol. 163, pp. 315–445.

Lowenfeld, A. F. (1981), 'Sovereignty, jurisdiction and reasonableness: a reply to A. V. Lowe', *American Journal of International Law*, vol. 75, pp. 629–38.

Maier, H. G. (1982), 'Extraterritorial jurisdiction at a crossroads: an intersection between public and private international law', *American Journal of International Law*, vol. 76, pp. 280–320.

OECD (1979), *Review of the 1976 Declaration and Decisions* (Paris: OECD).

Picciotto, S. (1983), 'Jurisdictional conflicts, international law and the international state system', *International Journal of the Sociology of Law*, vol. 11, pp. 11–40.

Poggi, G. (1978), *The Development of the Modern State: A Sociological Introduction* (London: Hutchinson).

Seidl-Hohenveldern, I. (1979), 'International economic "soft law"', *Hague Academy of International Law*, vol. 163, p. 169.

Steiner, H. J., and Vagts, D. V. (1976), *Transnational Legal Problems*, 2nd edn (Mineola, NY: Foundation Press).

UNCTAD (1975), *The Role of the Patent System in the Transfer of Technology*, Doc. TD/B/AC.11/19/Rev. 1.

United Nations (1982), Draft Final Act and Convention of the Law of the Sea, UN Doc. A/CONF. 62/121 and 122; repr. in 21 *International Legal Materials* 1245, 1092.

Vaitsos, C. V. (1976), 'The revision of the international patent system: legal considerations for a Third World position', *World Development*, vol. 4, no. 2, pp. 85–102.

Whiteman, M. W. (1963–70), *Digest of International Law*, 14 vols, US Department of State (Washington, DC: United States Government Printing Office).

Yntema, H. E. (1966), 'The comity doctrine', *Michigan Law Review*, vol. 65, pp. 9–32.

9

What about International Relations?

SUSAN STRANGE

If there is one common message from the preceding chapters, it seems to be that students of international political economy whether academic beginners or hoary-headed old hands need to broaden their outlook. They have been urged to become economic historians, to tackle technology, to fathom the intricacies of international finance, to grasp the elements of commercial exchange, to go back to the basics of demography. International political economy, it has been said again and again in these chapters, has a broader concern, a wider range altogether than the politics of international (that is, intergovernmental) economic relations. In the closeknit world economy of today transnational relations are so many and various that a narrow attention to international relations as it has been taught and studied for half a century or more will fail to enlighten its students about the real outcomes, the who-gets-what-and-why of world society.

The implication of the message seems to be that international relations as a field of social science is old-hat, an outworn fashion. Temporarily fostered by naïve hopes of progress through international organisations it has now been passed by with changing times. Interest in it has been superseded by the new vogue for international political economy, except perhaps for interest in strategic studies and the political aspects of military power and capability which is of perennial and absorbing interest both to governments and their armed forces, and to corporations likely to profit from defence budgets.

With that obvious exception, the preceding chapters of this book might well give the impression that international relations as a branch of social science is destined for a slow decline comparable to the failing interest in moral philosophy or Latin and Greek. If they did so, it would in my opinion be a great pity and the enterprise of making such a collection as this would have been misspent, a wasted effort.

On the contrary, I would like to develop the argument in a few brief concluding pages that if you wish to study international political economy there is no better starting-point than some knowledge of international relations. More than that, even: that the most essential and thus least easy foundation to dispense with is some familiarity or awareness of the habits and customs of states in their relations with one another. However this may have been acquired, through books or lecture courses or through direct experience in a foreign service, an international organisation or, I would add, by writing for a newspaper or journal concerned with international affairs, does not greatly matter. The essential 'feel' for the realities of power is what matters. Politics at any level being the art of the possible, it seems to me vital that anyone interested in the issues and problems of international political economy should have at some point and in some manner acquired a sense of what is, and is not, possible; of the feasibility of proposals for change and of the constraints which, by the nature of the international political system, limit the choice of action open to governments as they deal, in domestic policy-making and in international diplomatic negotiations, with the issues of the day.

I do not mean to dismiss altogether the prophets and visionaries whose conceptions of a better society sometimes help to lift our eyes from the everyday problems and inspire us with the energy and enthusiasm to reach out for a further goal. But they also sometimes distract us from attending to the immediate problems which, neglected or ignored, will make our predicament even worse than it is already. And there are times – such as the late 1930s and perhaps now – when blueprints of an impossible tomorrow really do take good minds and willing hands away from pressing issues of today and justify the saying that the best is the enemy of the good. And let me, therefore, as briefly as possible list a few reasons why I believe this claim for international relations to be justified.

Security the Prime Value

A very obvious point, but one which is surprisingly often overlooked is that – to put it crudely – defence is more important than economic growth, political ideology, or the legal principle *pacta sunt servanda*. More important, that is, to the state, to national government and those who shape these policies. Now you may argue if you wish that the state is merely the executive committee of the ruling class, but so long as states retain within their defined territory the monopoly of violence and with it (as part, indeed, of the bargain) the responsibility for maintaining security from attack and invasion from without as well as security within the territory, so long will the concern of governments with their security set very hard and severe limits on their choice of policies in other matters – be it trade, money, investment, education, or the management of agriculture and industry.

An appeal to the exigencies of security, in other words, takes priority over all other claims on state policy. In the last resort it cancels out every objection on other grounds. Nor is it hard to illustrate this point from the behaviour of states in international relations. Look back into the history of congressional approval of one of the most imaginative and radical initiatives ever taken in the foreign policy of the United States – the offer of Marshall Aid to Europe in 1948. Every record of that debate on Capitol Hill makes clear that despite all the arguments that were raised against the European Recovery Program, the administration won the day by pointing at the threats to American security from the social and political consequences of low economic performance, especially in France and Italy, and therefore of the need to act as a matter of natural security and defence policy more than for humanitarian reasons or to promote the interests of American industry and, more especially, large American corporations.[1]

More recently, the experience of the state of Israel in devoting something like 30 per cent of the gross national product to defence, and at the same time tolerating for years on end one of the highest inflation rates in the world, bears witness to the priority which societies organised on the basis of territorial states will give to the perceived need to defend that territory against hostile neighbours.

Of course, not all societies are in Israel's position and it might be argued that the priority of defence needs over all else is, therefore, the exception rather than the rule. But the point is that any state which *was* in Israel's position and which perceived its neighbours to be as hostile as Israelis do would behave similarly. History does not lack examples. Short of that condition of acute perceived vulnerability to external attack, states may not give defence needs such high priority. But that is because for the time being they do not perceive an immediate threat to their security, or they may decide that the strategy of the zebra melting inconspicuously into the background is better than that of the hedgehog armed all over with prickles and opt for a nuclear-free-zone policy, for instance. But my point still holds for a zebra policy. For that also requires that the state whatever its other preferences does not offend or provoke powerful and potentially aggressive neighbours. So the pursuit even of this inoffensive, neutralist strategy for the security of the state will still have priority over other considerations, of economic interest or minority rights or whatever.

The influence of this fundamental concern with security is easily forgotten in countries where there has been, for one reason or another, little perceived threat – postwar India, for instance – or where such threats as might exist have been taken care of by a more powerful protector – Japan or Canada are examples. And economists in my experience are particularly prone to forgetfulness of this basic fact about world politics. Yet the history of economic development in the United States, in Germany, in Japan – and even in Britain if you look at the sixteenth and seventeenth centuries – shows clearly the strong impetus to investment and growth given by the governments of all the leading economies through their defence strategies – including policies to protect and nurture basic industries, to educate people to work in defence-related sectors and to close technological gaps that jeopardise national security (Sen, 1984).

In discussions of issues in international political economy this uncomfortable and inescapable fact gives rise to many difficulties, some of them possibly insoluble in any rational or regular fashion. Take, for instance, the question of conditionality of stand-by credits from the International Monetary Fund (IMF). The Fund's disciplinary teams can devise conditions relating to the rate of domestic credit expansion, to the provision of consumer subsidies and other measures of social welfare and can insist that the applicant for its assistance comply with its norms and limits exchange controls or protectionist tariffs. What it cannot in the nature of the international system do is expressly to forbid that state to spend its scarce foreign exchange on the purchase of armaments or expressly demand that productive labour be freed from unproductive military service.

Or take the disputed issue of economic sanctions. If the United States decides, for defence-related reasons of foreign policy, to express its disapproval of the Soviet occupation of Afghanistan by imposing economic sanctions on the Soviet Union, and demands that the Europeans in their gas pipeline deal do likewise, it is no use the Europeans protesting that such action would violate those principles of free trade. Whether sanctions are right or wrong, useful penalties or empty rhetoric is not the point. The point is that the Europeans would not think of objecting on grounds of *economic principles* because they and the United States – and every other government in the system – accept the fundamental fact that security comes first, however its requirements may be perceived.

Economic Diplomacy

The second reason why international relations is a necessary subject of study for political economists is also rather obvious and also quite often overlooked. It is that as states become more involved in one way or another in their respective economies, and as their economies become more involved – 'integrated' – with one another through international trade, international production and the development of what is truly a global market for capital and credit, so the agenda for intergovernmental bargaining, in other words, economic diplomacy, continues to expand. But to understand economic diplomacy between governments it is a great help, to say the very least, to know something about diplomacy in general. 'Bargaining' is not necessarily the same thing either in the abstract or in other contexts like collective wage bargaining between capital and labour. In the abstract it is apt to lead to theories based on unrealistic assumptions such as rational behaviour in human beings or a known (or known and stable) ranking of motives or priorities of objectives in public choice. In other contexts it is easily forgotten that the limits set to threat and counterthreat, demand and counterdemand set by political authority or social convention within a state are apt to be very different from those governing negotiations between the diplomats of two states.

To make the point explicit it is more help in understanding negotiations over, say, a European Community Common Fishing Policy to know about negotiations between Allied governments during the Second World War than it is to know about bargaining in the context of political party coalition-building or bargaining in the context of corporate mergers. You have to look for different things in order to discover the compulsions likely to influence governments and the range of choices from which they feel free to choose and to be aware of a changeable political as well as an economic context in which their negotiations take place.

Tariff-bargaining in the context of the General Agreement on Tariffs and Trade (GATT) would make no sense at all if analysed from a purely rational basis. The opening of the negotiations is predicated on a common belief in shared interest in the removal of barriers to secure a more efficient allocation of resources reduces costs to the consumers. But the conduct of the negotiations is based on the exchange of 'concessions' that have to be 'paid for' (as if they represented a loss to consumers rather than a gain) by the offer of compensating concessions. The truth is that governments are under greater political pressure from producers to keep tariffs up than from consumers to bring them down. They, therefore, have to show that the other state or states has made equivalent sacrifices in order to justify having made life tougher for their own producers. The necessity of *quid pro quo* in the diplomatic game where more often than not either party is at liberty to walk out is familiar to diplomatic historians who after all are the intellectual forebears of scholars in international relations.

But whereas swapping of tariff concessions has been a familiar practice among governments at least as far back as 1860, many other issues now settled by state officials negotiating with other state officials were once left to the market or from time to time to intercorporate cartels usurping the power of the market to determine price and market shares.

Bargaining over steel imports is an obvious example. In the 1930s the French and German steel industries, with the steelmen from smaller continental European countries, got together and negotiated a market-sharing agreement among themselves. For entirely political reasons, and in the first place in order to find a solution to the longstanding territorial dispute between France and Germany over who should govern the Saarlanders (and their coal), the French and German governments intervened with the Paris Treaty of 1951 setting up the European Coal and Steel Community (Diebold, 1959). In 1967 for the first time the United States government entered the ring in defence of an ageing and uncompetitive American steel industry under merciless attack from Japanese exports (Hudson, 1977).

To cut a long and none too savoury story short, by the 1980s negotiation over shares of various steel markets, especially the American and the European, had become a regular feature of international diplomacy, both at the governmental level and at the corporate level through the meetings of the International Iron and Steel Institute. Altogether this bargaining was a messy business. Agreements even among the European community partners could not be relied on for long, especially when market conditions changed – usually in the early 1980s for the worse. And outcomes were not solely decided by such bargaining. The United States government allowed legal proceedings to be started by domestic steel producers against foreign exporters – even state-owned ones such as the British Steel Corporation – claiming financial compensation for competition they claim to have been unfairly subsidised (Strange, 1979; Strange and Tooze, 1981). Although price was at the bottom of such conflicts, the outcome was not decided by price, but by the bargaining strength of the participating governments and, in particular, by the power of the United States Treasury arbitrarily to fix a 'target price' high enough to prevent further erosion of the market shares still held, though with difficulty, by ailing American steel corporations.

Nor is such a multiple bargaining situation likely to prove a temporary phenomenon. Markets for steel which once had largely been supplied from local, national producers had become increasingly merged into one vast global market, thanks in part to the falling real cost of transport in relation to other costs and in part to the increasing subdivision of steel into a great number of special steels for specific industrial uses, and partly again to another aspect of technological progress which was the increasing size and capital cost of production units. As Meyer (1978) explained so clearly, the need to recoup investment capital in ever-larger amounts but in ever-shorter spans of time – before the chosen innovative process itself becomes obsolete – imposes on steel industries a hunger for foreign markets of a new and sharper kind.

Technological change is, of course, a major factor contributing to the seemingly endless proliferation of international organisations in which bargaining over technicalities easily becomes fraught with political significance (Jacobson, 1981; Williams, Ch. 5 above). Each of the transport and communications technologies in turn – railways, telegraphs, radio, air transport, satellites – has opened up a new area of inter-governmental economic diplomacy. Sometimes this diplomacy has to agree how to share a scarce resource (for example, radio wavelengths). Sometimes it has to decide on uniform rules of nomenclature (for instance, pharmaceuticals) or uniform processes of trade and payment. Sometimes an agreed formula is sought to limit or share the costs of 'externalities' (to use the economists' somewhat obscure term) such as pollution of air, rivers, or sea, or to reduce the risks to a tolerable level, as with the disposal of nuclear waste or the ocean transport of LNG or dangerous chemicals. Often the diplomacy is conducted simultaneously on a multilateral basis and on a bilateral basis between governments and sometimes on a sub-governmental, intercorporate level as well. The untangling of such overlapping processes is not always easy, but it would always be essential to understanding the situation to know about the relative power, and the perceived national interest, of the chief governments involved.

Concern for national security, for the balance of payments, for employment (especially when as with textiles, steel, or shipbuilding this is highly localised), all these are powerful magnets drawing states into international diplomacy over economic matters.

A good example from recent history is the concern of the United States with liberalisation of barriers on international trade in services, notably banking and insurance but also data processing, consultancy, and so forth. At the time the International Trade Organisation (ITO) treaty, the Havana Charter, was negotiated in 1948, in all its 106 articles covering every conceivable aspect of international trade, there was no mention of trade in services. The GATT which was retrieved from the abandoned ruins of the ITO was equally silent. The United States itself had never restricted the entry of foreign and especially British insurance companies and from the nineteenth into the mid-twentieth century these had both prospered on behalf of their shareholders and policyholders and contributed through their very large investments to the economic development of the United States. They were, indeed, the only large group of dollar-asset owners to escape the compulsory, wholesale government requisition of private British shares and other dollar assets by the Churchill government during the war. Others were sold to raise foreign exchange to buy arms, but the sales of insurance company assets would probably have so upset the stock market that it was not even contemplated. Yet despite its own open-door policy, the United States did not seem much concerned, when the OEEC was set up to administer Marshall Aid (and when all sorts of objectives of policy and conditional terms were written into the text); nor when the GATT was planning its procedures for trade diplomacy was there mention of trade in services. Only when opinion in the United States in the 1970s perceived that the loss of jobs in manufacturing was likely to be a permanent one, that the American surplus on visible trade could not be relied on to cover defence costs, capital outflow and other contingencies like short-term monetary movements, did Washington begin to raise the question of the impropriety of restrictions on free competition between national and foreign insurance companies. To this, European governments – Britain excepted – have mostly replied that the control and regulation of insurance, which even after state social security plans are introduced remains a major medium for intermediating savings and investments, is intimately bound up with domestic economic management and thus could not be open to free-for-all competition.

There, for the moment, the matter rests. The Americans have great influence in the OECD and GATT where the issue has been raised. But the Europeans have an equal determination to resist. It has already been under discussion for five or six years without much result except vague and noncommittal resolutions. Whether in the end American persistence or European (and Japanese) resistance will be victorious is hard to say. For once again we are talking not about quantifiable benefits for efficiency, nor abstract justice nor even the maximisation of security against risk to financial system, but about power.

Power in Political Economy

And the analysis of power and all its complex components is – and has always been – the prime concern of scholars in international relations. That, in fact, is my third argument in support of international relations as a foundation for the study of international political economy: that it directs one's attention straight away to the balance of power in any disputed or unsettled issue.

But lest I be misunderstood, I must try briefly to be a bit more explicit about what I understand by 'power' and what I think the study of international relations has to teach about it.

It used to be said in some of the older textbooks on the subject that in the international system of nation-states power consisted in the ability of state A to compel state B to do something it would not otherwise do: or conversely, to desist or refrain from doing something it otherwise would do. But in the world of today, for example, interest rates in state B rise or fall in accordance with American interest rates and these if not determined precisely by how the United States administration is conducting its finances and pursuing its monetary objectives, are certainly very substantially influenced by that conduct. If state A, for this purpose, is the United States, it is not enough to say that American power is only exercised when its government deliberately sets out to force, say, the Italian government to raise its interest rates. The concept of power, in other words, must comprehend the involuntary even unconscious

exercise of compelling authority, when that authority is no less re-
sistible than if the United States had issued an ultimatum backed by
military force.

It is not even enough to extend the concept to what you might call
'Godfather authority', that is, the power of A (the Godfather in Mafia
society) to make B an offer he can't refuse; or even to 'suggest' an action
which B then feels obliged to carry out. This kind of authority consists
both of an element of coercive power plus some element of willing
consent. And in assessing negotiations within the Western or within the
Soviet alliance in the 1980s, as in earlier periods, the changing extent and
limits of this 'Godfather authority' has certainly been of decisive importance in many circumstances. I would instance the authority exercised
by the United States over Canada in matters of foreign policy especially
in the decade or so after 1947, when the successful pursuit of American
aims was again and again assisted by independent initiatives voluntarily
undertaken, by Mr St Laurent and by Lester Pearson especially, in
NATO and at the United Nations. Canada acted as scout and broker, as
pacemaker and cheer-leader and did so not so much because Canadian
governments were responding to American coercion but because they
were acknowledging the validity and quality of American leadership.

But that sort of authority still does not explain or include the sort of
power indicated by the interest rate situation. Here the United States
did not require nor appreciate the European response: it was quite
simply indifferent, as European finance ministers and central bankers
did not cease to complain. What we have to introduce into the study of
political economy, in other words, is what the Marxists and dependency
theorists call 'structural power'.

By this I understand the ability of state A, through its domestic
as well as its foreign policies, to govern or influence the context or
environment within which B also has to take domestic and foreign
policy-making decisions. To call this context structure adds perhaps a
suggestion of permanence, of some predictability, even of deliberate construction, which I do not think is always fully justified by the facts. But
that it is an important – and perhaps the most important – aspect of power
in international political economy I have no doubt. Radical theorists are
also inclined when writing about structural power to concentrate
overmuch on the production structure, by which they mean the way in
which (and the terms on which) land, labour, capital and technology are
combined to produce goods and services. I believe that besides the
relations of production, the relations of security (that is, how military
force, law and authority are combined to maintain order and preclude
or limit the use of violence) are just as important. And so is the financial
structure and the 'knowledge structure', by which I mean the way in
which who-gets-to-know-what-and-how predetermines the extent of
choices, opportunity and risks for others beyond the territorial front-

iers of the political authority which most influences this important structure.

Actually when one looks at economic history, this structural or contextual power, though it has certainly increased in intensity and extent in recent years, is nothing new. Take the power of Britain 100 years ago over all those who ventured on the world's seas and oceans. Some coercive power was exercised by the British Navy but far more pervasive and longer-lasting, in fact, was the influence over others exercised through the provision of Admiralty charts, the regulation of ports and harbours in every part of the world, even the safety rules applied to British ships and the seamen in them.

Today the contextual power exercised through technology (Williams, Ch. 5 above) or through market domination (Rangarajan, Ch. 7 above) or through the monetary system (Calleo and Strange, Ch. 6 above), all have this in common: in important new ways they allow certain governments (and other institutions including large corporations, banks, foundations, even universities and scientific centres) to take decisions which either extend or restrict the range of choice available to 'sovereign' governments over their economic development. Some of these decisions will open up new opportunities to governments. Others will impose new risks, or redistribute familiar ones.

Thus the power over outcomes in international political economy cannot be limited to that exercised by governments; it cannot be perceived only from the topside, but also from underneath, by the perceptions of increased risks or restricted opportunities (or their converse) of those affected by it.

Some Other Observations

What else does a study of international relations (or international history) bring home that might be of value and service to the economist, the sociologist, the lawyer, or the man or woman in government or business?

Mostly it is commonsense. And were it not for the uncommonness of commonsense in much academic writing, it would not be necessary to reiterate such workaday observations. One such is that nothing lasts for ever, and few political relationships continue even for quite a short while without change. The frequency of 'diplomatic revolutions', by which is meant the changing of partners in international history, forewarns against taking any close alliance, or any bitter enmity as a fixture in the political context of economic policy-making. Recall that only five years elapsed between the Treaty of Brest-Litovsk and the Rapallo Treaty of 1922. Recall the drastic change in Sino-Soviet relations at the end of the 1950s. Recall the speed of the Nixon reconciliation with

China at the start of the 1970s. Immanuel Wallerstein has speculated on the possibility of a final break-up of NATO and its replacement by a European-Soviet accord and by a still closer Sino-Japanese-American axis.[2] He may be right or wrong, but the point is that it *is* possible.

Secondly, international relations teaches that the demise of the state as a form of political organisation with more authority than any other is not imminent: indeed, that it is a highly durable institution. The reason is simple: without a world government or a world empire (the difference is perhaps only semantic), the only source of security from robbery, violence and gross bodily harm at the hands of other societies that has so far been devised is the territorial state. It may be true that as states have added to their social responsibilities especially in the welfare field and in the production structure, they have diluted their capacities to perform effectively any one of their self-imposed tasks. Yet as Bruce Miller (1982) has observed in an excellent restatement of the 'realist' view of international society, the state is the ultimate protector of the individual and there is no visible alternative. This does not mean that the characteristics of state behaviour, or the basis of state power, may not change quite substantially. But so they always have; the possibilities of princely marriages are no longer capable of extending or limiting the power of the state; and neither territory nor population are so important as they were even a century ago. The viability of governments to deliver on their promises may, as Krasner (1978) has argued, weaken the state, but the weakness, if not reversed, is more likely over time to produce a takeover bid and the transfer of political power, *de facto* or *de jure*, to another government than it is to lead to the total disappearance of political authority defined (but not delimited) by a line drawn on a map. Total sovereignty within those territorial frontiers always was something of a legal fiction. All that has changed with the advanced integration of the world economy is the extent to which decisions both political and economic – and, indeed, cultural and social – taken inside one territorial state have immediate consequences for people living and working inside others. So it was in fourteenth- and fifteenth-century Italy but the system of international relations observed by Machiavelli and Giuccardini was not fundamentally different from our own, except that (1) the sources of transnational power are secular rather than religious or cultural, (2) that the instruments of military power are vastly more destructive and (3) that the geographical extent of the system is global rather than regional.

So commonsense on observation is especially necessary perhaps in relation to recent suggestions that political economy can and should be studied in terms of the struggle between social classes rather than the relations between states (Pettman, 1979; Wallerstein, 1979). So far as the statement is directing our attention to the basic who-gets-what, or *Cui bono?* question of all political analysis one cannot argue with it.

Almost all the poetry of the First World War, for example, makes the same point: the war may have been started by states, but it was the PBI (poor bloody infantry) and harmless civilians not government ministers or their generals who paid the bitter price for it. Brecht's *Mother Courage* had the same message.

But to say that the conflict of interest between classes in society *determines* outcomes is another matter. The best chance of their ever doing so, perhaps, was missed in August 1914. Never again was the international class consciousness of revolutionary parties and their sympathisers so acute. Now it has been irreparably dulled and blinded by the *embourgeoisement* of the workers in industrialised countries, the willing collapse of those who have the chance into the motherly embrace of corporate welfare systems, the discouraging examples of Soviet dissidents and Polish Solidarity, and now a scramble for market shares that makes employment a zero-sum game between labour unions in competing states and competing corporate enterprises.

One must conclude, I think, that although it is possible and desirable to ask how outcomes in international political economy affect people as social groups – and in that I would include all sorts of other social groups (such as those of sex or generation, of town or country, debtors and creditors, homeowners and tenants, and so on) as well as classes – it is still necessary to recognise that the key decisions and choices that affect them will have been made by states not by class leaders.

And that goes for the so-called multinational corporations. Powerful as they are, they must still obey the orders of governments for the simple reason that their presidents and managers, jet-borne though they perpetually are, still have homes and often wives and children and passports. They are thus vulnerable in the last resort, and they know it. So while much has been written about the effect of the large transnational enterprise on the sovereignty of the state, very little has been openly said about the impact of states on the behaviour and nature of the corporation. Wishing as they all say they do to be 'good citizens' of a multiplicity of states, corporation managers are having, I believe, increasingly to modify some aspect of their 'global strategy' in order to conform with the often conflicting wishes and demands of national governments. What was once a monarchy or a tight federal republic in terms of corporate organisation may be destined (at least in some sectors) to become a much looser confederation.

Finally, perhaps the most important lesson to be learnt from a study of international relations is the Socratic one of the depth and breadth of our ignorance. Students of political economy have this in common with those of international relations, that they are expected by definition to be polymaths able to draw on the insights and findings of a dozen different disciplines. Intellectual humility is inescapable. With it goes a proper hesitation to make firm predictions or didactic judgements.

Both seem to me lessons that some economists seeking to discern the realities of international political economy are apt to forget.

Where to Start?

Should any mature student of international political economy who has *not* had an intellectual infancy, so to speak, in international relations take any of the above to heart, where should he or she begin? On reflection I would say with the reading of international history, rather than with the perusal of textbooks. The names of some of the reputable textbooks, new and old, will be found in the References to this chapter (Holsti, 1978; Bull, 1978; Aron 1966; Miller, 1982; Jacobson, 1981; Duroselle and Renouvin, 1968; Morgenthau, 1954; Frankel, 1979; Reynolds, 1978).

For those disinclined to wade through texts essentially designed for undergraduates but who want to get their bearings in the subject, and discern the main divides and debates going on in it, I would recommend the British Open University's 'reader' (Smith *et al.*, 1981) put together for a course in world politics based on rival perspectives (realist, pluralist and structuralist) which gives a selection of major (or typical) writing. Shorter still but useful to newcomers is Taylor's (1978) overview of the literature.

Some might say better still go to the classics, to Clausewitz, Machiavelli, Thucydides especially. But I think this is a counsel of perfection which few would have the stamina to follow. It would also not substitute for a necessary acquaintance with the major developments of the international political system as it has developed since the Treaty of Westphalia (Morse, 1969) or since the Napoleonic Wars or at least the present century. International politics since the Second World War, on which many students are offered international relations courses, is really insufficient – as those now looking back to the 1930s for illumination of the effects of world depression on international relations or economic diplomacy are becoming very aware.

This historical background is necessary for several reasons, not the least important being the importance of 'tribal memories' on policymaking. Unless you are familiar with the ups and downs of Franco-German relations or of Japanese foreign policy in the 1930s or Latin American experience of the Monroe Doctrine, it is difficult to understand the emotions which lie behind and often explain contemporary policy decisions. Once more, I have included in the References a rather random selection of general international histories, peppered with a few 'case-study' works which allow a closer, more microscopic view of how states and statesmen behave, and how what they *do* so often differs from what they *say*. The bibliographies of macrohistories would offer a still wider choice.

And that leads me to a final observation, which is the importance, in international political economy, wherever you may start from – whether law, economics, international relations, or anything else – of knowing *something about something*. That is to say, the best preparation of all is to have looked closely at some specific issue or episode in sufficient detail that the interaction of politics and economics, which is so obvious when it comes to empirical detail, becomes self-evident. Familiarity with even one piece of micropolitical economy – provided it is constantly used as a point of reference on larger issues – is the best kind of intellectual inoculation against unrealistic assumptions, wild generalisations, or sentimental wishful-thinking.

Notes: Chapter 9

1　Block, 1977, takes the extreme view that Marshall Aid was really motivated more by American concern to 'open up' the world economy to American trade and investment than by fear of continent expansion of Soviet power to the West. Even if this were true (which I doubt), it does not affect the point that debate in Congress hinged on the security factor.
2　Immanuel Wallerstein, 'The end of Nato', *SAIS Review*, Winter 1982.

References: Chapter 9

Aron, R. (1966), *Peace and War: A Theory of International Relations* (London: Weidenfeld & Nicolson).

Block, F. L. (1977), *The Origins of International Economic Disorder* (Berkeley, CA: University of California Press).

Bull, H. (1978), *The Anarchical Society* (London: Macmillan).

Diebold, W. (1959), *The Schumann Plan: A Study in Economic Cooperation, 1950–59* (New York: Praeger).

Duroselle, J.-B., and Renouvin, P. (1968), *Introduction to the History of International Relations* (London: Pall Mall Press).

Frankel, J. (1979), *International Relations in a Changing World* (London: OUP).

Holsti, K. (1978), *International Politics: A Framework for Analysis* (Englewood Cliffs, NJ: Prentice-Hall).

Hopkins, T. K., and Wallerstein, I. (eds) (1980), *Processes of the World System* (Beverly Hills, CA: Sage).

Hudson, M. (1977), *Global Fracture* (London: Harper & Row).

Jacobson, H. (1981), *Networks of Interdependence* (New York: Knopf).

Krasner, S. (1978), *Defending the National Interest* (Berkeley, CA: University of California Press).

Meyer, F. V. (1978), *International Trade Policy* (New York: St Martin's Press).

Miller, J. D. B. (1982), *The World of States* (London: Croom Helm).

Morgenthau, H. (1954), *Politics among Nations* (New York: Knopf).

Morse, E. (1969), *Modernization and the Transformation of International Relations* (London: Collier Macmillan).

Pettman, R. (1979), *State and Class: A Sociology of International Affairs* (London: Croom Helm).

Reynolds, P. (1978), *Introduction to International Relations* (London: Longman).

Sen, G. (1984), *The Military Origins of Industrialization and International Trade Rivalry* (F. Pinter).

Smith, M., Little, R., and Shackleton, M. (eds) (1981), *Perspectives on World Politics* (London: Croom Helm).

Strange, S. (1979), 'The management of surplus capacity: or how does theory stand up to protectionism 1970s style?', *International Organization* (Summer).

Strange, S., and Tooze, R. (eds) (1981), *The International Politics of Surplus Capacity* (London: Allen & Unwin).

Taylor, T. (1978), *Approaches and Theory in International Relations* (London: Longman).

Wallerstein, I. (1974), *The Modern World System* (New York: Academic Press).

Wallerstein, I. (1979), *The Capitalist World Economy* (Cambridge: Cambridge University Press).

Waltz, K. (1959), *Man, the State and War* (New York: Columbia University Press).

Waltz, K. (1979), *Theory of International Politics* (Reading, MA: Addison Wesley).

Appendix: 1980 World Population Data

	Population 1980 (million)	Birth rate	Death rate	% under age 15	% over age 64	Total fertility	% urban	Per capita GNP (US $)
World	4,414	28	11	35	6	3·8	39	2,040
More developed	1,131	16	9	24	11	2·0	69	6,260
Less developed	3,283	32	12	39	4	4·4	29	560
Africa	472	46	17	45	3	6·4	26	530
Northern Africa	110	42	13	44	3	6·2	42	790
Algeria	19	48	13	47	4	7·3	55	1,260
Egypt	42·1	38	10	40	4	5·3	44	400
Morocco	21	43	14	46	2	6·9	42	670
Western Africa	141	49	19	46	3	6·8	21	460
Ghana	11·7	48	17	47	3	6·7	36	390
Ivory Coast	8	48	18	45	2	6·7	32	840
Nigeria	77·1	50	18	47	2	7·1	20	560
Eastern Africa	135	48	19	46	3	6·6	13	240
Ethiopia	32·6	50	25	45	3	6·7	13	120
Kenya	15·9	53	14	50	3	8·1	10	320
Tanzania	18·6	47	16	46	2	6·5	13	230
Middle Africa	54	45	20	43	3	6·0	29	300
Angola	6·7	48	23	44	3	6·4	22	300
Cameroon	8·5	42	19	41	4	5·7	29	460
Zaire	29·3	46	19	45	3	6·1	30	210
Southern Africa	32	39	11	42	4	5·2	44	1,380
South Africa	28·4	38	10	42	4	5·1	48	1,480
Asia	2,563	28	11	37	4	3·9	27	760

South-west Asia	98	40	12	43	4	5·8	46	2,280
Iraq	13·2	47	13	48	4	7·0	66	1,860
Israel	3·9	25	7	33	8	3·5	87	4,120
Saudi Arabia	8·2	49	18	45	3	7·2	24	8,040
Turkey	45·5	35	10	40	4	5·0	45	1,210
Middle South Asia	938	37	16	42	3	5·5	21	180
Bangladesh	90·6	46	20	44	3	6·3	9	90
India	676·2	34	15	41	3	5·3	21	180
Iran	38·5	44	14	44	4	6·3	47	—
Pakistan	86·5	44	16	46	3	6·3	26	230
South-east Asia	354	36	13	42	3	4·7	21	400
Indonesia	144·3	35	15	42	2	4·1	18	360
Philippines	47·7	34	10	43	3	5·0	32	510
Vietnam	53·3	41	18	41	4	5·8	19	170
East Asia	1,173	18	6	31	6	2·3	32	1,200
China	975	18	6	32	6	2·3	26	460
Japan	116·8	15	6	24	8	1·8	76	7,330
Korea, South	38·2	23	7	38	4	3·2	48	1,160
North America	247	16	8	23	11	1·8	74	9,650
Canada	24	15	7	26	8	1·9	76	9,170
United States	222·5	16	9	22	11	1·8	74	9,700
Latin America	360	34	8	42	4	4·5	61	1,380
Middle America	91	38	7	46	3	5·3	59	1,180
Guatemala	7	43	12	45	3	5·7	36	910
Mexico	68·2	37	6	46	3	5·2	65	1,290
Caribbean	30	28	8	40	5	3·8	50	1,160
Cuba	10	18	6	37	6	2·5	64	810

Appendix (Cont.)

	Population 1980 (million)	Birth rate	Death rate	% under age 15	% over age 64	Total fertility	% urban	Per capita GNP (US $)
Dominican Republic	5.4	37	9	48	3	5·4	49	910
Haiti	5.8	42	16	41	4	5·9	24	260
Tropical South America	198	36	9	42	3	4·6	60	1,430
Brazil	122	36	8	41	3	4·4	61	1,570
Colombia	26.7	29	8	45	3	3·9	60	870
Peru	17.6	40	12	44	3	5·3	62	740
Temperate South America	41	24	9	30	7	2·9	80	1,750
Argentina	27.1	26	9	28	8	2·9	80	1,910
Chile	11.3	21	7	35	5	3·0	80	1,410
Europe	484	14	10	24	12	2·0	69	5,560
Northern Europe	82	13	11	23	14	1·8	74	6,140
United Kingdom	55.8	12	12	23	14	1·7	78	5,030
Sweden	8.3	11	11	21	15	1·7	83	10,210
Western Europe	153	11	11	22	14	1·6	82	8,970
France	53.6	14	10	24	14	1·9	73	8,270
Germany, West	61.1	9	12	21	15	1·4	92	9,600
Netherlands	14.1	13	8	25	11	1·6	88	8,390
Eastern Europe	110	18	11	23	11	2·3	59	3,670
Germany, East	16.7	14	14	21	16	1·8	76	5,660
Poland	35.5	19	9	24	10	2·3	57	3,660
Romania	22.3	20	10	25	10	2·6	48	1,750
Southern Europe	140	15	9	26	11	2·3	60	3,290
Italy	57.2	12	9	24	12	1·9	67	3,840
Spain	37.8	17	8	28	10	2·6	70	3,520
Yugoslavia	22.4	17	9	26	9	2·2	39	2,390
Soviet Union	266	18	10	24	10	2·4	62	3,700
Oceania	23	20	9	31	8	2·8	71	6,020
Australia	14.6	16	8	27	9	2·1	86	7,920

Source: Population Reference Bureau, 1980 World Population Data Sheet, Washington, DC, 1980.

Contributors

DAVID CALLEO is Professor of International Relations at the School of Advanced International Studies, Johns Hopkins University in Washington, DC, and author of *The Imperious Economy* and many other books.

NICHOLAS DEMERATH is Emeritus Professor of Sociology at Washington University, St Louis, and is the author among other books of *Birth Control and Foreign Policy*.

ROGER TOOZE is a Lecturer at North Staffordshire Polytechnic and has also taught at the University of Southern California in Los Angeles. He is the organiser of the International Political Economy Group of the British International Studies Association.

L. N. RANGARAJAN is the present Ambassador of India to the Sudan. Previously he was Ambassador in Athens and before that for several years led the Indian delegation to GATT in Geneva.

SOL PICCIOTTO is a lecturer in Law at the University of Warwick.

DENNIS PIRAGES is a professor at the University of Maryland and author of *The Sustainable Society* and other books.

SUSAN STRANGE is Professor of International Relations at the London School of Economics.

ROGER WILLIAMS teaches at the University of Manchester Institute of Science and Technology and has acted as special consultant to the Canadian government.

DAVID WIGHTMAN has been, until recently, Professor of International Organisation at the University of Birmingham and the founder of its interdisciplinary School of International Studies.

Index